THE 6 ENABLERS OF
BUSINESS AGILITY

THE 6 ENABLERS OF BUSINESS AGILITY

How to Thrive in an Uncertain World

KARIM HARBOTT

Berrett–Koehler Publishers, Inc.

Berrett-Koehler Publishers, Inc.
1333 Broadway, Suite 1000
Oakland, CA 94612-1921
Tel: (510) 817-2277
Fax: (510) 817-2278
www.bkconnection.com

ORDERING INFORMATION

Quantity sales. Special discounts are available on quantity purchases by corporations, associations, and others. For details, contact the "Special Sales Department" at the Berrett-Koehler address above.

Individual sales. Berrett-Koehler publications are available through most bookstores. They can also be ordered directly from Berrett-Koehler: Tel: (800) 929-2929; Fax: (802) 864-7626; www.bkconnection.com.

Orders for college textbook / course adoption use. Please contact Berrett-Koehler: Tel: (800) 929-2929; Fax: (802) 864-7626.

Distributed to the U.S. trade and internationally by Penguin Random House Publisher Services.

Berrett-Koehler and the BK logo are registered trademarks of Berrett-Koehler Publishers, Inc.

Printed in the United States of America

Berrett-Koehler books are printed on long-lasting acid-free paper. When it is available, we choose paper that has been manufactured by environmentally responsible processes. These may include using trees grown in sustainable forests, incorporating recycled paper, minimizing chlorine in bleaching, or recycling the energy produced at the paper mill.

Library of Congress Cataloging-in-Publication Data
Names: Harbott, Karim, author.
Title: The 6 enablers of business agility : how to thrive in an uncertain world / Karim Harbott.
Description: First edition. | Oakland, CA : Berrett-Koehler Publishers, Inc., [2020] |
    Includes bibliographical references and index.
Identifiers: LCCN 2021000695 (print) | LCCN 2021000696 (ebook) | ISBN 9781523090051
    (paperback) | ISBN 9781523090068 (adobe pdf) | ISBN 9781523090075 (epub)
Subjects: LCSH: Organizational change—Management. | Organizational effectiveness. |
    Success in business.
Classification: LCC HD58.8 .H36375 2020 (print) | LCC HD58.8 (ebook) |
    DDC 658.4/06—dc23
LC record available at https://lccn.loc.gov/2021000695
LC ebook record available at https://lccn.loc.gov/2021000696

First Edition

26 25 24 23 22 21   10 9 8 7 6 5 4 3 2 1

Book producer: Westchester Publishing Services
Cover designer: Adam Johnson

For those leaders who are smart enough to know they need change, and brave enough to try.

Contents

INTRODUCTION
About This Book

It's not enough to do your best. You must know what to do, then do your best.

—W. EDWARDS DEMING

Business Agility and the Organizational Operating System

Business agility is a term that is used to mean many things. Its true definition is the ability to respond quickly and easily to change in order to maximize the delivery of value to customers in increasingly turbulent business climates. It is about adapting, improving, and innovating quickly enough to stay ahead of a constantly changing curve. It is a trait that increasingly separates the most successful organizations on the planet from all the rest. When organizations achieve this trait, it looks effortless. The rapid evolution, disruption, and continuous reinvention take place with the easy grace of a cheetah twisting and turning on the plains of East Africa. The following is a story about a company that has thrived for two and a half centuries. It has done so only because its forward-thinking leaders have continually evolved the company with the changing markets.

That company is GKN, a British aerospace space company founded in 1759. What is even more remarkable than an organization that is over 260 years old is that aviation pioneers the Wright brothers did not carry out their first successful flight until 1903, a full 144 years after the company was founded. How is this possible? The answer is that GKN was not always in the aerospace business. It began life as a coal mine before becoming Britain's largest producer of iron ore during the Industrial Revolution. By the start of the twentieth century, it was the world's largest producer of fasteners (bolts, nails, and screws). Soon after that, it began making parts for automobiles, and subsequently airplanes. In 2017, GKN provided services to some of the biggest aerospace companies in the world, generated revenues of $9.6 billion, and employed 58,000 people.[1]

Many have attempted to achieve similar levels of business agility by replicating particular tools, processes, and frameworks. What few understand is that merely adopting these ways of working without adapting the prevailing structures, policies, and mindsets of the organization is akin to installing an app designed for Android on an iPhone powered by iOS. The chosen practices are incompatible with what I refer to as the organizational operating system.

There are many great books providing details on the various frameworks, processes, and practices for increased agility. I have spent much of my career advising on their adoption. *This book is different.*

This book is less about specific ways of working, and more about how to create the underlying organizational operating system for business agility, a topic that is rarely addressed. In short, it is about creating the right environment for the myriad agile tools and techniques to stand a chance of working effectively, and in doing so, building organizations that are designed to thrive in an uncertain world.

Why I Wrote This Book

Many people dream of writing a book. I was never one of those people. I chose to study mathematics as my first degree, then became a software engineer largely so I would not have to write words. I continued in that vein, opting for a master's degree in innovation and entrepreneurship. Yet, in many ways, this book has been brewing in my writing-averse mind for more than 10 years. For much of that time I did not know it was going to be a book—but in recent years it became increasingly clear that I was heading down that path. So why, then, have I done the very thing I had spent most of my career avoiding?

Well, I have been on quite a trajectory over the past 20 years. In that time, I have worked with dozens of organizations on some of the largest transformation programs in the world. I have gotten a lot wrong, I have gotten a lot right, and I have learned more than I imagined possible. I have gone from software engineer turned project manager, working in a rather traditional, 120,000-person organization, to ultimately cofounding and leading my own company, which helps leaders and entire organizations adopt modern, progressive, and often unfamiliar ways of working. I see many organizations struggling to achieve results in their journeys toward agility, and many are making similar mistakes. I therefore wish to share what I have learned with as many people as possible to make an impact. I firmly believe that writing this book is the best way to reach a wider audience, to distill many years of learning and experience, and to help people who are on similar paths.

My Two Key Drivers

When I spent some time crystallizing what really drives me and identifying the essential problem I am striving to solve, I found that it came down to two things. These two things are why I do what I do, they are why I get out of bed every morning, and they are why I created the 6 Enablers model.

- **Driver 1: Increasing Organizational Agility.** The world is currently more complex, more interconnected, more turbulent, and therefore less predictable than at any point in our history. In order to survive and thrive in such an environment, an organization's ability to adapt quickly, easily, and cheaply becomes its competitive advantage. Most struggle to know where to begin on this front.

- **Driver 2: Increasing People's Engagement.** When it comes to work, large numbers of people feel disempowered, frustrated, and bored. They are unable to make the most of their potential because when it comes to contributing ideas, tapping into their creativity, and truly revealing their passion for what they do, they are stifled. Helping to shape environments where people not only work more effectively but also enjoy what they do is incredibly satisfying.

In short, I am passionate about helping to create high-performing, agile organizations that delight customers with great products and services, and I am passionate about helping to create truly people-centric organizations in which people love to work—organizations to which they can bring all of their capabilities and in which they can realize their potential every day. Everything I do in my professional life is in the service of these drivers. While they may appear different, in practice, the two cannot be separated.

Most organizations, particularly traditional ones, tend not to pay much attention to either. This is, frankly, unsurprising. Surviving and thriving in the twentieth century required efficiency and compliance rather than adaptiveness and creativity. The world has changed a lot since then, and now, in the twenty-first century, we need to reinvent organizations so that they can be effective in a very different business climate.

How This Book Works

This is not a book of recipes. Many crave such a book, but this is not it. With such diversity in business goals, cultures, capabilities, and strategies, there can be no recipe that is universally applicable. Those who claim to have such a recipe clearly misunderstand the complex and contextual nature of organizational change. Not everyone wants to make the same cake, and they certainly don't have the same ingredients and equipment. Instead, this book focuses on mindset, principles, and general patterns. It is a summary of what I believe are the important factors in increasing organizational agility and why they work. They are things to consider in a so-called *agile transformation*.

The book will provide examples, stories, knowledge, and tools that will help you on your way. Exactly how to apply them in each unique context will be down to those leading the change. On a topic this large, one cannot cover everything. Rather, I seek to highlight the areas that are often ignored but are nonetheless vital to creating high-performing, agile organizations. At the end of each chapter, I have provided a summary, some key practices, and further reading and resources for those who wish to explore the topic in more detail. At the end of each section within each chapter, I invite the reader to reflect on its particular context. I advise you to take the time to perform these reflections and to note down your answers somewhere safe. Having these reflections all together will be invaluable as you explore the final chapter and begin to consider populating the Business Agility Canvas.

In a way, each chapter is designed to be standalone. You can read any chapter and get a lot out of it. However, given the interconnectedness of the topics explored here, reading the book as a whole is recommended. Like an athlete pulling together a coherent, coordinated program of the right diet, physical training, technique, and tactics where all elements work together to achieve their goal, the final chapter shows how the 6 Enablers can be designed in a complementary way to achieve a business goal. My hope is that upon completing the book, people will be inspired to dive deeper into the areas that interest them most. There is no shortage of great material out there with which to continue the learning journey.

The days of agility being confined to IT are long gone. So who is this book aimed at? There are, I believe, two main groups who will benefit most from it. The first is composed of leaders seeking to create nimbler, more adaptive organizations—those leading agile transformations. For that group, this book will open their eyes to the kinds of changes *they* will need to make in how they show up each day as leaders, but it will also illuminate the areas of their business that need to be included and brought along. The second group consists of those who coach leaders through agile transformations—senior coaches and consultants who advise and coach at the organizational level to support these changes. The topics I will be covering are ones on which I very much hope members of this group will educate themselves so that they will be able to coach and advise successfully the leaders with whom they work. Too often I see many of these topics being ignored because they are just not on the radar. I hope to go some way toward making them visible.

What I will *not* be doing in this book is promoting any particular agile approach as superior. There is plenty of that in the agile space already. Most of the approaches out there work well in certain contexts. I will try to identify in which context some approaches *may* work well, and why. I will also avoid providing prescriptive recipes. Every organization is different, and each will have its own route to agility and high performance. What is important is that we tackle all of the areas that are crucial to creating an environment in which any chosen approach can work.

In chapters 1 and 2, I will start with a description of how the agile movement began and how it moved into the boardroom. I will also provide context around the *why* of agility from a business and leadership perspective. In chapter 3, I will outline the six main areas of focus for any organization seeking to move toward agility. Typically, only one or two of these areas are given attention, and this narrow focus leads to an extremely low success rate. Chapters 4 to 9 will be deep dives into the underlying principles behind the six domains identified in chapter 3. And finally, chapter 10 will pull it all together through the lens of the Business Agility Canvas. This will provide a steer on not only how to get started with a transformation but also how to achieve clarity and alignment around the vision, success criteria, key risks, key stakeholders, and key obstacles, as well as a coordinated set of high-level changes across the 6 Enablers of Business Agility to give your transformation the best chance of success.

I'm confident that this book will prove to be a valuable investment of your precious time.

CHAPTER 1

The Changing Business Climate

We are in one of those great historical periods that occur every 200 or 300 years when people don't understand the world anymore, and the past is not sufficient to explain the future.

—PETER DRUCKER

IN THIS CHAPTER, WE WILL EXPLORE

- the key differences between exploration and exploitation
- the concept of VUCA (volatility, uncertainty, complexity, and ambiguity) and its implication for the business climate
- the main drivers behind the emergence of agile ways of working.

Exploring and Exploiting: Two Key Organizational Activities

Think of the most commercially successful organizations around today. What makes them so successful? A superior product or service? Great business model? Efficient operations? The ability to continually innovate and create successful *new* products, services, and business models? For the most successful, it's likely to be all of the above. At the highest level, most organizations are undertaking two main types of work—*exploiting* current products and services and *exploring* new ones. Most will be more focused on one than the other, but both will be happening to some degree. The natures of these two activities are fundamentally different. They seek to achieve different outcomes, require different skill sets, and must be approached in different ways.

Traditional organizations tend to be designed to *exploit* known and understood products, services, and business models. Demand for these has been proved, often over many years. The strategy here is to compete based on the delivery of incremental improvements to existing products and services while simultaneously reducing costs and increasing efficiency. Processes are well understood, there is enough data to make accurate forecasts, detailed plans can be made, and performance can be assessed based on revenues, growth, and profit. These activities are largely understood and predictable, and success relies on effective execution toward a known goal. This pursuit is what we have come to expect from established organizations. An example of effective *exploiting* is Amazon's implementation of algorithms to improve the efficiency of picking and shipping items from its fulfillment centers. It offers the same service as before, but more cheaply, which allows Amazon to pass those savings on to customers, giving it a competitive advantage.

While many organizations have mastered the art of *exploiting*, few can claim to be effective at *exploring*. Exploring is the act of seeking out new products, services, customer segments, and even entire business models. The strategy here is to compete through innovation and sometimes the reinvention of the entire organization. It is an uncertain, unpredictable pursuit that tends to involve a lot of trial and error. As such, making predictions and detailed plans is often not possible. To return to our Amazon example, while it sought to *exploit* its core business model of online retailing, it also continuously *explores* new products, services, and business models. One example of this came in the form of the Kindle e-reader, a product innovation that revolutionized the publishing industry. Another example is a business model innovation, a cloud computing platform called Amazon Web Services (AWS). Launched in 2002 and relaunched in 2006, by the end of 2019, AWS had an annual revenue of over $30 billion.[1]

As we will see, the ability to effectively exploit *and* explore is more important than ever, but it was not always this way. Traditionally, organizations have been able to succeed largely through the mastery of exploitation. In the rest of this chapter, we will take a look at how the imperative to explore has increased over time, and the main reasons for that shift.

Reflection

What are the key areas in your organization engaged in exploiting existing customer offerings? What are the key areas engaged in exploring new customer offerings? How much focus and investment is spent on each? How does that compare with the most successful in your industry? Remember to keep your answers in a notebook for use in chapter 10.

The Twentieth-Century Organization: Exploiting with Efficiency

For most of the twentieth century, organizations survived and thrived by being expert exploiters, creating economies of scale, and relentlessly pursuing operational efficiency. Outfits that produced an as-good or superior product more cheaply than their competitors were likely to prevail. Thus, managers constantly sought to achieve the highest possible output, with the least investment of time, money, or effort. This was achieved largely through specialization, standardization, and the division of labor. In short, it was survival of the most efficient. The ability to exploit their existing products and business models effectively was the main concern, and so organizations were designed almost exclusively for this purpose.

The embodiment of the efficiency movement was Henry Ford, founder of the Ford Motor Company. On October 7, 1913, Ford and his team at the then-Ford plant in Highland Park, Michigan, launched what is arguably the greatest innovation ever in the field of manufacturing: the moving assembly line. Inspired by the overhead trolley used by Chicago packers to dress beef, the new process allowed the production time of the Model T to drop from 12 hours to 90 minutes, and for the price to drop from $850 to $300. This innovation eventually allowed for the production of a Model T every 24 seconds. By 1927, Ford had gone from just another small automobile manufacturer to selling more than 15 million Model Ts every year—half of all automobiles sold at the time.[2] It had masterfully exploited the Model T and had won at the efficiency game.

The assembly line method of production soon spread to other automobile companies, and then to almost every other consumer goods manufacturer. Meanwhile, Ford's contemporary Frederick Taylor was applying engineering discipline and the scientific method to the factory floor to measure and increase worker productivity. In his groundbreaking 1911 book *The Principles of Scientific Management*, Taylor outlined how to decrease unit costs and maximize efficiency by identifying "the one best way" to perform a task and ensuring that everyone followed that way. Taylor would study each task, breaking it down into small steps, painstakingly optimizing and documenting each step, and thus optimizing the whole task, much as a mechanic would improve the performance of an engine by tuning each component. Taylor summed up his approach: "It is only through enforced standardization of methods, enforced adoption of the best implements and working conditions, and enforced cooperation that this faster work can be assured. And the duty of enforcing the adoption of standards and enforcing this cooperation rests with management alone."[3]

The ideas of Ford and Taylor dramatically increased productivity and led to previously unseen levels of efficiency. The Ford and Taylor model of strict hierarchy and specialization resembled that of a finely tuned machine. The machine concentrated power and decision-making at the top, disseminated orders down the chain, and improved efficiency by eliminating inconsistent outputs. In order to do this, organizations sought to measure, control, and minimize variance. This gave rise to all sorts of initiatives, including what we now know as Six Sigma and Total Quality Management.

Businesses that became master exploiters by embracing the machine model tended to outperform the market throughout the twentieth century, and organizational design and almost all tools of management thus focused largely on this area.

Reflection

Which parts of your organization are optimized for exploiting with efficiency? Are those areas characterized by stability, predictability, and known outputs? How effective is your organization at exploiting existing products and services?

The Rise of VUCA: The Game Has Changed

Throughout the fifteenth century, the standard formation of European infantry soldiers was based on their principal weapon, the pike. In the early sixteenth century, the musket was introduced. Over the next 100 years, the pike slowly fell from favor and muskets and bayonets became the default infantry weapons. Rather surprisingly, however, the standard formation of infantry remained unchanged. It took two generations before anyone thought to ask the question, "Is this still the most effective formation for our infantry?" It quickly became apparent that the formation was optimized not for muskets but for pikes and bows. Soon after, the default formation was changed to something more suited to the new context.[4]

This is a phenomenon that can be observed all too often today in various contexts. The dominant paradigm is handed down from generation to generation, and very few take the time to question whether it remains appropriate in the current context. The fact that it was appropriate a century ago or more seems to be sufficient reason for it to remain unquestioned. Anyone who has ever heard, as a justification for a process remaining unchanged, the phrase "But we've always done it this way" will be familiar with this concept.

By today's standards, the twentieth century remained largely static in terms of innovations, which were few and far between. That meant most organizations were able to know in advance exactly the thing on which to be worked, what to exploit. When you know with near certainty that you are working on the "right thing," efficiency is a good indicator of effectiveness. The problem to be solved was how to produce a known output with the least possible input of resources. The cultures, structures, and policies—that is, the organizational operating systems—of many entities from this period were designed for just that.

As such, most large, traditional organizations are designed, and very well prepared, to solve the challenges of the twentieth century. But like the old aphorism about military generals always fighting the last war, the reality is that many organizations now find themselves in a very different business climate. A climate in which yesterday's solutions do not solve today's problems. A climate in which efficiency is rarely the most important goal. A climate in which knowing the "right thing" on which to work has become all but impossible. The organizations that will survive and thrive are the ones that recognize that a fundamentally different problem now exists; the ones that are able to reinvent themselves continually to solve those new problems; the ones that can master the art of *exploring* as well as exploiting.

Today's world can be characterized by the term VUCA. Emerging from the US Army War College in the early 1990s, VUCA described a post–Cold War, multilateral world that was more volatile, uncertain, complex, and ambiguous than ever before.[5] The term caught on in business after the 2008 and 2009 global financial crisis. VUCA, it seems, is the new normal. Here's what it means.

Volatility

It all started on the streets of Sidi Bouzid, in central Tunisia. A 26-year-old man named Mohamed Bouazizi was struggling to find a job. Refusing to join the "army of unemployed youth," he instead began supporting his family by selling fruit and vegetables.[6] However, he faced constant harassment from the local police, and his cart and goods were eventually seized, ostensibly because he lacked a permit. It turned out that very few street vendors had permits at the time, and it is not clear whether one was even required. This left Bouazizi $100 in debt and unable to make a living. On December 17, 2010, enraged at police corruption and unable to pay the required bribes, Bouazizi had had enough. He went to the governor's office in Sidi Bouzid and doused himself in gasoline, shouting, "How do you expect me to make a living?"[7]

Then he lit a match, and the world changed forever.

Nobody could have predicted the sheer pace at which events unfolded. Pictures of Bouazizi's immolation quickly appeared online, and within hours, angry crowds began to protest. He had inadvertently tapped into the anger of many people living across the Middle East at the time. Videos of the protest, taken on smartphones, soon went viral across the globe via YouTube and other social media platforms. As the police struggled to maintain order, the protests spread across Tunisia and into the capital. A mere four weeks later, the president of Tunisia, Zine al-Abidine Ben Ali, resigned and fled to Saudi Arabia, ending his 23-year rule. After another four weeks, the 30-year rule of President Hosni Mubarak of Egypt came to an end, closely followed by the end of the 42-year rule of Muammar Gaddafi in Libya and the 22-year rule of President Ali Abdullah Saleh in Yemen. Ten years on, at the time of writing, Syria remains in a bloody civil war.

Bouazizi's story, and that of the subsequent Arab Spring, demonstrates the volatility of the world in which we now live. Had these events happened just 10 years earlier, the effect would likely have been minimal. The most popular phone at that time, the Nokia 3310, had no video capability, and YouTube would not be founded for another four years. As it was, technology advances and the increased interconnectedness of the world supported the rapid spread of information, images, and videos and allowed the Arab Spring to build unstoppable momentum quickly.

This is just one example of how the pace of change in the world today is unlike anything we've witnessed before. The same phenomenon also plays out in the business environment. The Industrial Revolution of the eighteenth and nineteenth centuries transformed the world forever. The McKinsey Global Institute estimates that the pace of change today is roughly *10 times* what it was during that period, and at roughly *300 times* the scale. That means that the changes going on today have a whopping *3,000 times the impact* of the Industrial Revolution.[8] This all adds up to some startling statistics. If we consider the adoption rates for new technologies, we find that they have risen dramatically in recent years (figure 1). Electricity (invented in 1873) took 46 years to reach 25 percent of the US population. The telephone (1876) and radio (1897) reached the same milestone in 35 and 31 years, respectively. The World Wide Web (1991) took only 7 years, and the smartphone (2007) a mere 4 years.[9] The adoption rates of these last two technologies, it could be argued, led to the downfall of dozens of organizations—Nokia, Blockbuster, and Borders, to name but three. They all had their products, services, or business models rendered obsolete in a matter of a few short years, and they just could not respond quickly enough. Rapid adoption of

FIGURE 1

Years to reach 25 percent of US population

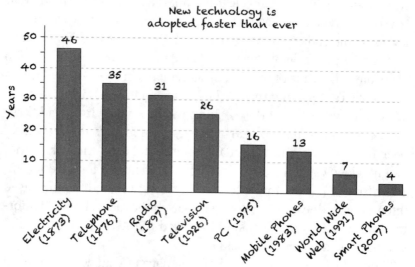

Source: Eric Ries, *The Startup Way: How Modern Companies Use Entrepreneurial Management to Transform Culture and Drive Long-Term Growth* (New York: Currency, 2017). COPYRIGHT: © Eric Ries, reprinted by permission of the author.

technology also led to the rise of nearly all of the most valuable companies today, including Apple, Amazon, Google, and Facebook.

Similarly, organizations once took decades to reach the mystical valuation of $1 billion or higher. It took Prada 98 years to reach that landmark. Harley Davidson and Whirlpool both took 86 years, with Nike and Starbucks taking 24 years apiece.[10] Even the mighty Google took 8 years. By contrast, however, WhatsApp and Dropbox took just 4 years, Square 2 years, WeWork 18 months, and Jet.com took a mere 4 months[11] (figure 2). All this means that the biggest threat to your organization could be entities that do not yet exist, leveraging a technology that has not yet been invented. In this context, many three-to-five-year strategic plans tend to be out of date before the ink dries. It seems that we now live in an age in which the only thing that remains the same is the relentless pace of change. Whether that change is social, technological, economic, environmental, political, or military, that trend looks set to continue. All this should make for uncomfortable reading for those leading the established market leaders.

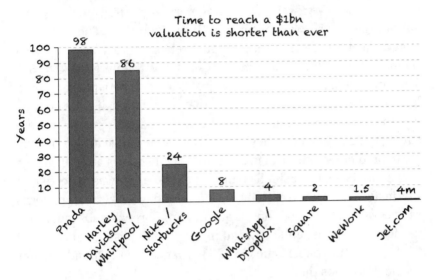

FIGURE 2

Years to reach $1 billion market capitalization

Time to reach a $1bn valuation is shorter than ever

Uncertainty

Right now, we have more information at our disposal than ever before. We have more technology and more computer processing power. And despite this, we have never been less able to make accurate predictions about the future. The faster the landscape changes, and the more interconnectedness there is, the less we are able to predict the future.

To illustrate this point, let us go back to 1961, when an MIT mathematician named Edward Lorenz was simulating two months' worth of weather patterns on the Royal McBee LGP-30, a cutting-edge computer at the time. He was using 12 variables to cover starting conditions related to temperature, wind speed, and so on. Lorenz, keen to examine some interactions in greater detail, set out to rerun one of the simulations. Given that computers in 1961 had a fraction of the processing power available today, he used a set of printouts for the 12 variables and started the simulation from the midpoint to save time. One hour and one cup of coffee later, Lorenz returned to be met with a result that diverged so much from his original that it was unrecognizable.

He was shocked. How could it be? Lorenz suspected a computer hardware issue, something that was not uncommon at the time. The computer, however, was functioning normally. After much investigation, the culprit was discovered. It was the data. The computer stored data to six decimal places, but Lorenz's printout only displayed them to three. Thus, the number 0.506127 was entered as 0.506.[12] This miniscule rounding error on just one of 12 data points should have had very little effect. Indeed, the prevailing belief at the time was that very small influences can be neglected. A tiny error in measuring the position of Halley's Comet in 1986 would cause a tiny error in predicting its arrival in 2061. And yet instead of a small change in the input causing a small change in the result as was expected, in this instance, it caused such divergence that the two weather patterns seemed as if they were chosen at random. Lorenz's subsequent investigation and insights led him, in 1963, to publish a paper called "Deterministic Nonperiodic Flow." This paper laid the foundation for the field of chaos theory.

In 1972 Lorenz delivered a talk titled "Predictability: Does the Flap of a Butterfly's Wings in Brazil Set Off a Tornado in Texas?" It is from here that the phrase "butterfly effect" derives. It is commonly used to describe how small changes in initial conditions can lead to disproportionate changes in outcomes. As we will see (in the *complexity* section next), unpredictable, nonlinear behavior is a hallmark of complex systems. It is the reason we can predict, with high levels of confidence, when my home city of London will see its next lunar eclipse, yet we still struggle to predict whether it will snow on Christmas Day. The former is an example of an ordered, predictable problem, while the latter is an example of a disordered, unpredictable one. As we operate increasingly in this latter, more complex space, the resulting inability to make accurate predictions leads many traditional, deterministic business practices to become less effective by the day.

Complexity

We all intuitively know that we do different types of work within the parameters of our businesses. We know that we should likely approach different types of work in different ways, but it's not often that organizations recognize this and use varying context-appropriate leadership approaches in different situations. Consider a team of neuroscientists working in a hospital. They are conducting clinical trials of a new, highly experimental drug. How much can they expect to know up front through analysis? How likely is it that their plan will remain unchanged as they progress—or that they will learn what works and what doesn't as they go? Now consider a team of network engineers laying high-speed cables throughout that same hospital. Would they approach their work in the same way? Would they be able to make, and stick to, more detailed plans? Is their work more predictable than the neuroscientists'?

We hear the words *complicated* and *complex* often in life. Many use them interchangeably, not really considering their deeper meanings. When used to describe the nature of systems, sharing their first five letters is pretty much where the similarity ends. In order to understand how to manage both complicated and complex systems, we must first be clear what each word means in this context.

The human brain is pretty well designed to understand complicated systems. Complicated systems are ordered. There may be many parts to the system, but each part is joined to the next in relatively simple, and understandable, ways. A car engine is a good example of this. Each part can be understood in isolation, and the interactions among the parts can be mapped out reasonably easily. Because of the small number of interactions, the whole can be understood by deterministically breaking it down into discrete parts. The whole is the sum of those parts. This means that, with some analysis, fairly good predictions can be made about the behavior of the system. Cause and effect can be understood in advance. Another hallmark of complicated systems is that behavior is linear. A change in the input will lead to a proportional change in the output. For example, if you deposit $1,000 in the bank and you receive 5 percent interest, your profit, after a year, will be $50. If you put in $2,000, your profit after a year will be $100. Hence we have a predictable, linear cause and effect that allows us to understand, in advance, the impact of making changes to the system. In short, there are unknowns, but they are *known unknowns*.

Complex systems are not so easily understood by the human brain. These systems are disordered. There are many parts, all interacting with many other parts, often in ways we cannot understand. With this dramatic increase in the number and frequency of interactions, it becomes all but impossible for anyone to understand the system. As we saw with the examples of the Arab Spring and Edward Lorenz, a hallmark of complex systems is the volatility and complete unpredictability of outcomes for a given change. One simply cannot comprehend the sheer number of possible interactions and outcomes. The behavior of the system is nonlinear in that a small change in input could yield a dramatically different output. Consider how differently a game of Scrabble would go if just one or two tiles were changed in one player's starting set. With a different starting word played, after each player took, say, 20 turns, the game would be utterly unrecognizable compared with what it would have been with the original tiles.

Complex systems cannot be understood by breaking them down into their constituent parts. This is because their behavior is not the sum of the system's parts, but a product of the myriad interactions among them. This is why a doctor investigating a patient's blurred vision cannot focus on the eyes in isolation. The root cause could be anything from myopia to high blood pressure to diabetes; diabetes is an inability to produce insulin in the pancreas, which in turn may be caused by a combination of genetic and lifestyle factors. The reductionist approach just does not take into account all the possible interactions leading to any given outcome. The doctor in this case will need to think more holistically.

All of this means that, when working in a complex system, seeking to predict cause and effect in advance, through analysis, is a fool's game. No matter how much one seeks to study a system, it will always yield surprises. Complex systems can only be understood through safe-to-fail experimentation. As economist and author Tim Harford once said, "You show me a successful complex system, and I will show you a system that has evolved through trial and error."

Table 1 gives a summary of the key differences between complicated and complex systems.

TABLE 1

Summary of complicated and complex systems

	TYPE OF SYSTEM	
	Complicated	Complex
Typical examples are . . .	Repeatable production and construction work	Creative design, development, and innovation work
The system works toward . . .	Known, stable outputs	Emerging, frequently changing outputs
Behavior is . . .	Largely predictable and linear—a small change in the input leads to a small, predictable change in the output	Largely unpredictable and nonlinear—a small change in the input leads to a large, unpredictable change in output
Risk is best mitigated by . . .	Up-front analysis and detailed planning	Small experiments, quick feedback, and frequent course correction
Competitive advantage is gained through . . .	Efficiency—creating a known output with as little input as possible	Adaptiveness—continuously seeking feedback and course-correcting toward an emerging output
Management processes tend to reward . . .	Conformity to the plan	Value delivery
The whole is . . .	The sum of its parts—the whole can be understood by understanding the constituent parts	The product of the many interactions between the parts—the whole can be understood only by observing the whole
The system contains . . .	Largely *known* unknowns	Many *unknown* unknowns

Ambiguity

With so much information at our fingertips, it seems rather counter-intuitive that we have less clarity about reality than ever before. Reality can be hard to understand, and many leaders feel as though they are operating in a fog. Gone are the clear black-and-white views, making way for shades of gray, multiple perspectives, different plausible interpretations, and no clear link between cause and effect. Despite information being available, overall meaning is often unclear. Ambiguity is often confused with vagueness. *Ambiguity* offers many specific, plausible interpretations of a situation—some obvious, some less so. When information is *vague*, however, it is very difficult to formulate any specific interpretations. This makes decision-making extremely difficult. More information is rarely the answer. The chances are that there are multiple good answers.

While a hallmark of ambiguity is an inability to form an accurate picture at the time, what can often be observed is a level of retrospective clarity. This is where a big event was not predicted at the time owing to the many interpretations of the data, but after the event, it appears so obvious that people wonder why it was not picked up. This often occurs with large terrorist attacks or financial crashes. There is so much data that it is difficult to see the forest for the trees in advance, but once the event has happened, people wonder how no one "joined the dots." Once the dots have been joined up, it seems obvious, but before that happens, it is merely a sea of seemingly unconnected dots.

The four terms that make up VUCA are, in reality, extremely closely related. It is impossible to separate one from the others. The higher the complexity—the more moving, interconnected parts there are—the higher the volatility, uncertainty, and ambiguity tend to be. The key here is that it is vital for leaders to understand the difference between work involving higher levels of VUCA and that involving lower levels. They must also be able to identify the nature of the work being done by teams and to select effective leadership approaches for *that type of work*. This contextual approach can dramatically increase a leader's effectiveness. As the old saying goes, if you only have a hammer, everything looks like a nail. Today's leaders need a whole toolbox, and they need to know which tool to use at which time. Much of the work being done today involves substantially higher levels of VUCA than was the case during the previous century. The business climate has shifted. The biggest mistake leaders can make is to continue to apply yesterday's deterministic thinking to today's complex, unpredictable challenges.

Reflection

What are some examples of VUCA for your organization? What is the impact of that? Are there some areas that are particularly uncertain and unpredictable? Do you foresee these areas increasing in the coming years?

The Modern Organization: Exploring with Agility

The dawn of the information age changed everything. Technological innovation and deregulation caused barriers to entry to fall dramatically. Suddenly, large sums of start-up capital were not necessary to enter a market. Whole industries could now be disrupted from a garage in Silicon Valley—or anywhere in the world, for that matter. This means that products, services, and even knowledge now very quickly become commodities. As customers are able to switch over to competitors at the click of a button, they must be courted and won over repeatedly with new and exciting products and services—products and services that solve their real-world problems. This hypercompetition leads to ever-diminishing margins and revenues. Thus, merely possessing the ability to exploit your current products expertly will not yield the results it once did. The modern organization must be able to explore new opportunities to delight its current customers and attract new ones, to innovate quickly enough to stay ahead of the curve, and to cultivate the capability to reinvent itself continually *before* crisis hits. Celebrate the successes of today, for sure, but recognize that these are now poor indicators of success tomorrow.

Humans evolved to survive as hunter-gatherers at a time when food was hard to come by. This is no longer the case, at least in the West, and that means that we are now maladapted for the modern world. This is a world in which food is plentiful and exercise is an optional extra. Most people live sedentary lives, sitting behind a desk. Because of that, our health suffers, and our instinct to consume food when the opportunity arises now works against what is best for us. The same has happened in business. Many large entities have leadership styles, cultures, structures, and processes rooted in the Industrial Revolution. They are perfectly adapted for an environment that no longer exists. This means that they are ill equipped to compete in this new business climate—a climate defined by high levels of VUCA, hypercompetition, and an imperative to innovate continually, to explore new opportunities and create new knowledge.

All of this means that the winds of creative destruction are blowing stronger than ever. In the early 1960s, organizations enjoyed an average stay of 61 years on the S&P 500 index of leading US companies. As of 2012, that figure had plummeted to just 18 years (figure 3).[13] Of the original list of *Fortune* 500 companies from 1955, only 60 remained by 2017.[14] That's a mere 12 percent. The rest have disappeared, having gone bankrupt, merged, or been acquired, or they survive but no longer make the *Fortune* 500 cut. In 2016 Pierre Nanterme, CEO of Accenture, noted that "digital is the main reason that just over half the Fortune 500 companies have disappeared since the year 2000."[15] That is a phenomenal turnover in less than two decades. At that churn rate, 75 percent of the current S&P 500 will have been replaced by 2027.[16] A major contributing factor to these figures is the inherent bias in organizations toward exploit work. In a hangover from an era in which that approach was successful, organizations find themselves optimized only to exploit their current offerings. They tend to be designed to resist change and to move slowly toward new opportunities or away from existential threats.

When you are working toward a known output, efficiency is a great proxy for effectiveness. That's why so many outfits are built, from the ground up, to favor this trait. When operating in a climate so fast-moving and unpredictable, making accurate predictions becomes all

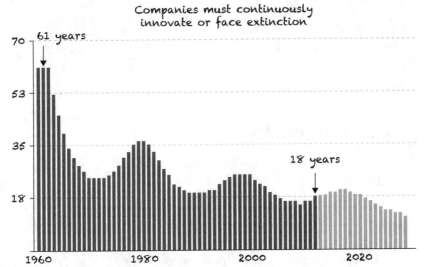

FIGURE 3

Average company lifespan on S&P 500 Index

Companies must continuously
innovate or face extinction

Source: Innosight, *Creative Destruction Whips through Corporate America*,
Executive Briefing, Winter 2012, https://engageinnovate.files.wordpress.com/2012
/03/creative-destruction-whips-through-corporate-america_final2012.pdf.

but impossible. Management pioneer Peter Drucker once said, "There is nothing so useless as doing efficiently that which should not be done at all." Today, the biggest challenge is knowing that you are working on *the right thing*. The organizations that achieve a competitive advantage are the ones that have the ability to respond more quickly, more easily, and more cheaply to *any* challenges that lie around the corner. Always to be working on the right thing, whatever that may be—this is the essence of business agility. With this in mind, leaders need to view their organizations less as efficient machines and more as complex ecosystems of many interacting parts, designed to adapt. To survive and thrive in this new climate, they need to compete every day for the customers they once took for granted. This requires a concerted effort not just to exploit current products but to master the art of exploring new ones, creating new knowledge, and putting the customer at the heart of everything they do. Like the double-faced Roman god Janus, they must be able to look simultaneously back at the past and into the future.

> **Reflection**
>
> Does your organization benefit from a stable or a turbulent environment? For which is it predominantly optimized? If stable, what might happen if it were forced to operate in a radically different landscape? How easily could it adapt?

Chapter Summary

- All organizations undertake two basic activities, exploiting their current products and services and exploring new ones.

- In the twentieth century, organizations succeeded by focusing predominantly on efficiently exploiting existing customer offerings. Given the relatively slow pace of change, they could often do this successfully for many decades.

- In the late twentieth century, the world became far more turbulent and unpredictable. Today organizations face far greater VUCA—volatility, uncertainty, complexity, and ambiguity.

- Technological advances, deregulation, and a greater interconnectedness led to lower barriers to entry to many industries. This drove up competition among organizations.

- Today, surviving and thriving is about more than efficient execution and exploiting. Organizations must now balance that equally with exploring the new, innovating, and delivering greater value to customers than ever before. This activity involves focusing not on efficiency but on agility.

Further Reading and Resources

Books

- Gary Hamel, *The Future of Management*, with Bill Breen (Boston: Harvard Business School Press, 2007)

■ Alex Osterwalder, Yves Pigneur, Frederic Etiemble, and Alan Smith, *The Invincible Company: How to Constantly Reinvent Your Organization with Inspiration from the World's Best Business Models* (Hoboken, NJ: Wiley and Sons, 2020)

Websites, Articles, and Videos

■ Please see www.6enablers.com/resources for more on this topic, including a downloadable reading list.

CHAPTER 2

Introducing
Business Agility

Whom the gods want to destroy, they send forty years of success.

—ARISTOTLE

IN THIS CHAPTER, WE WILL EXPLORE

- why it can take a long time for paradigm shifts to be accepted
- the emergence and evolution of the agile movement
- some real-world examples of business agility in action.

Breaking Out of the Status Quo: Beyond Belief Perseverance

In 1844, a Hungarian named Ignaz Semmelweis was appointed assistant to the professor at an obstetric clinic in Vienna. At the time, puerperal fever, also known as childbed fever, was plaguing maternity wards across Europe. While most women delivered at home, those who were hospitalized, owing to poverty or complications, faced mortality rates of up to 25–30 percent. There were various theories about the causes of the deathly fevers, ranging from overcrowding to poor ventilation.[1]

Semmelweis's hospital in Vienna had two maternity clinics. The first clinic had a mortality rate 2.5 times higher than the second clinic. The clinics were otherwise almost identical. The only observable difference was that the first was used to train student medics, and the second to train student midwives. After much investigation, Semmelweis concluded that the medical students, who were also performing autopsies, were transferring "cadaverous particles" from mothers who had died of puerperal fever to healthy patients whom they examined during labor. The student midwives in the second clinic were not involved in autopsies. In May 1847, he instituted a policy of using chlorinated lime for handwashing between autopsies and examinations. The result was that the mortality rate in the first clinic immediately dropped by 90 percent, from 18.27 percent to 1.27 percent. In March and August 1848, not a single woman in his clinic died in childbirth.[2]

One could be forgiven for assuming that Semmelweis was recognized by his peers for his life-saving work. However, while the younger medical staff at his clinics were largely supportive, his theories were ignored, rejected, and ridiculed by the wider medical community. Semmelweis's conclusions were at odds with the prevailing scientific and medical views of the time. Workplace politics of this sort saw Semmelweis removed from his post and hounded out of Vienna. He retreated back to his native Budapest. Although he was accepted in his homeland, the rejection of his theories took a toll on his mental health. In 1865 he suffered a breakdown and was committed to a mental hospital. He died there 14 days later.

Around 200 years earlier, 13-year-old Maria Sibylla Merian began collecting and keeping insects and caterpillars. One of the first naturalists to observe insects directly, Merian made detailed drawings and paintings of them. This was 1660, and insects were largely considered "beasts of the devil" that were "born of mud" through a process called spontaneous generation. Merian collected evidence contradicting these theories, having captured, though her observations, not just her subjects' anatomy but also their life cycles and interactions with other living things. She was the first to document that butterflies were born not of mud but of caterpillars. She went on to describe the life cycles of 186 insect species. Merian published her work on these subjects in two volumes, in 1679 and 1683, respectively.

Merian's work was largely ignored for a number of reasons. At a time when women who attempted to live much beyond the usual domestic sphere risked being jailed or even executed for witchcraft, Merian did not have the option of dedicating all of her time to her studies as a man of her class might have done. She had no formal scientific training, and self-trained naturalists were seldom taken seriously. She was thus dismissed by many prominent male scientists. As well, her first two books, which contained many great new insights, were written in German, while the official language of science at the time was still Latin. All of this meant that while Merian was considered a skilled artist and illustrator, her contribution to science has largely been forgotten.

The foregoing examples show us two things. First, any establishment tends to perpetuate the conventional wisdom of its time. Those who benefit from the current system usually have the most invested in that system. They therefore tend to resist change. Second, when people on the fringes challenge the status quo, when radical new ideas emerge from those from whom new, breakthrough theories are not expected, those people and theories are often not taken seriously. These ideas can remain on the shelf for decades, gathering dust and all but forgotten until the rest of the world finally catches up. The irony is that it often takes people from outside the system to make big leaps of progress. People who have a different perspective. People who are not weighed down by the burden of the dominant paradigm. People who can think differently enough to *shift* the paradigm. This is the power of the outsider's perspective.

All too often, breakthrough ideas are confronted by what's known as *belief perseverance*. This is the very human tendency to maintain one's beliefs despite credible evidence to the contrary. In fact, attempts to present evidence debunking someone's belief are likely to strengthen it. This is known as the *backfire effect*.[3] Physicist Max Planck noted that "the new scientific truth does not triumph by convincing its opponents and making them see the light, but rather because its opponents eventually die, and a new generation grows up that is familiar with it."[4] Never was this more apparent than with the theory of heliocentricity—that is, the belief that the earth revolves around the sun. The theory was proposed by Aristarchus of Samos in the third century BCE, but it would be another 1,800 years before Nicolaus Copernicus popularized it. This stubborn persistence is also apparent in business when radical new ideas emerge that threaten to shift the current paradigm.

Reflection

Are there beliefs that persevere in your organization despite strong evidence to the contrary? Are there vested interests that lead to some clinging to the status quo worldview? Are there people on the fringes who might have ideas worth exploring? If so, how could they be engaged?

The Three Waves of Agility: From 17 Software Engineers to the Boardroom

I believe that a similar pattern to those shown in the foregoing examples emerged when a group of pioneers created the agile movement. Now, this is not a book about software development; it is a book about business agility. One cannot, however, cover the topic of agility without first giving a hat-tip to the forward-thinking innovators who popularized the movement—those who saw that the status quo was not serving the customer well and that new ways of working were needed. Those management innovators just happened to be software engineers at a time when that particular group was often written off by executives as geeky, technical, and largely ignorant in the ways of management. Had they been professors at a prestigious business school, I believe the agile movement would have moved significantly faster than it has. As it is, it has taken us 20 years to get to this point, but the world now appears to be waking up to the need for a paradigm shift in how knowledge work is approached.

The following is a high-level overview of the emergence and evolution of the agile movement, from its beginnings with a small, largely inward-looking group of software developers focused on small teams, right through to CEOs of the biggest corporations on the planet today espousing wholesale business agility as the new competitive advantage. Certainly the seeds were sown some time before our starting point by innovators like W. Edwards Deming and Taiichi Ohno, both pioneers of the Toyota Production System, which later provided the basis for the Lean movement. I begin where I do because it marks the beginning of the formal agile movement, and to understand the

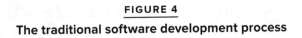

FIGURE 4

The traditional software development process

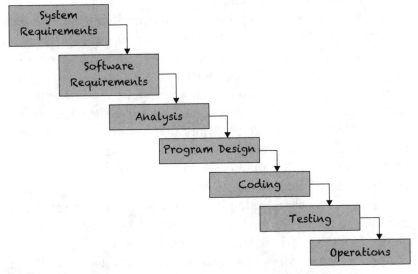

Source: Winston W. Royce, "Managing the Development of Large Software Systems," *Proceedings, IEEE WESCON,* August 1970, reprinted in https:// leadinganswers.typepad.com/leading_answers/files/original_waterfall_paper _winston_royce.pdf.

future of business agility, we must first understand the problem its pioneers sought to address.

Pre-Agile: Chasing Waterfalls

In 1970, an American computer scientist named Winston Walker Royce published a paper titled "Managing the Development of Large Software Systems."[5] In it, he laid out his personal views on managing large software developments based on his nine years of experience. Royce went on to explain how many people were approaching the problem at the time, outlining a linear process as seen in figure 4. The thinking was that if enough time and effort were spent up front working out the right thing to build to satisfy the customers' needs (the requirements), and then enough time was spent working out the best way to build the product (the design), then the implementation and testing would be pretty straightforward. The two key risks of building something the customer did not want and of building something that did not work as desired were, in effect, mitigated by much up-front thinking and planning.

While this made sense in theory, the big problem was that it did not work well in practice, and Royce knew it. As discussed in the previous chapter, in a world of high VUCA, the ability to make accurate predictions about what the customer wants and how complex systems should be built becomes all but impossible. When a system is *complicated* and largely stable and predictable (i.e., there are low levels of VUCA), the approach may work well. When a system is complex, unstable, and unpredictable, however, it will fail. No amount of up-front analysis will result in knowing all one needs to know to execute efficiently. That information will have to be discovered throughout the process, not just at the start. What is needed is the ability to experiment, receive feedback quickly, and then course-correct based on that feedback. In short, it is a matter of agility over efficiency.

Approaching *exploratory* work like software development with an *exploit* mentality is doomed to fail. Royce himself cautioned against the use of this sequential model, stating in the same paper that "the concept described above is risky and invites failure." Instead, Royce advocated a far more iterative approach, as many phenomena were "not precisely analyzable."[6] An iterative approach would mean going through the process multiple times and responding to the resulting feedback. Though he did not use the word, what he described was a more *agile* approach.

Another word Royce did not use was *waterfall*. This word, used to describe the sequential approach, came into use some 5 to 10 years after the publication of his paper. Despite never having used the term *waterfall*, and despite advising strongly against the use of the process, Royce is still often referred to as the father of the waterfall process. This was a most unfortunate and unintended consequence of his work.

Many believe that the reason the waterfall model became so widespread is its simplicity. Despite Royce's warnings, it is easy to understand, and it *seems*, at first glance, rigorous and disciplined. It was these factors that led the US Department of Defense in 1985 to develop the rather prosaically named DOD-STD-2167,[7] which, while it technically allowed for iterative approaches, was in reality heavily biased toward the waterfall model. This approach quickly spread across the public and private sectors throughout the United States and the rest of the world to become the de facto standard for managing software development, with governance models and organizational designs built around it. The lesson for us all here is this: Never publish a picture of a seemingly elegant, but ultimately flawed, model.

Agility Wave One: Team Agility

From February 11 to 13, 2001, 17 software engineers met at the Lodge at Snowbird Ski Resort in the mountains of Utah for the Lightweight Frameworks Conference. Their aim was to seek "an alternative to documentation-driven, heavyweight software development processes."[8] They could not have foreseen quite how much impact the few messages they crafted over those two days would have.

There had long since been consensus that the dominant approach to developing software, the waterfall model, was often ineffective. It could work for *simpler* projects, but for any nontrivial software endeavor, there were a number of challenges. It was too bureaucratic, was not responsive enough to (inevitable) changes, and meant that big decisions about what to build and how to build it had to be made up front, at the beginning of the process. Yet the beginning of any project of this sort is when the level of information held is the lowest it will be at any point. Waterfall also leaves no option but to defer key risks until the end of the process, when the testing happens. This tends to be an expensive way to find out that your product is not fit for purpose, and leads to much rework.

These challenges led small groups of people to begin to experiment with different ways of doing things. They created various frameworks that were more responsive to changing customer needs and derisked the process not through endless up-front analysis and planning but by delivering a working version of the product every one to four weeks, quickly soliciting customer feedback—and, crucially, course-correcting based on that feedback. These frameworks included Scrum and Extreme Programming (XP). Software engineers had discovered that when *complex* work was undertaken in environments of high VUCA, the key risks could only be mitigated through feedback and frequent course correction. These frameworks were termed "lightweight," in contrast to the heavyweight approach of the waterfall model—hence the convening of the Lightweight Frameworks Conference. Amazingly, these self-confessed "organizational anarchists" managed to agree on four value statements that united their approaches. These are outlined here.

Individuals and interactions over processes and tools. Consider a group of people working to build a product. They are disengaged and demotivated. Trust, collaboration, and communication are low. Team spirit is nonexistent. Now imagine that they have in place the most sophisticated tools and processes, all documented perfectly somewhere on a shared corporate drive. These ways of working have been crafted by a top management consultancy. How will this team perform? If they are working on simple work, probably adequately. But if they are undertaking creative knowledge work, the answer is, in all likelihood, badly. This is because when undertaking knowledge creation, the processes and tools are important, but team spirit, communication, collaboration, trust, mutual accountability, and many other factors are *more important*. Software development, product development, value creation, innovation—these are *people* problems. Organizations that put in place the conditions for high-quality integrations and team spirit significantly outperform their competitors. Steve Jobs went to great lengths to maximize these interactions while painstakingly designing both Pixar and Apple headquarters. Yet many organizations focus largely on processes and tools because those are easier matters to address. While these things are important, they do not yield anything like the same results.

Working software over comprehensive documentation. The feedback you get from documentation is nowhere near the quality of the feedback you get from a working version of a product—even if that product is incomplete. Getting to a working version, even if it is only a prototype, allows for all sorts of interesting conversations that would not otherwise happen. To give feedback on a cake recipe, one needs to taste the cake rather than read the list of ingredients. Documentation is still likely to be necessary, but it is less important than the product, which provides real value to the customer.

Customer collaboration over contract negotiation. I have never had anyone tell me that the key reason for the success of their new product or service is the contract they put in place. Contracts can be valuable when you know enough up front to put the right things in the contract—as with construction projects, for example. In the absence of that ability, and when the work is more creative and exploratory, contracts can easily inhibit learning and change, leading to inferior products. Collaborating closely with the customer, however, allows for the frequent collection of feedback, which can move you in a direction that solves the customer's real problem.

Responding to change over following a plan. Not generally renowned for his prowess in business strategy, former undisputed heavyweight champion of the world "Iron" Mike Tyson famously said, "Everyone has a plan 'till they get punched in the mouth." This insightful sentiment builds on that of President Dwight D. Eisenhower, who, in speaking of his military experience, noted, "In preparing for battle I have always found that plans are useless, but planning is indispensable." The most famous variation on this theme comes from nineteenth-century Prussian field marshal Helmuth von Moltke the Elder, who said, "No plan survives contact with the enemy." These quotes all stem from the same basic worldview. This view states that when the landscape on which we are operating is constantly shifting in ways we cannot predict, having a plan is all well and good, but the ability to replan continually, based on new information, is vital. If a plan is not working, there is little point in continuing to follow it. There is far more value in responding to change and creating a *new* plan. A *better* plan. A plan that is more likely to result in the desired outcome. In her book *Uncharted: How to Map the Future,*[9] Margaret Heffernan talks about "preparedness" instead of planning, doing everything today that you might need for tomorrow rather than following one set plan, and she urges us to resist the false promises of efficiency if we want to have a better chance of getting a future we want.

The four value statements just discussed were originally published as a manifesto for change in software development. The manifesto needed a name. After all, "lightweight frameworks expert" is not something most people want on their CV. A few names were bandied about, including *adaptive* and *responsive.* Ultimately it was the suggestion of my good friend and mentor that won the day. Mike

Beedle, whom we tragically lost before his time in March 2018, suggested that the word *agile* more elegantly captured the nature of these frameworks. The rest is history. The *Manifesto for Agile Software Development*[10] was born as a way for small teams to collaborate closely with customers to ensure that the most valuable items were always being worked on, even if what was determined to be valuable evolved over time and the final solution looked very different from what was anticipated at the start. The thinking here was that it is better to zig-zag toward a great solution than to travel directly toward an average, or bad, one. The full manifesto, complete with its 12 principles, can be found at www.agilemanifesto.org.

Agility Wave Two: Scaled Agility

The "scaled agility" movement was a response to the success of the agile movement. Organizations quickly noticed the increased effectiveness and business results of a more adaptive and responsive way of working to deliver software. But as large organizations became interested, the imperative to apply agility beyond just one team quickly became apparent. Some products are just too big and complex to be addressed by one team. Thus, patterns began to emerge around how to apply to teams of teams the values and principles that make single-team endeavors successful. This brought about a whole new set of challenges not seen before. In 2008, the influential book *Scaling Lean and Agile Development*[11] was released, leading to a host of so-called scaling frameworks that provided guidance on how to achieve agility at scale. While passions tend to run high over which approach is superior, I shall avoid that particular debate here and move on to the third act—the one that really excites me. This is the act that takes the concept of agility *far* beyond the realm of software development and IT, and applies it to the organization as a whole.

Agility Wave Three: Business Agility

While the agile movement has offered great value to many organizations, the people working in them, and their customers, its impact has, to this point, been limited. It is with business agility that I believe it will finally realize its potential. This will take the essence of what those 17 pioneers created and bring it out of its software development box and into the boardroom. As we have seen, with the rise of VUCA, making up-front predictions and detailed three-to-five-year plans, as well as focusing all attention on exploiting known products and services, is a risky strategy. The same qualities of responsiveness, experimentation, and relentless customer focus that underpinned the success of agile software development now underpin the success of entire companies. This is business agility, and it is the new competitive advantage.

Reflection

Does your organization seek to apply agile ways of working at any level? If so, is it at the team, program, or organizational level? Is there a need to achieve greater levels of agility?

Business Agility: Cautionary Tales from History

Once upon a time, two-ton wombats trundled across the Australian outback. Around the same time, one could also find mammoths and saber-toothed cats roaming freely across the continents. Before that, enormous dinosaurs were the kings and queens of their various domains. It seems that there is a tendency for successful species to evolve to be larger over time.[12] This should come as no surprise. Being larger allows an animal to cover more ground in order to find resources, catch prey, and overpower predators. All are key to a species' survival.

You might think, then, that species would have continued to grow slowly over time and that the earth would now be populated largely by giant creatures. This is not the case—because there is an opposing force at work, a force that has led to the extinction of many of the largest and most majestic creatures ever to walk the planet. In many cases, the animals that have filled the void they left are only a fraction of their size.

At first glance, this appears to make no sense—until we investigate mass extinctions. There is much hard evidence, in the form of teeth, bones, and other fossils, that for 260 million years dinosaurs ruled the earth. Then, starting around 66 million years ago, not a single trace of them can be found in the earth's layers of rock. It is as though all but the avian dinosaurs just fell off the earth. Along with them went many species of marine and flying reptiles. In total, about three-quarters of life on earth was simply wiped out. The generally accepted theory is that a meteor the size of a mountain struck the earth near the Gulf of Mexico, setting off a disastrous chain of events that led to dinosaurs' extinction. This is known as the Cretaceous-Paleogene extinction event.

The interesting finding is that many small mammals and birds survived this period. It appears that, in nature at least, size matters. While evolution tends to favor *larger* animals, extinction tends to give a break to *smaller* ones. In short, being large makes it easier to survive day to day, but much harder to survive any sort of dramatic change in habitat. Smaller creatures survive through scavenging and an ability to reproduce quickly, while their larger contemporaries struggle with long gestation and weaning periods, small populations, and an inability to adapt quickly. It seems that the very attributes that contribute to larger animals' evolutionary success can also lead to their fragility and ultimate downfall.

Historically, size has also mattered in business. During the twentieth century, economies of scale and efficiencies meant that the markets favored the larger organization. Much like the large predators just mentioned, over time these organizations became steadily larger and more successful—that is, of course, until the landscape changed dramatically. While less dramatic than the Cretaceous-Paleogene extinction event, the twenty-first-century business equivalent is, in its way, equally destructive. Consider the dawn of the mainframe computer, the personal computer, and the internet. Combine those with the dramatic increase in VUCA, and the business landscape looks unrecognizable. The position of large organizations begins to look increasingly precarious. Smaller, more nimble organizations tend to be far more adaptable under such conditions and, in turn, grow to become the new dominant players. They remain there until the business climate shifts again. Then, much like the *Tyrannosaurus rex* 66 million years ago, they find themselves perfectly adapted to an environment that no longer exists, and quickly decline. Thus the pattern repeats itself.

To illustrate the power of business agility, and the perils of a lack thereof, I shall elaborate two well-known examples from history.

Netflix versus Blockbuster

When Reed Hastings returned a copy of *Apollo 13* late to Blockbuster, he was fined $40 in late fees. Motivated partly by frustration at this treatment, Hastings and his colleague Marc Randolph founded Netflix in 1997. Aimed at capturing the small-section DVD rental market of people who wanted to receive and return DVDs via mail rather than through retail stores, Netflix had humble beginnings. It was, in effect, a mail-order company. It launched with 900 titles; by early 2000, this had swelled to 5,200.

Netflix's first innovation centered on its business model. Initially charging 50 cents per DVD rental, Netflix switched to a subscription model, charging $15.95 for up to four movies at a time. In 2000 the price increased to $19.95, and all late fees and return-by dates were removed. At the time, the company's revenues were a little over $1 million annually—but the subscription model would take it to $500 million within five years, and $1 billion in another three.[13]

In that same year, Blockbuster, the market leader in the industry, had revenues of $5 billion, with around $800 million (16 percent) of that coming from late fees.[14] Having been valued at $2.63 billion in an IPO a year earlier,[15] Blockbuster was in a dominant position. In just two years, the new CEO, John Antioco, had reversed a decline and had turned the once-struggling giant around. His strategy was to continue exploiting its business model to reduce costs and increase efficiency in the service of drawing maximum profit out of its customer base.

With that in mind, Hastings suggested that Netflix and Blockbuster join forces. He proposed a plan whereby Netflix would run the online part of the business and the current Blockbuster management team would focus on the stores. In declining this offer, Antioco's dismissive assessment of Netflix's future is probably not something he enjoys pondering: "The dot-com hysteria is completely overblown."[16] It was at that point that the conversation turned to

Blockbuster *acquiring* Netflix. Once the figure of $50 million was lobbed at Antioco, however, the conversation ended. Blockbuster had a successful business model. It didn't see the need to invest in its future or change much.

By 2004, however, Antioco had become convinced that Netflix was indeed a threat. In response, he proposed ending late fees (at a cost to the company of $200 million per year) and investing in Blockbuster's online business (at a cost of $200 million initially). He was finally seeking to balance exploiting the current business model with exploring a new one. Ultimately it was one of his lieutenants, Jim Keyes, who opposed him. It all ended in 2005 when Antioco was removed as Blockbuster's CEO and Keyes took over, reversing the changes Antioco had made to increase profitability. Keyes simply did not see the logic in making an investment of $400 million when Blockbuster's business model was, in his view, robust. In 2008, upon being asked about the biggest threats to Blockbuster, Keyes gave this response: "Neither RedBox nor Netflix are even on the radar screen in terms of competition."[17] Blockbuster would file for bankruptcy just two years later.

Over the next six years, Netflix continued along its subscription-model route and expanded its mail-order DVD rental business. By 2006, it had 6.3 million subscribers, a seven-year compound growth rate of 79 percent, and profits of $80 million. It was helped by incremental improvements to its website, with initiatives such as Cinematch, a ranking algorithm that offered personalized movie suggestions based on viewing history. This all served to provide a superior user experience.

The year 2007 proved to be massive for Netflix. Despite huge growth and a tried-and-tested business model, it did something risky. Over the next few years, it would disrupt itself and cannibalize its own business model.

In a prime display of exploring new opportunities while continuing to pursue growth traditionally, in 2007, Netflix invested $40 million in data centers and in licensing a few titles that customers could stream on demand. More titles soon followed; these were initially included for free with subscriptions, with more expensive subscriptions getting access to more content. Growth surpassed expectations, and the share price rose from $3 in 2007 to $42 in 2011. Then, in a surprise move, it created a two-tier subscription model. One tier was for mail-order DVD rentals, and one, at a much lower price, was for streaming only. By December of that year, however, the market was spooked; Netflix's share price was below $10, and profits were down by 50 percent.

Then an interesting thing happened. The lower streaming price meant that Netflix began to appeal to a wider customer base. This increased subscribers and allowed the company to buy more content, expand globally, and, ultimately, begin to create its own content. At time of writing, Netflix has 158 million paid subscribers across 190 counties. Only 2.73 million subscribe to its legacy DVD rental service.[18] Its share price is trading at $315, giving it a market capitalization of $138 billion.

Had Netflix continued to focus solely on its core business, which was at the time growing quickly and becoming ever more profitable, by now it would probably have disappeared, having been outmaneuvered by the likes of YouTube. Instead, it decided to invest in a model that could totally undermine its own core business model—and thus reinvented the entertainment industry. In 22 years, Netflix has gone from a mail-order DVD company to an online streaming company to creator of original content. It is just this kind of dual focus on *exploiting* and *exploring*, coupled with a willingness to cannibalize one's own products, services, and models, and to respond rapidly to a changing world, that is a hallmark of business agility.

Fujifilm versus Kodak

Kodak was formed in 1888 by George Eastman and Henry Strong in Rochester, New York. A relentless innovator, Kodak was known for its pioneering technology, its first slogan being, "You press the button, we do the rest." Kodak successfully pursued the razor-and-blades strategy, whereby a product (in this case, cameras) is sold relatively cheaply in order to make a large margin from complementary products (in this case, film, chemicals, and paper). Almost immediately, the money began rolling in for Kodak, and it quickly became the market leader in the United States. This dominant position lasted for decades and, in 1976, the company held 90 percent of the market share for film, and 85 percent for cameras.[19]

While Kodak held a near monopoly in the United States, another company was in a similarly privileged position in its native Japan. Founded in 1934 in response to a government plan to establish a domestic photographic film manufacturing industry, Fujifilm quickly developed expertise in a wide range of photography-based fields. It was this technological expertise that allowed Fujifilm to compete with Kodak. Color film is manufactured via a particularly complex process. Willy Shih, a former vice president of Kodak, recalls that film rolls "had to be coated with as many as 24 layers of sophisticated chemicals: photosensitizers, dyes, couplers, and other materials deposited at precise thicknesses while traveling at 300 feet per minute."[20] The required technological sophistication meant that very few outfits were able to master the manufacturing process, and, for decades, the business of color film was dominated by the duopoly of Kodak and Fujifilm.

In a world of high barriers to entry, minimal competition, and high margins, organizations can easily slip deep into pure exploit mode—a mode of unimaginative leadership and complacency, a strategy of seeking to protect one's position by building a moat and retracting the drawbridge. This approach is all well and good while it works, but sooner or later the winds of creative destruction will begin to batter even the most seemingly unassailable castle. This is precisely what happened to this particular duopoly at the dawn of the twenty-first century. The seed, however, had been sown some 25 years earlier by Kodak's very own engineers.

In 1975, a 24-year-old Kodak engineer named Steve Sasson created the world's first digital camera. Weighing in at eight pounds, the camera took 23 seconds to take a 0.01-megapixel, black-and-white image. Sasson's bosses were initially dismissive of the technology, believing that no one would want to view their photographs on a television. They were aware, though, that "filmless photography," as they initially called it, was a threat to the lucrative film and postprocessing business. Keen to avoid cannibalizing a profitable business model, they were slow to pursue the new technology, choosing instead to focus on their core business of analog photography. In fact, as late as 2000, film sales still accounted for 72 percent of Kodak's revenue and 66 percent of its operating income, compared with 60 percent and

66 percent, respectively, for Fujifilm. In 2001, film sales peaked, then quickly began to tail off, leading to 30 percent year-on-year drops in demand. By 2010, worldwide demand was less than 10 percent of what it had been only 10 years earlier.

The photography market had not disappeared; people were still very much taking pictures. It had merely shifted toward digital photography. The issue for Kodak and Fujifilm was that, compared with the complex process of producing color film, it was relatively easy to produce digital cameras and the memory needed to store photographs. The barriers to entry, and thus the moat protecting their fat profit margins, no longer afforded the protection they once did. Kodak's and Fujifilm's core business model had been rendered obsolete, and the business of selling digital cameras did not even come close to making up for it. It was for this reason that, in 2006, Antonio Pérez, then CEO of Kodak, peevishly called digital cameras a "crappy business."[21]

The threat had been looming for 30 years, but now, more than ever, survival was not guaranteed for Kodak and Fujifilm. Could either one adapt quickly enough—or would they both, like so many apex predators before them, go the way of the saber-toothed tiger?

In fact, both companies predicted the rise of digital photography to a certain extent themselves. The issue was how to respond to the threat in a way that would create new revenue streams and business models ahead of the curve. The key to survival would be diversification—to *explore* new ways to leverage their technological expertise to move into new markets with new products and services.

Kodak did make some attempt to reinvent itself as a digital company. As early as the mid-1980s, it increased its R&D budget to 10 percent of sales and quickly began integrating digital features into its product lines in the form of photo enhancement software, video systems, and scanners. By 1996, it had released its first professional-grade point-and-shoot digital camera. By 2005, Kodak was the market leader for digital cameras in its native American market. Despite this, the executives at Kodak just could not imagine a world in which film played no part in photography, and they were concerned about the low profit margins of the new technology. This led them to move too slowly and to continue to focus predominantly on film processing.

During a 1990 meeting with then CEO of Microsoft Bill Gates to discuss closer integration between Kodak products and Windows, Kodak chairman Kay Whitmore managed to fall asleep; he was fired in 1993.[22]

The first decade of the twenty-first century marked a long, painful decline for Kodak, one that saw its once sky-high revenue and profits collapse. It ultimately filed for bankruptcy in 2012.

During this same period, Fujifilm faced the same precipitous drop in demand for its core products and service, color print processing. As late as 2000, it believed that there would be a gentle, 15-to-20-year decline in demand for film, in which time it could continue to milk its cash cow while seeking to innovate and diversify. What it did not count on was volatility being a hallmark of the twenty-first century. Unfortunately for Fujifilm, the market moved far more swiftly than anyone predicted, and, within a decade, film went from accounting for 60 percent of the company's revenue to, effectively, zero. The president of Fujifilm recalls, "What we could not account for in our projections was the speed of the digital onslaught. The photographic film market had shrunk much faster than we expected."[23]

Despite this sharp decline, Fujifilm managed to grow its revenues in that period by 57 percent, while Kodak saw a 48 percent fall.[24] This was quite remarkable, and achieved through diversification. Fujifilm's R&D department spent some 18 months auditing its capabilities and mapping them to new markets. The outcome was that it became clear to leadership that Fujifilm's expertise could be relatively easily adapted to cosmetics, pharmaceuticals, and other types of products. Leveraging its technology, it was able to invest at just the right time in the LCD screen market. Fujifilm engineers were able to create FUJITAC, an advanced approach to creating LCD panels for televisions, computers, and smartphones that lets light from the backlight pass right through the screen. With one of the few films in the world with this capability, Fujifilm's share of the market for LCD polarizer protective films is roughly 70 percent.[25]

The move into cosmetics was a less intuitive one. Ostensibly, film processing and skincare have very little in common. The thing that links the two is collagen. Gelatin, a cooked form of collagen, is the chief ingredient in film. Collagen also happens to make up 70 percent of human skin. Fujifilm had deep expertise in preventing oxidization, the process that leads to both the fading of photos and the aging of skin. In 2007, Fujifilm launched its Astalift line of skincare products. A similar move into the drug and chemical business broke Fujifilm's reliance on its previous revenue sources and allowed its revenues to soar in the face of what could have been a turbulent time. The ability to invest in the search for new products, services, and business models ultimately allowed it to evolve quickly as the world changed around it—something that Kodak, for all its good intentions, was unable to do. As of January 2020, Fujifilm had market capitalization of over $21 billion.

> ### Reflection
>
> What market or technology trends could disrupt your main business model? How quickly could you respond if disruption occurs? What new capabilities might be needed to pursue new products and services?

No Sacred Cows: Disrupting Yourself

A common theme in these stories, and many like them, is the willingness of the most successful and enduring organizations not only to seek out new opportunities but also to disrupt their *own* business models. Cannibalizing one's own sales can be a difficult decision to make, but as Kodak, Blockbuster, and countless others can testify, failing to do so can lead to the downfall of once-great businesses. Apple cofounder Steve Jobs puts it like this: "If you don't cannibalize yourself, someone else will."[26]

Jobs got the opportunity to practice what he preached in 2007. When Apple launched the iPhone, Jobs knew full well that it was likely to kill the iPod. This was a gutsy move given that in the previous year, the iPod had accounted for 50 percent of Apple's revenues. In 2014, the iPod Classic was discontinued, and Apple stood tall as the most valuable company on the planet by market capitalization. Apple had stayed ahead of the curve by evolving before it even needed to. Its competitors were left struggling to respond.

Reflection

Would your organization be prepared to cannibalize its key products and services in pursuit of new ones? What are the risks of not doing so?

Chapter Summary

- With traditional business practices so deeply entrenched in business, many modern approaches have, until now, not been taken seriously, particularly when they emerge on the fringes.

- While the agile movement began as an effective approach to building software with single teams, the values and principles behind it have evolved to be applicable to entire organizations.

- Business agility, as a means for organizations to innovate, and to adapt quickly in an increasingly fast-moving world, has become the new competitive advantage.

Further Reading and Resources

Books

- Steven Denning, *The Age of Agile: How Smart Companies Are Transforming the Way Work Gets Done* (New York: AMACOM / American Management Association, 2018)

- Darrell Rigby, Sarah Elk, and Steve Berez, *Doing Agile Right: Transformation without Chaos* (Boston: Harvard Business Review Press, 2020)

Websites, Articles, and Videos

- Please see www.6enablers.com/resources for more on this topic, including a downloadable reading list.

CHAPTER 3

The 6 Enablers of Business Agility

I found that the key was agility, agility, agility. We needed to develop speed, nimbleness and athleticism to get the consumer experience right.

—SATYA NADELLA, CEO, MICROSOFT

IN THIS CHAPTER, WE WILL EXPLORE

- why so many attempted agile transformations fail
- why it's necessary to focus on the whole organization when seeking greater agility
- the 6 Enablers of Business Agility model and how each enabler contributes to improved business outcomes.

Why Agility Initiatives Fail: A Narrow Focus

Most large-scale change initiatives fail. In fact, research undertaken by global strategy consultancy McKinsey shows that 70 percent of change initiatives fail to achieve their stated goals.[1] There are many reasons for this that I will discuss in chapter 10. Having been involved with change initiatives employing agility for over a decade, I have seen varying degrees of success and, indeed, failure. My instinct tells me that the failure rate for agility-based change initiatives is higher than 70 percent. As well as the usual reasons change initiatives fail, I believe there is one that is specific to these kinds of changes—something that is continually missed by those leading the change. Something that, in my years working with organizations, has become all too apparent. It is a matter of scope and focus.

To illustrate the point, let's head to the Melanesian islands in the southwestern Pacific during World War II. These islands had been cut off from the Western world, with the indigenous populations having never seen foreigners, never mind manufactured goods. As the Pacific became a major theater in the war between the Allies and the empire of Japan, these islanders' lives would be changed forever. Thousands of troops began landing on the islands—first the Japanese and, later, Allied forces. Large quantities of supplies were brought to the island. Tents, clothing, weapons, medicine, and canned food were all delivered via airdrops and airlifted in via airstrips. The deliveries came in such quantities that the troops often ended up sharing them with the locals who tended to act as their guides.

Over the course of the war, the islanders came to rely on this cargo, which changed their lifestyles for the better. When the war came to a sudden end in 1945, the flow of material goods into the islands abruptly ended. With airbases abandoned and no more cargo being delivered, cults began to form around charismatic individuals known in Melanesia as "big men." These "cargo cults" sought to encourage the delivery of Western cargo, which, during the war, had so enriched their lives. They did this by ritualistically imitating the behavior of foreign servicemen in the hope that the cargo would return. The cargo cult followers cleared often valuable arable land to create makeshift landing strips. They constructed wooden control towers, carved headphones out of wood and coconuts, and even fashioned full-size replicas of planes out of straw. Cult devotees would then man these religious structures and even light fires, spending hours directing the nonexistent air traffic. In short, they reproduced the actions they had witnessed the American troops performing during the war—actions that they incorrectly believed were responsible for the deliveries. They were not, of course, privy to the bigger picture.

This form of sympathetic magic often involves imitating the actions of others in order to bring about desired results—in this case, the delivery of mass-produced Western goods. Rather predictably, the actions of the islanders did not result in the appearance of cargo.

It is not a huge leap to see how this is relevant to business change. Across the globe, I see the same thing happening with "agile transformation" initiatives. There is a growing trend for organizations to try to become more agile without achieving much actual agility. The focus in such cases is mainly on implementing many of the practices associated with the agile movement, practices an organization's leaders may have seen in more nimble, innovative outfits. These leaders may even support some of those practices with some training. There is then an expectation that these team-level work practices will be sufficient to bring about the desired results. After all, they seemed to be doing so at that more innovative, nimble start-up.

This is a prime example of the logical fallacy *post hoc, ergo propter hoc* (after this, therefore because of this). This is, for example, what happens when bad luck is encountered after one walks under a ladder and the observer falsely concludes that the bad luck was *caused* by walking under the ladder. In fact, the misfortune merely occurred after that particular event, and there is no causal link whatsoever between the two. Similarly, the results at that enviable start-up had little to do with team-level practices and a lot to do with a variety of other things. When, inevitably, a nonagile organization does not see the benefits of adopting such practices, there is a feeling of disillusionment around the concept of agility itself. There are murmurs of, "We tried agility; it doesn't really work here." Very soon the transformation runs out of steam. But is it really the case that agility, however the term is being used, doesn't work there—or are they, like the islanders of Melanesia, simply not seeing the bigger picture?

Having been involved with myriad agile transformations over the past few years, I have found that the reasons for the failure have become increasingly evident. Coaches and consultants are focusing narrowly on one small piece of the puzzle—work practices—while often unwittingly ignoring many vital areas of the business that are either key enablers of or impediments to success. If these areas are not brought into sharp focus, the chances of significant improvement are virtually nil.

For example, picture a good, solid, reliable family SUV. It's comfortable and has great safety features and plenty of space. This vehicle is designed for the needs of family life and serves that purpose admirably. Now imagine you have signed up for a road race through the Stelvio Pass in the Alps of northern Italy, near the border with

Switzerland. This legendary mountain pass sits 9,045 feet above sea level and contains 60 hairpin turns. It is frequently ranked as the ultimate test of both driver and machine. Would it make sense to take the SUV on that race? I rather suspect you are picturing something a little sportier, and probably red. Because, in fact, it would be sheer folly to attempt that drive in an SUV. Even if superficial changes, like putting on new tires and adjusting your driving technique, were employed, the vehicle is just not designed to give you the necessary results, and it therefore will never do so. To compete seriously here, one needs something designed, from the ground up, for that environment. Only when the design is fundamentally rethought will you be likely to get the performance you really desire. And some stunning views to boot.

This tinkering-at-the-edges approach is, unfortunately, how many organizations approach initiatives to increase agility. They imitate successful organizations in ways that are largely superficial and non-disruptive, all the while eschewing the bigger, more fundamental changes that actually lead to great results. This is known as *doing* agile rather than *being* agile. The former is shallow and focused on practice; the latter is profound and focused on values and principles.

Just as with the cargo cults, practices alone do not lead to success. For that, the root causes of an organization's problems must be addressed.

Reflection

Is your transformation focusing principally on work practices? If so, what areas of the organization could be preventing greater success?

Introducing the 6 Enablers of Business Agility: Taking a Holistic Approach

Why didn't an established digital photography company create Instagram? Why didn't an established taxi company create Uber? Why didn't an established music company create iTunes? It's not that the people in these organizations don't have great ideas. They do. I would argue that it is because these organizations are not *designed* to create new and exciting innovations, even when the ideas are there. Their finance departments are not set up to invest in initiatives with high uncertainty and a questionable return on investment. Their leadership and cultures are such that they are unlikely to view failure as a necessary stepping-stone to success. These organizations tend to be designed around functional silos set up for exploit-type activities. They are built to execute with efficiency, not to explore with agility, with all the messy collaboration and uncertainty the latter implies. As such, they find it extremely difficult to create new things, and no amount of tinkering around the edges will change that.

Over a decade ago, I began coaching teams that developed software products. It was a great role, and it was immensely satisfying to help teams improve their effectiveness, create better products, and operate with increased agility with a view to responding more quickly to constantly changing customer needs.

As the years rolled on, however, I became increasingly frustrated. I found that during the frequent reflections on how to be more effective in the future—a common agile practice—the areas identified as needing improvement were increasingly beyond our control. The obstacles to becoming a more effective team no longer resided at the team level. We had bumped up against what I call *organizational impediments*—the structural challenges that prevent teams from being more effective and agile. Continuing to optimize at the team level was now akin to tuning the engine of our little red sports car in the hope that it would go faster while sitting in a traffic jam, unable to move. In such an instance, making the *car itself* faster doesn't help, because the car is not the limiting factor. In order to make the car travel faster, the things in its way need to be removed. This would allow the already fast car to travel faster.

An example of the kind of *organizational impediments* teams encounter is team structures. This means not being able to form truly cross-functional teams because of an inability to break down organizational silos. This leads to an absence of key skills on the team and very little collaboration across functions. And that is a recipe for slowing everything down. Another impediment is the inability to respond to in-flight feedback from customers because the scope has been signed off up front and cannot be changed. The governance process thus does not allow the kind of course-correcting actions required when one operates in a high-uncertainty environment and receives ongoing feedback. Challenges like these tend to take a long time to resolve, and resolution is almost always driven from the top.

Having spent time advising organizations on how to work and innovate more effectively, I have been in a position to observe exactly what it takes to make a great team and to create great products that delight customers. As I began to transition away from hands-on team-level coaching toward working with leadership on larger-scale agile transformations, I began to think about all of the areas an organization would need to address to achieve true agility. All the areas that need to be invited into the change process. All the areas that have hamstrung organizations with which I've worked over the years through adherence to twentieth-century thinking.

It turns out that achieving true business agility has an impact on almost all parts of an organization. Yet many who embark on an agile transformation have little appreciation for the sheer reach the effort must have in order to succeed. Confining the changes to one department, often IT, will certainly not yield much benefit at all. If I achieve nothing else with this book, I hope to give people an insight into the areas of their organizations that will have to undergo significant change to enable greater agility. I hope this book will help leaders to go into these endeavors with their eyes open, truly aware of all the changes that will be necessary.

The question I wrestled with for some time is how to group these areas together in a coherent way that makes clear the scale of the challenge but also provides a structure within which to work. The groupings I outline here were not dreamed up in a lab. This has not been an academic exercise. What I have listed here is the result of dozens of iterations, years of experimentation, continuous feedback, and much adaptation. This model was developed in the trenches, and it has proved invaluable to countless entities. It covers all of the main areas that need to be addressed in order to make great progress toward business agility. While others may, and do, slice and dice

FIGURE 5

The 6 Enablers of Business Agility

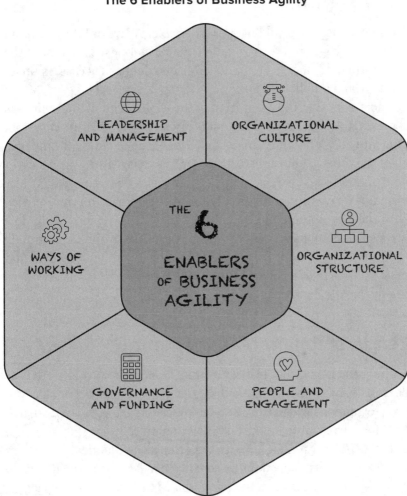

FIGURE 5

The 6 Enablers of Business Agility

things a little differently, I choose to group the enablers as follows (figure 5):

- Leadership and Management
- Organizational Culture
- Organizational Structure
- People and Engagement

■ Governance and Funding

■ Ways of Working

In my experience, all but the last enabler, Ways of Working, tend to be largely ignored during agile transformations. This is why the transformation success rate, however one defines success, is unacceptably and stubbornly low.

I do accept that the separation of the enablers along these lines is somewhat arbitrary. One cannot address any enabler in isolation. They are all highly interconnected, and each enabler will influence all of the others. I have made these divisions largely to raise awareness of the things that should be on the radar when leading a transformation. I do this to ensure organizations embark on this journey with their eyes open and do not seek to achieve results in shallow ways such as by merely imitating the practices of the latest trendy start-up. I also accept that there are many key mindset shifts that must precede making changes in each of the 6 Enablers. For now, let's briefly explore each enabler.

Leadership and Management

I often hear it said that leaders should support or "buy into" the agile transformation initiative. I disagree. I have been part of plenty of transformations where the most-senior leaders buy into the change—and that turns out to be the last involvement they have. Buying into a change is rarely enough. In my experience, a great deal more than words of support is needed. The change needs to be *actively driven* by leadership. The leaders themselves need to go through deep learning and growth in their roles. They need to transform the way in which they lead, and learn new cognitive and emotional capacities to foster a whole different set of behaviors across their organization (or department). *It all starts with leadership.*

There are many ways in which leadership and management of a truly agile organization are virtually unrecognizable when compared with the traditional versions of those roles. Vital shifts include those from directive to supportive leadership, from centralized to decentralized decision-making, and from focusing on the work to focusing on direction and creating an environment for success. This is done not just through words but also through new behaviors, structures, and policies that encourage the changes to happen. These kinds of changes just cannot be driven from the bottom up. *Leadership and Management* will be explored in greater detail in chapter 4.

Organizational Culture

In the *13th Annual State of Agile Report* (2019), the number one challenge in adopting and scaling agility was once again cited as "organizational culture at odds with Agile values." This was the top pick of 52 percent of respondents.[2] Culture mismatches consistently appear as the *number one* inhibitor of increased agility. Many will talk of the importance of addressing an organization's culture, but few will have a structured approach to assessing and shifting that culture. The first step is to understand the current and the desired culture of an organization. There are many frameworks for assessing this, and we will explore a few of them later in this book. Once this step is complete, the desired culture will be revealed to be either well aligned or in conflict with the achievement of greater levels of agility. If the desired culture is in conflict, then I would question whether the push for transformation should go ahead; leadership obviously values different things and should perhaps not attempt greater agility. This can prevent the waste of a lot of time, money, and effort. In such a case, it may be wiser simply to help people improve within the parameters of their values, whatever those may be.

If it is decided that the culture does indeed need to be shifted, this must be carefully planned. One does not change a culture simply by *trying* to change it. Culture is a product of the behaviors, values, and beliefs of the people involved in an organization or department. Cultures can only be shifted by changing behaviors. These new behaviors must be supported by new policies, metrics, structures, and leadership styles. Only then will the culture shift. This is a key enabler of agility, and it must not be ignored. *Organizational Culture* will be explored in greater detail in chapter 5.

The culture of an organization is akin to a shadow on a wall. It cannot be changed directly. To change a shadow, it is the item causing it, or the light source, that must be changed. Similarly, culture is itself a product of the other five enablers. The current and desired culture will, however, greatly influence the changes that are made in the other areas. For this reason, it must remain a key enabler of agility.

Organizational Structure

Few things affect an entity's agility like the organizational structure. Picture yourself on an oil tanker. You may be able to travel fast, but there is very little you can do to change direction quickly. Try as you might, the ship is designed, from the ground up, for something else. Now imagine yourself as part of a flotilla of speedboats. It's now much easier to change direction—much easier to respond to changes, much easier to be agile. It's less about what *you* are doing and more about the *system* in which you are operating.

Organizations are the same. The design of organizational systems tends to have a disproportionate effect on how those systems perform—far greater than do the people working within them. The types of organizational design changes that tend to increase agility are things like shifting from functional silos (such as finance, marketing, and engineering) to collaborative, cross-functional teams with vastly reduced handoffs. Others include a shift from traditional hierarchies, which are often slow to respond, to networks of interconnected teams responding to constantly changing events on the ground. Value creators must be brought closer to customers and business stakeholders to allow for greater collaboration.

Leaders must decide which characteristics they wish to see exhibited by the value-delivery system and (re)design it with those in mind. Organizational design and structural changes can be difficult, disruptive, and, for some, unnerving. On the other hand, they are often disproportionately significant in the pursuit of the desired outcome. Given that leadership can change organizational design directly in a way that it cannot do with organizational culture, and that organizational design changes are so important, this remains one of the most powerful instruments in the toolbox of greater agility. *Organizational Structure* will be explored in greater detail in chapter 6.

People and Engagement

In modern business, the rules of the game have changed. There is no longer any doubt about the link between employee engagement and business results. Whichever data you look at, the results are the same: companies with engaged employees significantly outperform their competition.[3]

Many organizations still use Industrial Revolution–era management approaches—approaches that manage for compliance and conformity. Instead of managing for these things, however, the most effective entities manage for initiative, passion, and creativity. This helps them attract and retain the most effective employees and will bestow a huge competitive advantage in today's complex knowledge economy.

Is it any wonder that in the 2017 *State of the Global Workplace Report*[4] by Gallup, only 15 percent of people polled indicated that they were "engaged" in their jobs? Organizations are wasting human potential and are not getting the best out of their people. This is bad for people—and bad for business.

To create high-performing, adaptive organizations, actively managing for engagement is a must. This involves reinventing many outdated HR policies for the twenty-first-century knowledge worker. *People and Engagement* will be explored in greater detail in chapter 7.

Governance and Funding

A question I hear all the time is this: "How can we be agile when we need to sign off the scope, cost, and timelines up front, and those things cannot be changed without revisiting the business case?" The answer, of course, is that you can't. This is akin to asking how one can respond to change while simultaneously *not* responding to change. It makes no sense.

I'm sorry. I don't like giving that message. But to give a different one would be disingenuous. A waterfall-based governance model that insists on big up-front analysis and design, the creation of detailed business cases, strict change control, and the funding of large batches is not a model designed for agility. Quite the opposite, in fact—it is designed for rigidity and predictability. It makes a whole load of assumptions that do not tend to hold water in the face of complex developments—assumptions like, "We can know what to build in advance," "Things won't change much as we progress," and "It's safe to place big bets and validate our assumptions once the money is spent." This is fundamentally incompatible with agility. It is also not how you build great products in such a complex, fast-changing space.

Changing how money is invested from predicting and planning to experimenting and adapting is a huge mindset shift. Placing many small bets and course-correcting based on feedback is the least risky way to proceed, but organizations need to be set up for that. Most are not. Transitioning from investing in large projects to investing in long-lived products and taking a venture capitalist approach to allocating funds will unlock true agility. Movements like Beyond Budgeting can also be a huge help. Bringing in finance, risk, compliance, project management, and other governance functions to shift to an approach that enables greater agility is a long and difficult process. Many have ignored it and have failed to become agile. Many have done it and are reaping the benefits. As ever, when it comes down to it, you just need to follow the money. *Governance and Funding* will be explored in greater detail in chapter 8.

Ways of Working

Ways of working is the enabler on which most organizations place the majority of their focus. Whether it is implementing formal agile frameworks or improving engineering practices, this tends to be the starting point for most seeking increased levels of agility. People spend a lot of time arguing over which frameworks or practices are "good" and which are "bad." The fact is that focusing purely on ways of working without addressing the other five agility enablers will all but guarantee that "agility doesn't work here." In short, it doesn't matter which approach you use; if you focus only on this element, you will fail. The reason you will fail is that the organizational and leadership changes needed to create an environment of success, the organizational operating system, will not have been made. This is akin to trying to grow a beautiful rose in a desert. It just will not, and cannot, thrive until the conditions are right.

The various frameworks available can be very valuable when applied in the right context. Your organization's culture will lend itself to a certain approach. Any "coach" or consultant who advises that you start with a particular framework without understanding your workplace's context, culture, desired outcome, and attitude to change is someone who probably doesn't have the experience to advise you on your transformation. I see this all too often, and it is a failure of our industry. Processes, practices, and frameworks are important, but they will not achieve results in isolation. *Ways of Working* will be explored in greater detail in chapter 9.

Putting It All Together

There are many models out there that seek to address similar issues to those covered in this book. One I particularly like and with which I feel highly aligned is from the Corporate Rebels.[5] After traveling the world and meeting with the most progressive leaders and organizations on the planet, they identified eight habits[6] that seem to be a common thread among the most effective organizations. The eight habits are the following:

- from profit to purpose and values[7]
- from hierarchical pyramids to a network of teams
- from directive leadership to supportive leadership
- from predict and plan to experiment and adapt
- from rules and control to freedom and trust
- from centralized authority to distributed authority
- from secrecy to radical transparency
- from job descriptions to talents and mastery

Each of these areas, along with accompanying patterns, will be covered as we progress through the 6 Enablers.

Helping to cultivate high-performing, agile organizations that are also engaging workplaces and a delight to customers is what gets me up each morning. It is only right that we seek to educate leaders to understand the business benefits of increased agility and employee engagement while making clear the scale of the challenge involved in achieving it. It is not merely a case of teams changing their ways of working, like a car switching out one of its tires. That is a small piece of the puzzle. There are big organizational changes involved in creating the organizational operating system in which teams can be successful in the high-VUCA world of the twenty-first century. To bring together and visualize these changes, I will introduce the *Business Agility Canvas* in chapter 10. The canvas will ensure clarity and alignment about the *why*, *what*, and *how* of the transformation. The journey will be long, hard, and disruptive, but the rewards for making it are substantial. I'd go as far as to say that the long-term survival of many organizations depends on it. To increase your chance of success, broaden your focus from processes and practices to include the whole picture. Create a holistic approach to growing your organizational capability, and see how much more effective you can be.

Reflection

Are all six enablers contributing to your organization's achieving greater agility? If not, which need more focus?

Chapter Summary

- Many agile transformations focus narrowly on Ways of Working while ignoring the other five agility enablers.

- The other areas on which to focus are Leadership and Management, Organizational Culture, Organizational Structure, People and Engagement, and Governance and Funding. These form the underlying organizational operating system on which work practices are built.

- Only when all six enablers are addressed holistically and in a coherent and coordinated way will organizations have a real chance to increase their agility.

Further Reading and Resources

Books

- Joost Minnaar and Pim de Morree, *Corporate Rebels: Make Work More Fun* (Amsterdam: Business Contact, 2020)

Websites, Articles, and Videos

- Please see www.6enablers.com/resources for more on this topic, including a downloadable reading list.

CHAPTER 4

Leadership and Management

Right now, your company has twenty-first-century, Internet-enabled business processes, mid-twentieth-century management processes, all built atop nineteenth-century management principles.

—GARY HAMEL

IN THIS CHAPTER, WE WILL EXPLORE

- the circumstances in which management emerged, and the problems it sought to solve
- the mindsets of the early management pioneers
- why traditional management approaches have become ineffective in many contexts
- some modern approaches to managing effectively in high-VUCA environments.

The Birth of Management: The Emerging Imperative

At the top of my road in suburban North London lies a traditional village green. The green dates back over 250 years to when the area was largely rural. Although now around half its original size, the green remains in use to this day and gives the area the feel of a village, which belies its location within a city of almost 9 million people. Rather pleasingly, a cattle trough still stands at one end, although today it houses flowers rather than the cattle feed it once held. During a recent game of hide-and-seek on the green with my two daughters,

I found myself hiding in a structure that I had barely noticed before, never mind questioned, despite the fact that I have lived in the area for some years. The structure was a red box with a single door. Inside, there was barely enough space for one person. Affixed to one of the inner walls of the red box was a smaller, black box with a long cord attached to it. Once my daughters found me, the conversation quickly turned to what on earth I was hiding in. It was, of course, an old-fashioned public telephone box. The model, designed in 1924, is a British design icon and, although increasingly rare, it is instantly recognizable around the world. After I explained what the phone box was, my elder daughter asked why people couldn't just "use the phone in their pocket." A reasonable question for a seven-year-old who has never known a world without mobile phones. Explaining a world in which people were not in easy and continual contact seemed to leave both my daughters rather befuddled.

My girls just could not imagine a world in which mobile phones did not exist. Likewise, most people struggle to imagine a world in which *management* did not exist. It feels as if it has always been there—an omnipresent force that few notice and even fewer think to question. The idea of a time when it was not there is an alien concept. Yet there *was* a time before management, a time when there was no need for formal processes and large-scale planning and coordination. While some forms of management are as old as *Homo sapiens* itself, what we know as management is a relatively new concept. Before we can begin to envisage the future of management, we must first understand its past.

In 1890, the average American company had four employees.[1] The country's economy was largely agricultural. Outside of a handful of organizations like the church and the military, there was little need for formal management. Skilled and unskilled workers alike had a good idea of what needed to be done in their jobs, and just got on with it. The limited planning, coordination, and direction required were informal, and mostly performed by more experienced workers alongside their usual work.

Few could have imagined how things would change over the course of the next three decades, a period that marks the latter part of the Second Industrial Revolution. The end of the nineteenth century saw rapid technological advances that included the dawn of the internal combustion engine, energy sources such as electricity, and communications such as the telephone. Aided by these advances, captains of industry such as Henry Ford (automobiles), John D. Rockefeller (oil), Cornelius Vanderbilt (steamships and railroads), James Duke (tobacco), and Andrew Carnegie (steel), among others, were able to build giant organizations. This culminated, after a merger in 1901, in US Steel becoming the first billion-dollar company ($43 billion at 2001 prices).[2] As the size of organizations grew dramatically, so too did the need for more formal methods of organizing large groups of people. During these three decades, management as a formal discipline, and the concept of managers—those whose job was purely to manage—would be defined, and would transform productivity across both industries and continents.

While there are many definitions, in this book I use the term *leadership* to refer primarily to an organizationally focused activity concerned with cultivating vision, values, culture, and structures, as well as setting direction. I use the term *management* to mean ensuring that work gets done in the right way and within set rules. In short, leadership is about strategy and culture, while management is largely about execution.

Early Management: Back to the Pioneers

To understand early management theories, it is important to understand those who shaped them. We will now explore three key contributors to the field and their associated approaches to management. It is important to consider their theories in the context of the work being done at the time.

Frederick Winslow Taylor: Scientific Management
Born in 1856 in Philadelphia, Taylor had a privileged upbringing. The son of a Princeton-educated lawyer, he attended the exclusive Phillips Exeter School, where his intellectual prowess and strong work ethic saw him lead his class. In 1874, he comfortably passed the

Harvard entrance exam, and intended to follow in his father's foot-steps and study law. Unfortunately, Taylor's intensive study habits had caused his eyesight to deteriorate quickly. This led to a career pivot in which he declined his place at Harvard and took up an apprenticeship as a patternmaker and machinist at a small manufacturing company in Philadelphia called Enterprise Hydraulic Works. Taylor fell in love with the factory environment and gained precious shop-floor experience. He called this time "the most valuable part of my education."[3]

Upon finishing his apprenticeship in 1878, Taylor took up a job as a machine-shop laborer at Midvale Steel Works. He did not remain at that level for long, however. He was quickly promoted through the ranks, moving through shop clerk, machinist, gang boss, foreman, maintenance foreman, and head of the drawing office, until he was ultimately appointed chief engineer.[4] In 1883, having pursued his studies at night, Taylor received his degree in mechanical engineering from Stevens Institute of Technology.

At the time Taylor was put in charge of the factory floor, managers had little to do with shop-floor workers and the work was rarely standardized. Technological advances had led to the use of highly sophisticated machines able to operate with scientific precision, but the processes and means by which workers were operating them were anything but scientifically rigorous. In fact, there was little thought given to it at all. Taylor noticed that, left largely to get on with it in whichever way he saw fit, each worker carried out his work in different ways—some more efficiently and some less so—and thus output varied wildly. He also believed that employees were engaging in what he called "soldiering," the act of giving less than one's full effort to the job. This only exacerbated variations in output. He stated, "The natural laziness of men is serious, but by far the greatest evil from which both workmen and employers are suffering is the systematic soldiering which is almost universal under all of the ordinary schemes of management."[5]

While much thought was going into creating ever more advanced machines, almost none was directed at increasing *productivity*, a word that was not yet in common use. The study of how people worked had not kept pace with the study of the technology with which they worked. Hence, Taylor believed, productivity was far lower than it should have been, and labor costs were therefore far higher. It seems hard to believe, with all the tools, techniques, and management consultancies available today, that so little attention was given to how work was performed. Taylor made it his mission to address this productivity gap through a rigorous study of work. As a mechanical engineer, he wanted to get scientific about it. At the time, this was pretty radical. Instead of seeking to *make* workers go faster, he would *show them how to* do so. In the words of management guru Peter Drucker, "Frederick W. Taylor was the first man in recorded history who deemed work deserving of systematic observation and study."[6]

Thus began Taylor's pursuit of efficiency and productivity. He believed that, for every task, there must be "one best way" to perform it, a way that would be faster and more efficient than all other ways. He studied each task in detail. Relying on the reductionist approach of an engineer, he broke each task down into its constituent steps. Armed with a stopwatch and notepad, he experimented with many ways of performing each task, an assistant noting down the time taken for each variant. He shaved seconds off each step and, upon putting them all back together, had achieved dramatically increased efficiency. Once this work was documented on instruction cards in simple steps, workers simply had to follow those steps. They were then expected to meet strict output guidelines. Taylor called this approach "scientific management." Gone were the rules of thumb that for centuries had been left to workers' judgment. In their place were prescription and measurement.

In many ways, this was a dehumanizing approach, turning proud workers into mere cogs in a machine. But this machine was efficient and productive. Thus, despite resistance from the shop floor, the march to productivity was inevitable. Taylor's scientific management was based on four key principles:

■ Use methods based on a rigorous, scientific study of the work rather than the old rules-of-thumb methods.

■ Actively select, train, and develop workers for tasks rather than letting them train themselves.

- ■ Provide detailed instructions on how to undertake each task and supervise workers' performance closely, rather than leaving workers to find their way.

- ■ Separate the work such that managers perform the thinking and planning, while workers perform the task itself.

Having helped Midvale Steel Works become an industry leader, in 1890 Taylor began applying scientific management across many other industries. After helping to reduce the cost of overhauling boilers from $62 to $11 at Midvale, he went on to help decrease the number of workers required at a pig iron plant from 600 to 140 and reduce labor costs from $30 per ton to $8 per ton at a paper mill, among many other examples of efficiency and productivity gains.[7] Workers resented his methods as much as factory owners loved them. The workers' attempts to strike, however, were futile. Taylor merely replaced the more experienced workers with cheaper, less skilled ones; after all, all they had to do was follow the prescribed steps to get the same results. Workers had become fungible "resources" who could be swapped out at will by managers.

Taylor saw it as the job of a manager to find the "one best way," document it in detail as a series of simple steps, and ensure that workers followed those steps to the letter—with the ultimate goal of squeezing the most out of each worker. Thus the concept of *best practice* was born. This marked the beginning of the separation of managers and workers. Taylor stated, "There is no question that the cost of production is lowered by separating the work of planning and the brain work as much as possible from the manual labor,"[8] telling workers, "I have you for your strength and mechanical ability. We have other men paid for thinking." In 1911, Taylor published his work in the landmark book *The Principles of Scientific Management*. More than anyone else in history, Taylor revolutionized the world of work. The principles underpinning his work can still be found today in almost every large organization on the planet. He legitimized management as a discipline and drew a hard line between managers and workers, between rule-makers and rule-followers, between thinkers and doers. That is a line that only now, 110 years later, is beginning to blur.

Max Weber: Bureaucratic Management

While much of Taylor's work was concerned with individual tasks and how workers could perform them with maximum efficiency, others were, around the same time, concerning themselves with entire organizational systems—systems such as business and government departments and how to manage them effectively. One of the most influential of these thinkers was Max Weber. Born in 1864 in the province of Saxony in the Kingdom of Prussia—modern-day Germany—Weber grew up at a time when industrialization was effecting great change in both business and society. The son of a prominent and wealthy civil servant, Weber and his family were immersed in both politics and academia. Weber was a bright child who excelled at school. He went on to study law at the universities of both Heidelberg and Berlin before working as an academic in the fields of sociology and economics.

Weber visited the United States in 1904 in order to study its economy, and capitalism more broadly. He was struck by how much more competition and innovation were encouraged there than in his homeland. He was deeply concerned that, in Germany, authority was based on connections and social standing rather than knowledge and experience. He believed that organizations would be more efficient if they were based on "rational authority"—that is, if authority was given to the most competent. He called such "rational" organizations *bureaucracies*. In fact the word *bureaucracy* is a pairing of the French word *bureau*, meaning "desk," and the Greek word *kratia*, meaning "power"—that is, ruling from a desk.

Weber documented six characteristics of a bureaucracy:

- *Hierarchy*: Managers are organized into layers. Each layer controls the layer below and is, in turn, controlled by the layer above.
- *Specialization*: Tasks are divided into simple categories based on specialization. Workers focus only on their narrow area, and there are clear roles and responsibilities.
- *Formal selection*: Workers are selected and promoted based purely on their technical skills and competence.

- *Rules and regulations*: Managers set formal rules and workers stay within these rules. This ensures uniformity and predictability.

- *Impersonality*: There is no special treatment. Rules apply equally to all workers.

- *Career orientation*: Workers are protected from arbitrary dismissal, and management and ownership of the organization are separate from each other.

As was the case with Taylor's work, Weber's ethos spread quickly through all types of businesses and remains, to this day, recognizable in the way in which most are run.

Henri Fayol: Administrative Management

Like Weber, Henri Fayol was interested not just in tasks but in how to manage entire entities. Born to a French family in Constantinople (now Istanbul) in 1841, Fayol's father was an engineer in the French military. The family moved back to France in 1847, at a time when France was undergoing many of the social and industrial changes observed by Weber, and Fayol attended the mining academy École Nationale Supérieure des Mines in Saint-Étienne, graduating in 1860. He began his career, aged 19, at a mining company. He swiftly rose through the ranks to become its managing director, in charge of over 1,000 people. The story goes that Fayol came to a key insight after a horse broke its leg in a mine. Fayol wrote a voucher ordering the replacement of the horse, but the stablemaster point-blank refused the voucher, as it had not been signed by the company's director, who was absent. The refusal led to the shutdown of the mine, and a day's production was lost.[9] Fayol viewed this as a failure of management to plan and organize the work properly, and began to think about improved ways in which to manage.

Today, Fayol is best known as a management theorist and important contributor to the field of management. Like Taylor, Fayol believed that managerial practices were key to predictability and efficiency in organizations, and he spent much of the early part of the twentieth century studying such practices. Building on Taylor's work, in 1916 Fayol published a summary of his theories of administrative management in the book *Administration industrielle et générale,* which was translated into English in 1929 as *General and Industrial Management.* Fayol defined five functions of management:

- *Planning*: Looking into the future to understand objectives, goals, and forecasts, and creating a structured plan of action to achieve them
- *Organizing*: Creating the structures for people, arranging for materials and tools to be in place, and bringing things together to execute the plan
- *Commanding*: Providing direction to workers so that they know what to do
- *Controlling*: Tracking, measuring, keeping things on track, reducing deviations, and making improvements
- *Coordinating*: Ensuring all divisions and departments work together to achieve the plan

These functions were supported by 14 principles, which included division of work. This led to increased specialization, and to centralization, which places power with top-level management. As with Taylorism, Fayol's work and its principles are visible in many businesses today.

Over the remainder of the twentieth century, the principles defined by these three men, and many other management pioneers, would provide the foundations on which the dominant paradigm in the field would be built. This paradigm held that it is the job of management to extract the maximum output for the least input of time, energy, and money. It was a paradigm of hierarchy, of rules, of specialization, of managers thinking and planning while workers merely perform tasks, a paradigm so widely applied and so rarely questioned that almost all of the techniques we have explored here can be found, in one way or another, in organizations across the world today. While advances in management during these early years brought huge benefits and contributed to record productivity growth, for many years now, they have been holding organizations back.

Reflection

Are there examples in your organization of authority being concentrated in the hands of a few leaders and managers? Are there instances where that has proved problematic?

Reinventing Management: What Worked Before. . . .

Over the course of my career, I have worked with dozens of organizations. I have been on both sides of a traditional management structure and at various levels of the hierarchy, from worker to executive. Almost all of those places were run using a combination of scientific, bureaucratic, and administrative management principles. They almost all strove to maximize efficiency, productivity, and predictability through some sort of standardization and prescription.

Such things are great when both your output and your process are known in advance and are unlikely to change—when your biggest problem is producing a known output for the minimum possible input of time and cost. They're great when "the machine" is merely complicated (rather than complex) and can be understood simply by breaking it down into its constituent parts and analyzing each in isolation. That is why these techniques worked so well during the Second Industrial Revolution, from the mid-nineteenth to the early twentieth century, when Taylor, Weber, and Fayol were most active in creating their theories and principles. Because the work being done at that time was largely predictable, stable, and easily understood, VUCA was low, competition was even lower, and innovation was not the goal. The problem these management pioneers were seeking to solve was how to get large numbers of people to turn up, carry out their simple tasks as per detailed instructions, and stay within the rules. They were masters of *exploiting* their existing products and services. Thus, large parts of management became about compliance with rules and processes. But we mistake, at our peril, an approach that works well in a given context with one that works well univer-

sally. These techniques continue to work well only if the context remains unchanged.

Abraham Maslow once famously said, "I suppose it is tempting, if
the only tool you have is a hammer, to treat everything as if it were a
nail."[10] Since the early days of the management innovators, precious
little progress has been made. Most traditional organizations approach management in largely the same way they did 100 years ago.
Managers are equipped with a set of tools and techniques, and these
get applied to almost all contexts, with little regard for suitability. The
point is not that traditional approaches to management are *bad*
per se. Quite the opposite. In their day, they yielded extraordinary results, although one could argue that the human costs were high. The
problem is that, a century later, the landscape has changed beyond
recognition. High-VUCA environments, the increase in knowledge
work, and the shift away from exploiting and toward exploring have
seen once-effective techniques fail miserably. When seeking to manage knowledge work, innovate, and achieve business agility, traditional approaches are, time and again, found wanting. Like the UK's
Challenger II—a tank designed for peacekeeping missions in urban
areas and that subsequently broke down when deployed to fight in
sandy, desert-based conflicts—nineteenth- and early twentieth-
century management techniques are now being applied in a context
for which they were not designed and are utterly unsuited.

The mid-twentieth century gave rise to another revolution—the
digital revolution—and the industrial age rolled into the information
age. Mechanical and analog technologies gave way to digital technologies leading to home computers, the internet, and smartphones.
Suddenly the largest organizations in the world were not paying employees merely to follow orders mindlessly and carry out repetitive,
manual work. They were paying them to *think*. Peter Drucker coined
the phrase "knowledge worker" in 1966.[11] Knowledge work differs
profoundly from more traditional manual work. Manual work involves carrying out simple, routine tasks in a repeatable manner,
often guided by tight prescription. Manual workers are often regarded as faceless and interchangeable. Tayloristic management
practices transfer all thinking to managers, which leaves workers

merely to execute according to instructions. It is this approach that famously led Henry Ford to ask, "Why is it every time I ask for a pair of hands, they come with a brain attached?"[12]

Knowledge work is different. Knowledge workers go to work to think, not to *do*. They are not necessarily managers, but they do engage in nonroutine, creative problem-solving and make large numbers of decisions based on large amounts of data and information. Knowledge workers are often engaged in creative work—work in which solutions are largely unknown and emerge as the work progresses. During this process, many decisions are made. It turns out that maximizing the productivity of knowledge workers is all but impossible with traditional management approaches, not to mention hard to measure. Here, I explore three key reasons for this change.

Increased Work Complexity

There is a parable that originates in the Indian subcontinent. It has been traced back to the middle of the first millennium BCE. A group of blind men encounter a strange animal they are told is called an elephant. The men are curious and wish to inspect the animal the only way they can—by touch. So they all set about feeling the animal. The first man's hand lands on the trunk. He declares, "This animal is thick like a snake." The next man's hand feels the animal's ear. He says, "It is like a fan." The next man feels its leg and declares, "It's like a tree trunk." All of the men in the story are correct in what they say, but each is unable to comprehend the big picture and ends up jumping to the wrong conclusion.

The same is true when individuals attempt to understand complex systems through reductionist techniques similar to those Taylor used. They worked for him and his contemporaries because managers could master a small number of repeatable tasks with minimal variables in play. Everything could be measured and optimized, and they could be confident that things would remain the same the next day and the day after that. They could see the whole elephant and be sure that the elephant would never move or change.

Complex knowledge work is different. One cannot understand the whole merely by understanding the constituent parts—because the whole is not the sum of the parts; it's a product of the many interactions among them. Research suggests that the number of chunks of information humans can hold in their head at any time is between five and nine.[13] For focused attention, it becomes four.[14] There are now frequently far too many variables and interactions for one person to comprehend fully. There is no longer "one best way," and if there were, one person would not be able to find it. The concept of best practice stops making sense with complex work. There are many possible solutions, and these can only be understood through experimentation, fast feedback, and small adaptations. This can only be done by those *doing the work*.

And to make matters worse, with knowledge work, the same problem is rarely solved twice. Every day is a new challenge with a new set of possible solutions. Prescriptive instruction cards might help with yesterday's problem, but not today's. No manager can possibly have the cognitive capacity, knowledge of all activities, or physical presence to make all decisions. They simply cannot see the whole elephant. That can only be done by those doing the work, those who truly understand the context and who have the tacit knowledge to make sound decisions. Taylor's hard line has blurred.

Increased Frequency and Urgency of Decisions

When simple, repeatable work is undertaken—for instance, in factories, such as Midvale Steel Works, where Taylor developed his theories—the number of decisions required on a daily basis is low. Once the "one best way" is found and all workers understand instructions, it is simply a matter of efficient execution of those instructions. The analysis and thinking have been done in advance, by managers. Workers must simply carry out the tasks, while managers ensure compliance. When the work is sufficiently simple, this can easily be done by a small number of managers.

But what happens when the work is creative? When the solution must be discovered through some level of investigation and trial and error? When decisions are required not just up front but *throughout* the process—sometimes on a minute-by-minute basis? Take, for example, a surgeon. She may begin a surgical procedure with a plan, but upon opening up the patient, she may find that she must quickly adapt that plan. Who is best placed to make that decision? The hospital manager, sitting in an upstairs office, remote from the information? Or the surgeon, with all her experience, and the information at her fingertips and the ability to act on it swiftly? When the patient's blood pressure drops suddenly, fast and effective decision-making is vital. Pushing the information up to the managerial authority and waiting for a command to be pushed back down to the surgeon becomes impractical, ineffective, and, in this case, dangerous. The authority must be pushed to where the information is to allow swift and effective of execution.

Widespread Disengagement

The third reason traditional approaches to management begin to fail is a very human one. Separating the thinking from the doing essentially reduces people to faceless, fungible programmed computers, mindlessly executing tasks to predefined rules. Unsurprisingly, this is a not particularly fulfilling existence for the vast majority of people who carry out work. Disengagement, boredom, and demotivation are hallmarks of an overly controlling management style. This leads to the very behavior Taylor described as "soldiering," in which people give less than 100 percent. Can anyone blame them? People do not do their best work when a manager with a clipboard and a stopwatch is behind them. The issue here is not the people; it's the environment that has been created and in which they must operate. One hundred years ago, people rarely moved companies. Today, people rarely stay for more than a few years. Attracting, and keeping, the best talent is now very much a problem for big organizations. As Steve Jobs once said, "If you want to hire great people and have them stay working for you, you have to let them make a lot of decisions and you have to be run by idea, not hierarchy. The best ideas have to win, otherwise, good people don't stay."[15] The concept of engagement will be discussed in detail in chapter 7.

What's clear is that, in recent years, there has been a blurring of the line between work and management of work. Those who are using a known and stable process to create a known and stable product in a known and stable market will still see much value in traditional management methods. Those who are not will require an entirely new approach to leadership and management. Twenty-first-century leadership is about setting vision and direction, creating the right culture, then tapping into the collective intelligence of people to solve complex problems. It focuses less on compliance, and more on creativity and growth. Leaders must now create an environment in which people do the exact opposite of what Taylor and Ford wanted them to do: *think.*

Reflection

Are there times in your organization when managers find it hard to get on top of the complexity of the work? Can managers sometimes be a bottleneck to decision-making? Are decisions that are made sometimes a source of frustration for teams? Are there examples of those carrying out the work appearing disengaged or demotivated?

Twenty-First-Century Leadership: Some Emerging Approaches

Stephen Richards once said, "If you do what everyone else does, you will get what everyone else gets." Organizations seem to understand this on some level. There is always a lot of talk about innovation, and many attempts to employ fresh new technology. There is even a desire to create new products and services. Few would disagree that innovating is a useful endeavor. Few would shy away from launching a new product or service purely because no one else is doing it yet; indeed, being first is the very point of innovation. Yet this desire to innovate rarely carries over into the field of management itself. It seems that doing new things with technology and products is welcomed, but when it comes to how organizations are structured and run, innovation is to be avoided at all costs. Suddenly, we feel safer with best practices—doing things the way everyone else does them. Why go out on a limb? No one gets fired for buying IBM, right?

Except that management innovation is precisely how some organizations create such a large competitive advantage. In his book *The Future of Management*, Gary Hamel identifies what he calls the Innovation Stack (figure 6). At the bottom of the stack, and having the

The Innovation Stack

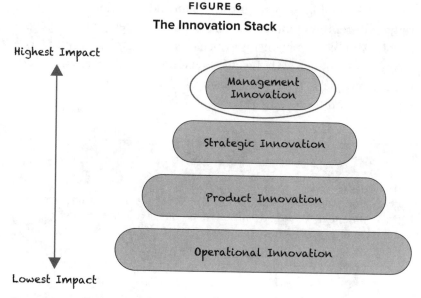

Source: Gary Hamel, *The Future of Management*, with Bill Breen (Boston: Harvard Business School Press, 2007).

least impact, is operational innovation—making improvements to how the work is done, in traditional management style. This rarely yields much of an advantage. With the current vast networks of partners and consultants cross-fertilizing new ways of working among clients, these innovations are diffused almost instantly, leaving minimal competitive advantage for the innovating organization.

The next level up in the Innovation Stack is product innovation. While there is no doubt that launching a great new product will yield a short-term advantage, it is often only a matter of time before others get inspired and produce very similar items. It did not take long for manufacturers to introduce touch-screen smartphones that looked very similar to the iPhone or bagless vacuum cleaners that looked similar to those of Dyson, and Tesla's 2008 Roadster has spawned a vast array of electric vehicles. There is an inevitability about this, given how notoriously difficult patents are to enforce.

The third level up is strategic innovation. This is when a whole new business model emerges that challenges the incumbents. Think about how Southwest Airlines and Ryanair disrupted air travel, or how

Uber managed to become the world's biggest provider of personal transport without owning any vehicles. It is not Uber's *product* that has caused its user base to swell to 110 million.[16] The digital technology behind its website and app has been around for years, as have taxi services. Instead, it is its innovative *business model*, which effortlessly connects those who need a service to those who can offer a service, that has allowed it to disrupt an entire industry. This has provided a significant advantage in the medium term—but, as Uber, Southwest Airlines, and countless others have discovered, business models can also be copied over time.

Finally, at the top of the stack is management innovation, a bold new approach to leading organizations that can produce lasting results. This includes General Electric bringing discipline to its scientific discovery approach, Ford creating new models to manage what was at the time the largest company in the world, General Motors' pioneering divisionalization, and Toyota's creation of the Toyota Way. These innovations are particularly difficult to decode, especially in cases in which they are largely cultural. This leaves competitors scratching their heads, wondering how they do it and why copying their working practices does not yield the same results. Here I discuss three recent, and not-so-recent, management innovations and the contexts in which they emerged.

Directed Opportunism (Stephen Bungay, The Art of Action)

In 1806 the Prussian army, built up by Frederick the Great, was feared and admired in Europe. A well-oiled, disciplined machine, it had seen much success. The French army, by contrast, consisted largely of citizen conscripts left over from the revolution. They had very little time to train or to become disciplined and tended to engage in an unordered swarm, with each man taking the action he saw fit. When the two armies came together at the twin battles of Jena and Auerstedt, the result was as surprising as it was decisive. The French stunned the Prussians on both fronts. In the wake of the Prussians' crushing defeat, General David Scharnhorst led a group dedicated to understanding how it had happened and identifying the changes that would have to be made to avoid a repeat.

They found that the Prussian army needed to get cleverer and faster. They had initially sought to overcome uncertainty through centralized control and process. This led to slow decision-making and left the men compliant but demotivated. By contrast, the French troops were highly decentralized and were expected to use their own initiative. They could make swift, context-based decisions and, as such, were highly motivated. They were able to overwhelm the Prussians with an unmatchable speed. In response, the Prussians sought to transform from the ground up how they recruited, trained, and operated.

Field Marshal Helmuth von Moltke the Elder is far from a household name. *Auftragstaktik*, his lasting legacy, is far from a household word. His impact, however, and that of his work, is felt in militaries and other entities across the globe. Upon taking command of the Prussian army in 1866, he began espousing the cause of independent thinking and action over obedience. In 1869, he issued a document called *Guidance for Large Unit Commanders*. Its principles for higher command remained unchanged for 70 years and are reflected in both US and NATO doctrine to this day. This doctrine contains Moltke's somewhat counterintuitive approach to closing the three gaps and thereby reducing organizational friction.

To close the knowledge gap, he emphasized the importance of planning only what *could* be planned and accepting uncertainty and the need for timely decision-making in flight once more information was available. He noted that "in war, circumstances change very rapidly, and it is rare indeed for directions which cover a long period of time in a lot of detail to be fully carried out."[17]

To close the alignment gap, he emphasized communicating as much of the higher intent as is necessary to achieve the purpose. This understanding of what is to be achieved and why would allow for more effective lower-level decision-making and would prevent actions misaligned with the intent.

To close the effects gap, he emphasized that everyone should make their own decisions and act within predetermined bounds. He knew that when VUCA is high, plans have to evolve continually based on emerging circumstances. Once intent is clearly understood, those on the ground, where the information lies, can respond by adjusting their actions but remaining aligned with the intent. This is where

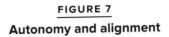

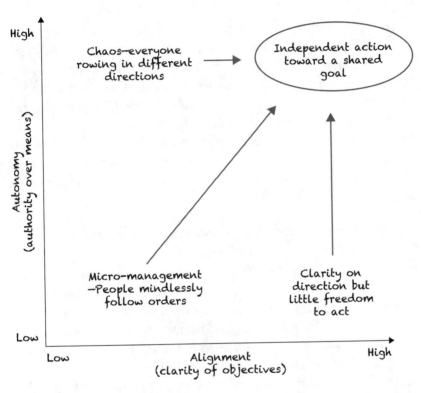

FIGURE 7

Autonomy and alignment

Moltke's most famous quotation comes from: "No plan survives first contact with the enemy."

The great insight Moltke had was that alignment and autonomy were not trade-offs. More of one does not necessarily mean, as was the thinking at the time, less of the other. Instead, he observed that the more alignment one has, the more autonomy one can grant; the former enables the latter (figure 7). He espoused the idea that leaders should concentrate on communicating intent, what is to be achieved, and why—the complete opposite of what Taylor would go on to advise. It would then be up to others to decide the "how" with the benefit of information acquired on the ground. They would define the actions necessary to achieve the intended goal. This approach increases organizational intelligence and resilience, as it does not rely on the presence of a small group of brilliant people at the top. In 1870, an increasingly confident Prussian army, led by Moltke, took on the French army once again, reversing the result of Jena-Auerstedt in a decisive victory.

Auftragstaktik slipped into the English language as the term *mission command*, and it is now official NATO doctrine. It was first applied on a large scale in the 1991 Gulf War. In 1981, the late Jack Welch, CEO and chair of GE, adopted a version of the approach, calling it "planful opportunism." In *The Art of Action*, Stephen Bungay used the term "directed opportunism" to describe mission command for commercial organizations. This approach can be summarized in three steps: (1) Decide what really matters. (2) Communicate that message as clearly and succinctly as possible. (3) Give people space and support to execute effectively.

Intent-Based Leadership (David Marquet, Turn the Ship Around)

In December 1998, in Pearl Harbor, Hawaii, Captain David Marquet was due to take command of the nuclear-powered submarine USS *Olympia*. He had spent 12 months doing nothing but studying the ship's every detail. At the last minute, however, Marquet was switched to another submarine, USS *Santa Fe*. He had a mere three weeks to study it—nowhere near enough time. This was the worst-performing submarine in the fleet, with by far the worst retention rate—in 1998, just three of the crew had reenlisted, with no officers retained. Upon assuming command, Marquet would be entirely accountable for everything that happened on that failing $2 billion submarine. He would need to have it ready to deploy in only six months, and he would have to do that *without* the one thing he needed most: supreme technical competence.

Nuclear submarines are the epitome of what Marquet calls the "leader-follower" model. This means information is passed up the chain to the decision-making authority, who, in turn, sends commands back down to be executed. This leadership style is underpinned by, in this case, deep knowledge of the ship. Performance is only ever as good as the orders given at any point. This is an approach that leads to rampant disengagement, as people passively follow orders from above. As Marquet discovered the hard way during a training drill on the *Santa Fe*, his crew would even attempt to carry out orders that made no sense rather than question them. They were just not *thinking*. The system discouraged it. Ordinarily Marquet could have given precise and correct orders, but this was not an ordinary situation. The ship was completely unfamiliar to him. His lack of technical expertise meant that he had to lean more heavily on the crew for explanations of how the ship worked. He had to *give* control to others.

The model that emerged on board the *Santa Fe* in place of the passive leader-follower model was the active leader-leader model. As one would do with directed opportunism, Marquet replaced low-level orders with *intent*. He sought to stop taking control and creating followers, and to start giving control and creating leaders. This meant that Marquet held back the urge to step in when problems or challenges presented themselves. When a leader provides a solution, it robs people of the opportunity to find it for themselves—and thus to think, and to grow into tomorrow's leaders. By stepping back and waiting, Marquet invited his officers to state their intentions, a prerequisite for which is *thinking*. This was empowering and engaging, and tapped into the minds of his entire crew, meaning that 135 people were thinking, rather than just one or two.

Upon hearing the words, "Captain, I intend to . . . ," Marquet quickly had to determine two things: Was it the right thing to do given their mission? And was it safe? He asked these questions so often that the answers were soon presented as part of the statement of intent. Echoing what Field Marshal Moltke had preached 150 years before, control can only be given once people have the requisite technical competence and alignment with the overall mission. The mantra on board the *Santa Fe* became, "Don't push information to the authority, move authority to the information." This shifted psychological ownership of the ship's fate to the officers. The officers were now thinking like captains. Many more leaders were being created.

USS *Santa Fe* passed all inspections and was deployed within six months of Marquet assuming command. In 1999, 36 of its crew reenlisted, and 100 percent of its officers were retained. The submarine was rated the best in the entire US Navy. And all that happened under the command of a captain who barely knew the ship. He achieved this remarkable feat by tapping into the potential of everyone on board and creating leaders at all levels. He did it by *giving* control, not taking it. Such is the power of management innovation. While not a traditional environment for an experiment of this kind, the story of USS *Santa Fe* goes to show that if this kind of turnaround can be achieved when 135 human lives are on the line and when operating with huge complexity and volatility, it can be done in any organizations willing to try.

Leadership Agility (Bill Joiner, Leadership Agility)

In 1970, Bill Joiner and his colleagues began a long-range, three-phase research project into human ego development stages, leadership, and the emotional and cognitive capacities of hundreds of managers and leaders around the world. Their aim was to understand the various behaviors of great leaders. This, alongside three decades of coaching, consulting, and training across the globe, has helped them to build up a detailed picture of what makes effective leaders and how to help people on that journey. The result was the Leadership Agility framework, and the view that there is an ever-increasing imperative for leaders to progress through these stages.

Joiner found a striking correlation among leadership agility, organizational agility, and business performance. He puts this down to two things. The first is, once again, the increased pace of change in the world—a phenomenon Joiner attributes to globalization, deregulation, technology, and social, economic, environmental, and political change. As described in earlier chapters, this makes the world far less predictable than it once was. The second thing to which Joiner points here is the increased complexity and interconnectedness of both work and organizations. This means that it is all but impossible for a small group of people to perform all problem-solving and strategic planning themselves—to see the whole elephant. Leadership agility is, in essence, about becoming more effective at responding to the growing complexity, interconnectedness, and pace of change in the world, and helping to create organizations that can do the same. Business agility cannot be separated from leadership agility. The latter must precede the former.

The Leadership Agility framework consists of five development stages. Stages cannot be skipped, and progressing to the next stage means learning new emotional and cognitive capacities that underpin new behaviors. These capacities are retained, meaning that leaders operating at the highest level will retain the abilities of the lower levels. The following is an overview of the most common *three* stages.

- **Expert leadership:** Experts are the tactical problem-solvers. They focus on making small, incremental improvements to existing strategies within their unit. They believe that their power and legitimacy come from deep technical expertise and their positional authority. They tend to be strong command-and-control micromanagers with a low tolerance for conflict and feedback. Expert leaders can be effective when operating in stable environments with low complexity. Roughly 45 percent of leaders operate at Expert level or below. (Ten percent operate at pre-Expert level.)

- **Achiever leadership:** Achievers are strategic and outcome focused. They believe that their power comes not only from expertise but also from motivating others to contribute to larger objectives over a longer timeframe. Achiever leaders tend to be more effective in moderately complex, medium-paced environments. They can cope with occasional changes in strategy. They tend to seek buy-in for strategy, but are unlikely to be open to input from their team. They have a moderate tolerance for conflict and feedback. Around 35 percent of leaders operate at Achiever level; they are often executives.

- **Catalyst leadership:** Catalysts are visionaries with a facilitative and culture focus. They believe that a leader's job is to nurture the organizational culture and empower those around them and facilitate their development. They encourage openness, transparency, and participation. They actively encourage feedback and input from others, genuinely believing that bringing people into the process will lead to better solutions and higher engagement. Much like the captain of USS *Santa Fe*, they believe that the only way to succeed in environments of high complexity and fast-paced change is to expand capability and culture, and give over control such that teams, and the organization, can respond to any strategic challenges that may arise. In short, they believe in business agility. Roughly 10 percent of leaders operate at Catalyst level.

Reflection

Does your organization focus on management innovation or keep to what is considered standard practice? Are there opportunities to decentralize decision-making? What benefits might that bring? At what level are most leaders operating in your organization, Expert, Achiever, or Catalyst?

Agile Leadership: Three Key Mindset Shifts

What is clear from the foregoing examples is that recent management and leadership innovations share some common traits, but also are preceded by a shift in mindset. They take a different perspective of people and how complex knowledge work is best approached. These changes can be summarized as three key mindset shifts of agile leadership (figure 8).

Mindset shift 1: Focus less on the work, and more on the culture, strategy, structures, and policies. Leading in high uncertainty is about recognizing that those delivering the value to customers know best how to do that. Too often, organizational policies get in the way of delivery. Agile leadership is a lot like gardening. Flowers and plants cannot be made to grow; they do so only if the correct levels of sunlight, water, and nutrients are combined with fertile soil. Great gardeners focus on creating the best possible environment, then just let the magic happen. The leader's job is to set the direction and to support teams by designing and improving systems inside which they can be highly engaged and truly effective. As W. Edwards Deming once said, "A bad system will beat a good person every time."

Mindset shift 2: Decentralize as much of the decision-making as possible. This stems from a belief that, when undertaking complex knowledge work, it is those *doing the work* who know best how to achieve a given objective. A common fear is that giving control will

FIGURE 8

Three key mindset shifts of agile leadership

result in people all going in different directions. This is avoided by ensuring that there is crystal-clear alignment about the outcomes, and indeed the constraints inside which those outcomes must be met. The leader's job then is to decide what most needs to be achieved, clearly communicate and reinforce that message, and let self-managing teams decide how best to make that happen. With that in mind, seek to decentralize and distribute authority to where the greatest information lies (figure 9). This will result not only in faster decisions but also better decisions and highly engaged teams.

Mindset shift 3: Encourage and support the growth and development of those around you. Great leaders make a point of ensuring that those around them are always improving. They see it as their role to support their growth and development. After all, if teams are now expected to take more ownership of achieving outcomes, they must have the skills they need to do so effectively. It is up to leaders to ensure that those skills are in place, and to fill any gaps. Only when there is alignment around desired outcomes and the requisite capabilities are in place can more control be given. Resist the urge to solve problems for people. Help people to grow such that they can solve them for themselves. Great leaders create more leaders. As Adam Grant wrote

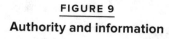

FIGURE 9
Authority and information

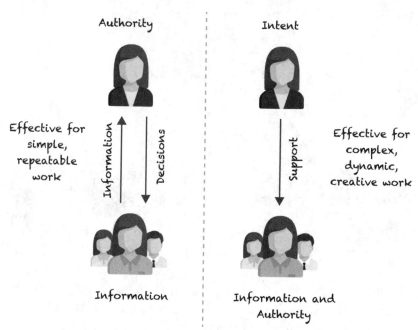

in the forward of *The Trillion Dollar Coach*, "To be a great manager, you have to be a great coach. After all, the higher you climb, the more your success depends on making other people successful."[18] This sums up perfectly leadership and management in the twenty-first century.

Mastering these mindset shifts is a journey. It is a journey on which many have embarked before, and on which a great many will need to embark in the future. It is not about copying what other organizations do. What works in one context may not work in another. Organizations must take an experimental, evolutionary approach. It takes a different way of thinking, and the development of new skills. It often goes against much of what is still taught about management and leadership, so unlearning behaviors is as important as learning new ones. Organizations seeking to evolve must start by recognizing that everything starts with the leadership mindset. Once that is in place, the journey can begin, ideally supported by a structured leadership development program.

> **Reflection**
>
> How would leaders in your organization feel about the three key mindset shifts of agile leadership? If there is fear and resistance to embracing these mindset shifts, what is behind that? How might the fear be reduced? Is there a plan in place to develop leaders who can embody these behaviors? How could some of these shifts be slowly built into everyday interactions?

Chapter Summary

- Management as we know it emerged during the Second Industrial Revolution, when levels of VUCA were mostly low. It largely involved separating thinking, planning, and decision-making from execution.

- Traditional management approaches are fine when the work can easily be understood by people removed from the execution and few decisions are required; however, once work gets complex, unpredictable, and creative, decision-making must be pushed to where the information lies: with those doing the work.

- In high-VUCA environments, distributed decision-making will lead to faster and more effective decision-making.

- In order for leaders to give over control, there must be high levels of alignment about what is to be achieved, and technical competence regarding how to achieve it. It is the leader's job to ensure those things are in place, alongside supporting organizational cultures, policies, and structures.

Key Practices for Business Agility

- Consciously shift the focus from how the work gets done to creating the environment for teams to be effective.

- Spend the majority of time on creating the right culture, structures, and policies as well as clearly articulating the strategy for alignment, the organizational operating system.

- Embrace uncertainty by optimizing for fast feedback and frequent course correction, rather than rigid plans and efficiency.

- As much as possible, decentralize decision-making, with the authority flowing to teams and those closest to the work and the customers.

- Spend time coaching and mentoring those around you, and invest in their development and growth.

- Embark on a structured leadership development program, and continually seek feedback on your effectiveness with a view to develop and grow in the role.

Further Reading and Resources

Books

- David Marquet, *Turn the Ship Around! A True Story of Building Leaders by Breaking the Rules* (London: Penguin Portfolio, 2013)

- Bill Joiner and Stephen Josephs, *Leadership Agility: Five Levels of Mastery for Anticipating and Initiating Change* (San Francisco: Jossey-Bass, 2007)

- Eric Schmidt and Jonathan Rosenberg, *Trillion Dollar Coach: The Leadership Handbook of Silicon Valley's Bill Campbell* (New York: Harper Business, 2019)

- Simon Sinek, *Leaders Eat Last: Why Some Teams Pull Together and Others Don't* (London: Penguin, 2011)

- Stephen Bungay, *The Art of Action: How Leaders Close the Gaps between Plans, Actions and Results* (London: Nicholas Brealey Publishing, 2011)

- Steve Denning, *The Leader's Guide to Radical Management: Reinventing the Workplace for the 21st Century* (San Francisco: Jossey-Bass, 2010)

Websites, Articles, and Videos

- Please see www.6enablers.com/resources for more on this topic, including a downloadable reading list.

CHAPTER 5

Organizational Culture

> I came to see, in my time at IBM, that culture isn't just one aspect of the game—it is the game.
>
> —LOU GERSTNER, FORMER CHAIRMAN AND CEO OF IBM

IN THIS CHAPTER, WE WILL EXPLORE

- the impact culture can have on organizational effectiveness
- how to define an organization's current and desired culture
- which culture types are most aligned with business agility
- how to shift organizational culture subtly.

Why Culture Matters: Lessons from a Failing Car Plant

In the 1960s, General Motors (GM) had over 50 percent of the US automobile market. In the decades since, that number has consistently been eroded by its competitors, at home and abroad. In 2015, that market share was just 18 percent. One story in particular sheds some light on what's been happening for the past five decades. The story begins in the early 1980s in a GM-operated plant in Fremont, California. To say that this was a troubled plant is to put it rather mildly. The Fremont Assembly plant was the worst-performing plant at GM. It had the worst productivity and the worst quality in the whole of GM. And labor relations were even worse.

Bruce Lee, who ran the Western Region of the United Auto Workers Union (UAW), goes further. Even though labor relations were pretty bad in the US car industry as a whole, Lee admits the workers at Fremont were awful. In fact, they were widely considered the worst workforce in the US automobile industry.[1] It really was a case of anything goes in the plant back then. People would drink, smoke, and gamble on the job. Anything was for sale, even drugs and sex. Workers would also intentionally sabotage cars. This ranged from anything from leaving loose bolts, bottle caps, and half-eaten tuna sandwiches behind panels, to scratching cars, to committing acts that were outright dangerous. One worker left bolts loose on the front suspension of over 400 cars.

Workers were trying to hurt the company by attacking the product. They could get away with this behavior only because of the strength of the UAW. The union's strategy was to drown management in grievances. Whenever managers tried to address any issue, they would be hit with another grievance. Soon there was more time being spent on grievances and strikes than there was on making cars, and it was virtually impossible to fire anyone. In 1982, there were over 5,000 grievances raised. With that safety net, absenteeism soared to over 20 percent. On any given day, one in five workers just didn't show up for work. All this was perhaps the inevitable result of the collision between Fredrick Winslow Taylor's scientific management and the labor union movement. Rather unsurprisingly, by 1982, managers at GM had had enough. The plant was closed, and 5,000 people were laid off.

But for a series of unlikely events, the story could easily have ended there. The next year, however, GM began speaking to Toyota, its competitor, about a joint venture. Government emission guidelines meant that GM was required to make small cars, but it was losing money on them, and the ones it made were of poor quality. Toyota could help it to build high-quality, profitable small cars while teaching it Toyota's much-admired Toyota Production System. This was akin to Coca-Cola offering to share its secret recipe. GM was keen to learn Toyota's secrets. From Toyota's perspective, looming import restrictions meant that it would need to learn how to build cars on US soil. GM could help with this. So it was that these two competitors entered into a joint venture name New United Motor Manufacturing Incorporated (NUMMI).

The chosen site was the recently closed Fremont Assembly plant. Lee, still representing the UAW, was invited to sit down with Toyota chairman Eiji Toyoda. Lee strongly believed that the workers themselves were not bad people; they just happened to be stuck in a bad system. Lee insisted on being allowed to hire the first 50 employees himself. Reluctantly, both sides agreed to this demand. Toyota managers in particular had always believed that their system could turn "bad" workers into "good" ones, so they thought this was reasonable. Lee's hires, however, would turn out to be the most militant and disruptive employees from the plant's previous incarnation. When NUMMI opened in 1984, 85 percent of the workers had been working at the Fremont Assembly plant when it closed. It would have taken a brave person to predict success at this point.

In the run-up to the opening, workers were flown to Japan in small groups to learn the new system of making cars, the Toyota Production System. They worked side-by-side for two weeks with their Japanese counterparts, learning how things were done there. Upon returning to Fremont, they were ready to begin a new chapter in their stories. It was a yellow Chevy Nova that first rolled off the assembly line at NUMMI. Instantly, the numbers were significantly better than before. Defect rates were among the lowest in the United States, and equal to those of cars coming out of Japan. An increase in output led to plummeting costs and a productivity rate that was the best at GM. It is estimated that it would have taken double the workforce to produce the same output under the old system. Absenteeism, once running at 20 percent, was dramatically reduced to just 2 percent, with morale reaching record highs. For the first time in years, people were enjoying coming to work. Being part of a team that solved problems together was empowering. People went from being ashamed of the quality of their cars to feeling proud. Some even left their personal contact details in the windshields of cars in parking lots, asking for the owner's opinions of the car.

It is clear from the NUMMI story that culture can have a massive negative or positive impact on the effectiveness of an organization. In their book *Corporate Culture and Performance*, authors James L. Heskett and John Kotter describe an 11-year study in which they analyzed the performance of firms. The results were staggering. They observed that among the firms in the study that did *not* have a performance-enhancing culture, stock price growth was, on average, 74 percent and net income growth was 1 percent over the 11 years.

Compare that with firms that *did* have performance-enhancing culture and the numbers jump to 901 percent and 756 percent, respectively.

What is clear is that culture matters. What is also clear is that cultural challenges are one of the biggest impediments during so-called agile transformations. As was mentioned in chapter 3, in the *13th Annual State of Agile Report,* released in 2019, the most common answer to the question asking about "challenges experienced when adopting & scaling agile" was, "Organizational culture at odds with agile values." That answer was chosen by 52 percent of respondents. It is the same challenge in virtually every organization I visit, and often, very little is done to address it. As is the case with many other obstacles to agility, it is largely ignored. The truth is that the kind of cultural turnaround seen at NUMMI is rarely seen in the corporate world. What makes NUMMI even more remarkable is that it was achieved with the same workers using the same machinery in the same plant that, just two years earlier, had been failing so badly. This story illustrates just how powerful this nebulous concept of culture can be, while demonstrating that large shifts in culture are indeed possible under the right conditions. In the coming sections, we will dig a little deeper into these concepts and how managers at NUMMI were able to achieve seemingly miraculous results in such a short time.

Reflection

How much attention is paid by leadership to organizational culture in your organization? Are people aware of the impact a strong culture can have on business performance?

Modeling Culture: Making Tangible the Intangible

In many ways, the man who brought the concept of organizational culture to the world's consciousness was Edgar Schein, a former professor at the MIT Sloan School of Management. But ask 10 leadership gurus to define culture and you'll probably get 11 different answers. The modern term *culture* is based on a term introduced by the ancient Roman orator Cicero, *cultura animi*, a metaphor from agriculture for the development of a philosophical soul. Over 2,000 years on, it remains a rather tricky concept to pin down. The definition I tend to use is one from Robert Quinn and Kim Cameron. They describe culture as "the set of taken-for-granted values, underlying assumptions, expectations, collective memories, and definitions present in an organization."[2]

The words that jump out at me here are *values, assumptions, expectations*, and *definitions*. It's a description of the collective ways of thinking, and the unwritten rules about how work gets done, within an organization. As such, culture forms a key part of the underlying operating system of an organization. It's not always noticeable, yet it yields a big impact on results. The legendary management guru Peter Drucker famously stated that "culture eats strategy for breakfast." What he meant by this is not that strategy is unimportant, but that, as we saw in the NUMMI story, culture is simply *more* important. In fact, I would go as far as to say that nothing can overcome a bad culture, and that there's nothing a good culture cannot overcome. More than any other of the six enablers of agility, culture has an impact on, and is affected by, almost every other part of an organization. As Schein wrote, "When we examine culture and leadership closely, we see that they are two sides of the same coin; neither can really be understood by itself."[3] I am inclined to agree, and I would add that the same is also true for people and engagement, an element that covers many HR aspects of business agility. Leadership, culture, and HR are so closely interconnected that there is no mutually exclusive, collectively exhaustive way to cover these topics. I have made the split based on many years of experience teaching and consulting in the business agility space, but do bear in mind that overlap will exist.

There are myriad culture models out there, from the Culture Web (Gerry Johnson and Kevan Scholes) to the Schneider Culture Model (William Schneider) to the Laloux Culture Model (Frederic Laloux) and many more. Having experimented with many models, I have found that the most effective model when advising organizations on how to increase business agility is the Competing Values Framework (CVF). There are many reasons for this. First, this framework is underpinned by over 40 years of deep academic research on organizational effectiveness. Second, it has been used and validated in over 10,000 organizations.[4] Third, it is simple to use, with only six attributes representing organizational effectiveness. It also has a lightweight assessment tool that can easily be administered within an organization or department. This makes the tool highly practical and delivers real insight to leaders. This combination of scientific rigor, breadth of use, and practical applicability makes the CVF, for me, by far the most effective model.

The CFV itself is actually rather simple; there are two primary dimensions. The first is the Stability-Flexibility dimension. Some organizations consider themselves effective if they exhibit a large degree of stability and control. Organizations that build for this tend to have clear structures, rules, plans, and budgets. They believe that the world can be understood, predicted, and tightly controlled. These tend to be entities with a high proportion of work in the exploit domain. Some organizations have the opposite perspective. They believe that they are effective if they exhibit large degrees of flexibility and adaptability. Organizations that build for this tend to focus more on people and activities than on processes and structures. They can respond quickly to changing circumstances. They hold a belief that the world cannot be predicted or controlled. These places tend to perform a large amount of work in the explore domain.

The second primary dimension is the Internal-External dimension. Organizations with an internal orientation tend to focus mainly inward on collaboration, integration, and coordination. Those with an external orientation focus mainly on the market, customers, competitors, and technology trends.

The competing nature of each pair of values (Stability-Flexibility, Internal-External) means that you cannot adhere to both at the same time. There is a tension. More of one means, by definition, less of the other. Together these two primary dimensions form four quadrants that represent distinct sets of indicators of organizational effectiveness (figure 10). They are the core values on which judgments are based. Each quadrant has a different perspective on value drivers, leadership types, theories of effectiveness, and approaches to change. I discuss the four quadrants here.

FIGURE 10
The Competing Values Framework

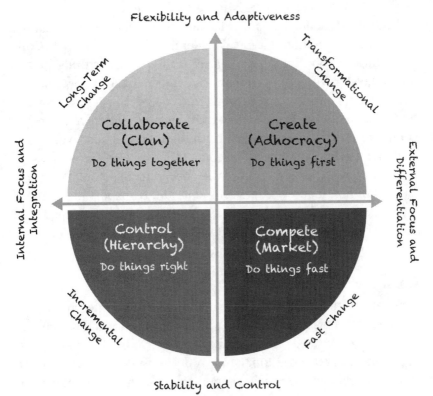

Source: Kim S. Cameron, Robert E. Quinn, and Jeff DeGraff, *Competing Values Leadership: Creating Value in Organizations*, 2nd ed. (Cheltenham, UK: Edward Elgar, 2014).

Control Culture

Control cultures are structured and process-oriented in nature. Rules and procedures direct what people do. The most important thing is to keep the organization running smoothly. Valued traits here are efficiency, standardization, predictability, and consistency of outcome. There is often strict governance, a strong respect for positional authority, clear lines of decision-making, and the close guarding of information. Emerging in the late nineteenth and early twentieth centuries, these types of organizations were based on the Internal Process Model of management and the work of the early management pioneers I discussed in chapter 4, Frederick Taylor, Max Weber, and Henri Fayol. In particular we see on prominent display Weber's six characteristics of a bureaucracy: hierarchy, specialization, formal selection, rules and regulations, impersonality, and career orientation. A typical leader in a Control culture is a micromanaging coordinator who closely monitors everything. Based on the Leadership Agility framework described in chapter 4, such a person would be described as an Expert Leader. His or her approach to change tends to be extremely cautious and incremental, and to comprise a series of baby steps. Until the 1960s, almost every book written on management was based on this type of culture.[5]

Control cultures can typically be observed in sectors like medicine, banking, insurance, government, and transportation. These have historically been relatively slow-moving and highly regulated industries in which consistent outputs are vital, the cost of mistakes is high, and the imperative to innovate is low.

Compete Culture

Compete cultures are competitive and results-oriented in nature. Most important is reputation and success. People are highly competitive and goal focused. Valued traits are growth, market dominance, achievement, and speed to market. A desire to deliver value to customers quickly and to watch competitors closely keeps the focus external. There is often a focus on hiring the best talent and putting pressure on them to move ahead through growth and promotion. An emphasis on winning keeps people together. Emerging in the early part of the twentieth century, Compete cultures are highly aligned with the Rational Goal Model of management. A typical leader in a Compete culture is hard-driving, directive, and competitive. They make hard demands on, but also greatly reward, employees. Based on the Leadership Agility framework described in chapter 4, this person would be an Achiever Leader. Here, change tends to be enacted quickly, but it may often be superficial.

Compete cultures tend to be found in sectors like sales, consultancy, accountancy, and the service industry. These have historically known moderate rates of change and complexity, and value market share and profitability in particular.

Create Culture

Create cultures are dynamic and entrepreneurial in nature. There is a highly creative environment with a propensity for risk-taking. Experimentation, learning, and innovation are their lifeblood, and launching successful new products and services is celebrated. Freedom, initiative, and rule-breaking are commonplace in these environments, coupled with the safety to make mistakes. There is often a strong sense of vision, high levels of transparency, and the free flow of information. Create cultures are highly aligned with the Open Systems Model of management. Typical leaders in a Create culture are visionary, innovative entrepreneurs. They lead by inspiring with a strong vision and capturing people's imaginations. They are inclined toward risk and embrace uncertainty. Based on the Leadership Agility framework described in chapter 4, a leader in this culture would be described as a Catalyst Leader. The approach to change here tends to be transformational. Radical change is welcomed, and will often be implemented in a big-bang fashion.

Create cultures tend to be found in technology-driven industries, start-ups, fashion companies, and disruptive services. These tend to be subject to high rates of change and complexity. They are climates in which creating *new* knowledge and original products and services is vital to ongoing success.

Collaborate Culture

Collaborate cultures are friendly and people-oriented in nature. They tend to feel like a large family with a strong sense of community. There are high levels of loyalty, trust, and participation. Teamwork, collaboration, and consensus are common. Teams are highly autonomous, are cross-functional, and solve complex problems together. In a fast-moving environment with high complexity, great value is placed on the growth and development of people and teams who can then respond to whatever strategic challenge arises. Emerging largely from the middle of the twentieth century on, Collaborate cultures are highly aligned with the Human Relations Model of management. A typical leader in a Collaborate culture is a mentor, facilitator, and team-builder with a strong people focus. Based on the Leadership Agility framework described in chapter 4, this person would be a

Catalyst Leader. The approach to change here tends to be long term. Collaborate cultures will happily invest in the future.

Collaborate cultures tend to be found in sectors like health care, education, and not-for-profit, and in family-owned businesses. These also tend to exist in environments of speedy change and high complexity. Work involves problems that can best be solved by teamwork and shared values, beliefs, and goals, along with high levels of engagement.

Table 2 gives a summary of the four culture types. An important point here is that all quadrants have value and every organization has its own unique mix of all four quadrants. This mix will outline

TABLE 2
Summary of the competing values framework culture types

	Control	Compete	Create	Collaborate
Approach	Do things right: eliminate errors	Do things fast: compete, move fast, play to win	Do new things: create, innovate, envision the future	Do things together: build teams, people matter
Value drivers	Efficiency, uniformity, predictability, consistency	Market share, growth, profitability, goal achievement	Innovation, new products and services, creativity, agility, transformation	Development, growth, cohesion, communication, participation
Decision-making approach	Detailed analysis—be certain up front	Fast decisions—analytical problem-solving	Experimentation—try lots of things and learn fast	Collective wisdom—participative
Environment in which this is effective	Stable, low-change contexts in which consistent, predictable outputs are vital	Contexts of moderate change and complexity in which market share and profitability are particularly valued	Contexts of fast change and high complexity in which creating new knowledge and products is vital	Contexts of fast change and high complexity in which problems are best solved by teamwork, shared values, and high engagement
Leader type	Micromanager, coordinator—Expert Leader	Hard-driver, competitor—Achiever Leader	Visionary, entrepreneur—Catalyst Leader	Mentor, facilitator—Catalyst Leader
Compatibility with business agility	Low	Low to moderate	High	High

FIGURE 11

A typical Competing Values Framework profile

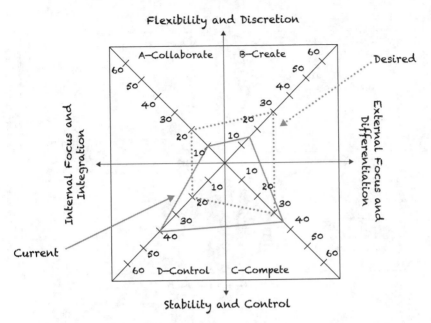

an organization's culture profile. See figure 11 for a typical profile of a large, traditional organization.

There are no good or bad cultures. There are, however, some culture types that tend to be more effective in certain domains and industries. It is not, unfortunately, always so black and white. Should a technology-driven bank be predominantly in the Control or the Create quadrant? This is where the concept of subcultures comes in. Different departments may have different culture types. This is to be expected. Within a bank, it would make sense for the legal and compliance departments to have a strong Control culture, while sales and marketing might sit in Compete, with the digital and technology side sitting in Create. Unfortunately, all too often a one-size-fits-all set of policies, structures, and practices is imposed across an organization. This leads to a one-size-fits-all *culture*. The bias tends to be toward Control and Compete, the exploit domain–friendly cultures. Hence, most organizations often encounter an inability to innovate and to adapt to changing circumstances.

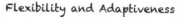

FIGURE 12

The agile values on the Competing Values Framework

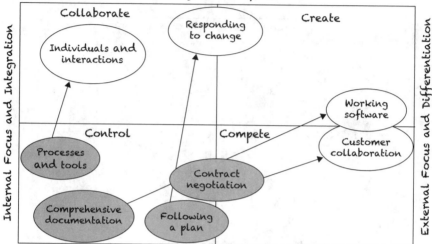

If we map the four value statements of the *Manifesto for Agile Software Development* (see chapter 2) to the CVF, we see that the majority of items the authors encouraged us to focus on less (processes and tools, comprehensive documentation, contract negotiation, following a plan), sit in the bottom left, Control quadrant (figure 12). If we then map the corresponding items the authors encouraged us to focus on more (individuals and interactions, working software, customer collaboration, responding to change), we find that the net direction of travel is up and to the right. What this is saying is that to achieve business agility, to master the explore domain, to be more innovative, and to survive in a high-VUCA landscape, organizations need to dial back the Control and Compete focus, and dial up the Create and Collaborate focus. This should not come as a surprise given that this represents an increase in adaptability and customer focus.

What I do find surprising is that many organizations that embark on an "agile transformation" have strong Control and Compete cultures as their current profile, and seem to have no desire to change. What this says to me is that the things they value most are stability and control. Why, then, try to adopt a model designed for the exact opposite, adaptability? Is it any wonder, in such cases, that there is friction, resistance, and an unwillingness to make the necessary structural changes? These places do not make the necessary changes because they do not truly value the outcome those changes will deliver. By moving toward flexibility and adaptability, they are moving *away* from stability and control, the things they value most. This is not an acceptable trade-off to them, and that is when the organizational antibodies, as I think of them, move in to destroy the change agents. This is why so many transformations fail. Agile transformation without corresponding cultural transformations will create nothing but frustration.

When it comes to any kind of attempt to increase agility, I tend to see the same three big mistakes made repeatedly. I have seen them in almost every organization with which I've worked. I see them among independent consultants and particularly among the large consultancy firms. Along with failing to address all six enablers of agility, these three things represent some of the biggest failings in the industry. I believe that they all stem from a lack of awareness of how to assess culture, and an inability to make the context-based decisions necessary for successful transformation.

The first mistake is pushing agility on any entity or unit that places a higher value on stability. Like a personal trainer who designs a training regime without understanding your health goals, this is a particularly dangerous mistake. Someone who wishes to build strength and muscle will not cut calories and run 10 miles per day. Pushing a solution that does not move the client toward something that he or she truly values is doomed to fail. Many clients ask for increased agility, but when you dive deeper into their core values, it becomes obvious that this isn't, in fact, what they really want. Recognizing this, and proposing something that will help them reach their stated outcomes, will save them a lot of time, energy, and money. Anything else just will not serve that client well.

The second mistake is the prepackaged solution. I see many consultancies move from client to client with their preferred model for increasing agility. Some of these approaches are out-of-the-box frameworks, while others are a Frankenstein's monster of many different frameworks and techniques stitched together. Some of these may work well in a particular context, while others may work well in a completely different context. The problem is assuming that what works well in one type of culture will work equally well in another. The likelihood is that it will not. Out-of-the-box solutions are attractive for sure, but they are only of use if aligned with the core values, and desired outcomes, of the organization to which they are applied. The chances are high in any given case that a different approach would serve the client better.

The third mistake comes down to approach to change. Passions run high in the debates about whether big-bang change (*kaikaku*, to use the Japanese term, whose roots lie with Toyota) is best, or whether a more incremental approach (*kaizen*) will elicit less resistance. The fact is that both sides are right, and both are wrong. It's a case of the old consultant's answer of "It depends." Each culture type has a different attitude to change. Mostly, I see people trying for big, revolutionary change in Control cultures. With their cautious outlook and incremental approach to change, however, transformation will prove far too risky for them. They will rarely go for that. They like small, toe-in-the-water changes and an evolutionary approach. Begin with approaches that do not initially disrupt established organizational structures, policies, and job titles. Likewise, suggesting an incremental approach to change to people in a Create culture will frustrate them. They have an appetite for revolution, not evolution. These cultures are much more open to the more disruptive change to established cultures, structures, and ways of working.

Packaged solutions and standard adoption playbooks completely ignore this aspect of culture. To avoid these mistakes, use a culture assessment to check whether agility really is valued by the entity with which you're working, find an approach that is aligned with those values, and use an appropriate change approach to get there. All of this involves experience, thinking, and cocreation of the solution with the client, rather than a copy-paste approach. Add a genuine focus on all six business agility enablers, and I believe success rates will be substantially higher. We will cover how to set up changes for success in chapter 10.

> ### Reflection
>
> What do you believe is the dominant culture type in your organization? Which culture type do you believe should be dominant? How aligned with business agility is that culture type? Given your dominant culture type, what is likely to be your organization's approach to change?

Shifting Culture: Changing by Not Changing

Understanding the need to shift the culture in an organization or department is relatively easy. It is also easy enough to map the current and desired culture. Moving toward one culture type and away from another, however, is anything but easy. The first thing to say is that culture is not under the direct control of anyone within the organization. Much like a shadow on a wall, culture is a result, a lagging indicator. To change a shadow, one cannot change the shadow directly; one can only change the things that cause the shadow, and subsequently the shadow will shift. Similarly, to change a culture, one cannot change the culture directly; one can only change the things that cause the culture, and subsequently the culture will shift. Both are a representation of something else. It is those other things that are under direct control of leadership. It is those other things that are the levers of culture change. Only through these indirect levers, can a new culture emerge. John Seddon puts it this way: "Attempting to change an organisation's culture is a folly, it always fails. Peoples' behaviour (the culture) is a product of the system; when you change the system, peoples' behaviour changes."[6] As we will see in chapter 7, employee engagement has the same property. It is also not a lever that can be pulled directly; it is a result of the pulling of many different levers.

Returning to the NUMMI story from earlier, we can get a sense of the most effective way to shift the culture of an organization quickly. How were NUMMI managers able to take a group of workers, some of whom were behaving in a borderline criminal way, and get them to work together, and even take pride in their work? How could the worst car plant in the United States become the best in just one year? The plant itself, the equipment, and many of the workers all remained

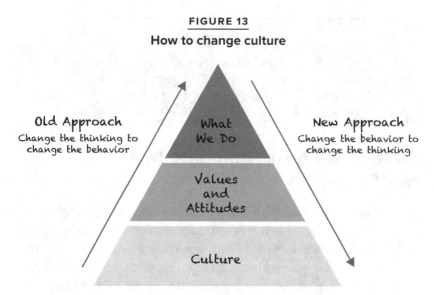

FIGURE 13

How to change culture

Old Approach
Change the thinking to
change the behavior

What
We Do

Values
and
Attitudes

Culture

New Approach
Change the behavior to
change the thinking

Source: John Shook, "How to Change a Culture: Lessons from NUMMI," *MIT Sloan Management Review*, January 1, 2010, https://sloanreview.mit.edu/article /how-to-change-a-culture-lessons-from-nummi/. © 2010 from MIT Sloan Management Review/Massachusetts Institute of Technology. All rights reserved. Distributed by Tribune Content Agency, LLC.

the same. We can consider all of that the hardware of the plant. What changed was the *culture*. We can consider that the software. A change in the software allows for a different outcome entirely, even with the same hardware. These same constraints also existed on the USS *Santa Fe*. It, too, went from worst to best with the same crew operating the same submarine. It, too, ran different software on the same hardware with extraordinary results. The question then becomes, How can the software, the culture, be changed?

John Shook, originally from Tennessee, moved to Japan in the early 1980s to pursue his fascination with Japanese management approaches. He was hired by Toyota to train the American GM workers in the Toyota Production System. Shook gained valuable insight into how the NUMMI culture was so radically shifted. In his influential article "How to Change a Culture: Lessons from NUMMI,"[7] Shook describes his attempts to capture what he had learned by creating a pyramid model (figure 13), which turns out to be very similar to a model created by Edgar Schein himself. Schein observed that the traditional approach to culture change is bottom-up. It begins with seeking to change the way people think, which in turn changes their values and attitudes, which leads, finally, to people starting to do the right things.

What Shook observed happening so effectively at NUMMI, however, was the exact opposite. Managers began by changing behaviors—what people *do*. They knew that, when seeking to change culture, the first step is to identify the desired behaviors, then to change systems, structures, and incentives to elicit those behaviors. As a result of behaving in a different way, people gain new insights, which leads to a change in values and attitudes. Finally, culture shifts as a result of embedding those new behaviors and habits.

To illustrate this point, we will explore what has become a symbol of Toyota's different culture and its commitment to building in quality. It's a thin, nylon rope that hangs above its auto assembly line on hooks. It's called the Andon Cord. While GM spoke of high quality, the behaviors it incentivized and rewarded led to the opposite. At the time, the cardinal rule in most US plants pre-NUMMI was "Never stop the line." Whatever happened, whatever issues was encountered, the line had to keep moving. There were even incidents of people falling in the pit and the line just carrying on. If someone saw a problem and stopped the line, that person was fired. No questions. The system, put in place by Henry Ford back in 1913, was designed to maximize output. If there were quality problems, someone else would deal with those later. Workers in the old Fremont Assembly plant spoke of engines installed backward, missing steering wheels, and faulty brakes all rolling off the line. The problem for the workers was that, even if they had wanted to resolve the issues, there was no way to do so. They couldn't stop the line, so the problem simply moved on to the next workstation. Fixing all the quality issues at the end piled on the costs, and the workers often did even more damage taking the cars apart to fix things.

When Toyota partnered with GM, they didn't address this issue by spending weeks extolling the virtues of quality. They implemented a system that led to changes in behavior. That system involved the Andon Cord. In Japan, when workers at Toyota detected an issue, they pulled the Andon Cord. They would then get help from a team leader within a minute. If the problem could not be resolved, the entire line was stopped until the issue was addressed. When GM managers questioned the wisdom of giving the workers the right to stop the whole line, Toyota managers replied that upon a worker's discovery of an issue, stopping the line became not a right but an obligation. This change led workers who, only a year before, had deliberately sabotaged the cars they were making to feel such a sense of pride that they left their phone numbers on the windshields of cars they had made when they came across them in parking lots. It also led to NUMMI having the highest quality levels in the US auto industry. Similar behavioral changes were implemented in the areas of teamwork and of continuously improving how the work got done.

Captain David Marquet, whom I discussed in chapter 4, made a similar observation to John Shook while on board the USS *Santa Fe*. He observed that behavioral changes, even small ones, had a big impact on the culture of the ship. Marquet, displeased by crew members' frequent use of the word *they* when referring to each other, declared, "There's no 'they' on the *Santa Fe*."[8] The fact that that rhymes probably helped it stick, but to drive the point home, a rule was implemented whereby no one could use the word *they* when referring to fellow crew members. Marquet felt that the term reinforced a sense of us-and-them on board. Of course, removing *they* from the lexicon left *we* as the next most sensible option. Suddenly it was "*We* didn't pressurize the fire hose," and "*We* didn't change the batteries on the thermal imager." Roughly six months later, a senior officer arrived to inspect the ship. He immediately declared to Marquet that it displayed the most amazing culture of teamwork and feeling together he'd ever seen. Marquet joked that they did not have a culture, they simply had a rule.

What is clear from both of the foregoing examples is that *action* must come before anything else. This makes sense in terms of the way the human brain works. As anyone who has tried to form a new habit will know, the mere awareness of something's value doesn't change anything in terms of a person's behavior. When it comes to dumping bad habits and establishing new ones, the issue is rarely a lack of knowledge. Functional MRIs show that it's our *actions*, and the associated emotions, that form and reinforce neurological pathways. The more frequently new actions are performed, and the accompanying positive stimuli are received, the more likely it is that those actions will continue to be performed. For example, an awareness of the benefits of good health is not enough to motivate most people to establish healthy habits. *Starting* to exercise, then receiving the positive stimuli of endorphins, as well as generally feeling and looking better, will make it more likely that a person will continue to exercise. Over time, as new perspectives emerge, values and attitudes toward being healthy will begin to shift. This may then even manifest itself in other new behaviors, such as eating better, and thus the process begins again. This is why the culture changed so dramatically at NUMMI and on the *Santa Fe*. It wasn't talking about changing the culture that caused the shift; it was implementing and reinforcing new behaviors. A new culture then emerged, like a shadow following the movement of an object on a sunny day.

Moving beyond Words: Creating an Environment for Agility

Increasing an organization's agility almost always requires a corresponding cultural transformation, and cultural transformation requires changes in behavior. As can be observed from the NUMMI and *Santa Fe* examples, as well as thousands of others, behavioral changes require myriad changes to the environment in which the work is done. These can be summarized as five key levers for shifting behaviors, and thus culture.

- *Structures*: The make-up of teams, and how members collaborate with each other, and other teams
- *Policies*: The rules which govern behavior, be they around expenses, dress code, or how money gets invested in products, or how decisions get made
- *Incentives*: What gets rewarded in terms of pay, bonuses, and progression
- *Metrics*: What gets measured, tracked, and therefore valued
- *Leadership behaviors*: The observable actions of leaders and managers

These levers of culture change will be present to varying degrees across all six enablers. In most organizations, these things tend to be most influenced by those in senior leadership positions. Thus culture change must be driven from the very top. It is not something to be delegated. Bottom-up culture change is unlikely to take root, as new behaviors will not be supported, enabled, or reinforced by associated policy changes. Leaders must also embody these behaviors. As Ben Horowitz puts it in his book *What You Do Is Who You Are*, "For a culture to stick, it must reflect the leader's actual values, not just those he thinks sound inspiring. Because a leader creates culture chiefly by his actions—by example."[9]

With that in mind, we will now explore some common patterns for culture change using the aforementioned five levers. To bring these to life, I shall use the example from the culture profile shown in figure 11, as moving slightly away from Control and Compete cultures toward Create and Collaborate cultures is a common aspiration. Let's bear in mind that dialing down a culture type does not mean abandoning it altogether. Each culture type has value, and all organizations need *some* element of each. Even the most innovative companies sitting largely in the Create quadrant need to get their supply chain and operations running smoothly and efficiently, an element more native to Control culture. The question is, how much change is just enough? That will be different for every entity. Now, let's discuss how to move the needle in a direction that will support business agility.

Dialing Down Control Culture Traits

It is interesting to observe the ways in which this happened on the USS *Santa Fe*. It sounds a lot like, when Captain Marquet took over, there was a strong Control culture on the ship.[10] There was a strict chain of command, many rules and regulations, and decision-making based on process rather than thinking. Now, a nuclear submarine will always need a healthy dose of Control culture traits, but with the decentralization of decision-making and an increased focus on developing people through greater clarity and technical competence, the ship seemed to shift significantly into Collaborate mode. The easiest win in a strong Control environment like this is to look for unnecessary rules and procedures and remove them. It's amazing what a little less control, and a little more trust, can do. On the *Santa Fe*, one of the first decisions Marquet sloughed off was signing off on the ship's menu. Why would the captain need to decide what type of rice was served with dinner?

Starting small is a hallmark of the incremental change approach, which works well in Control cultures. This can include things like relaxing dress codes or time tracking, removing unnecessary reporting and signoffs, and consciously pushing decision-making to where the information is. This helps remove the drive for standardization among teams. It may be neater for all teams to work in the same way and use the same tools, but it is often also ineffective. Empower teams to find the best processes and tools for the job rather than enforcing uniformity. A little less focus on process and a little more on cooperation will go a long way. Expert leaders must seek to expand their repertoires and move toward Achiever and then, ultimately, Catalyst models of leadership.

Dialing Down Compete Culture Traits

One key reason organizations end up with such a large dose of Compete culture is the ubiquitous measuring of Compete-friendly metrics. Increased growth, profitability, and market share are all good, measurable goals, but the more qualitative side can easily get forgotten amid the scramble to hit the number. This can lead to cutting corners and, in extreme cases like Enron, some questionable or even outright unethical behavior. Focusing on such metrics is often a case of making meaningful what we can measure because we cannot measure what is meaningful. Measuring and tracking engagement, growth, collaboration, and ideas are far more difficult. The benefits are big, but extremely challenging to represent on an accountant's spreadsheet. With a bias for fast results, these longer-term investments that have no direct cause-and-effect benefit can easily be overlooked.

This is what happened when John Sculley forced out Steve Jobs at Apple in 1985. Sculley, a marketing expert, shifted Apple from an innovative Create culture to a culture with a large dose of Compete. Initially, the numbers looked great as the company successfully exploited its existing products and services, but that short-term thinking, and a refusal to explore the next product, led it to come within

90 days of insolvency. Upon his return in 1997, Jobs had to shift the culture back radically to something with more of a Create emphasis. This got people innovating again, and saw Apple become the most valuable company on the planet.

To dial down Compete, focus on human as well as market needs. Focus more on teamwork and collaboration than on individualism and internal competition. Incentivize the growth of people as well as the growth of sales. Communicate values a little more and short-term profit a little less. If this is done well, then profit will result from your efforts to build great products and services.

Dialing Up Create Culture Traits

Between 1975 and 1988, US senator William Proxmire issued monthly Golden Fleece Awards to officials whom he deemed to be wasting public money. The first award went to the National Science Foundation for its $84,000 study on love. While Proxmire's intent may have been noble, Pixar president Ed Catmull, in his 2014 book *Creativity, Inc.*, speaks of the "chilling effect on research"[11] of attitudes like Proxmire's. There is no way of knowing the value of a great deal of research up front. If people are too afraid to take risks and ask open-ended questions, progress will be impeded.

A similar, albeit less formal, process tends to take place in organizations. Failure is punished, so people don't take risks. When people don't take risks, learning and innovation don't happen. People play it safe—and this impedes creativity. A hallmark of Create culture is the freedom to experiment, take risks, and even break rules. Some tangible ways to foster this kind of culture are providing strong vision, carving out time and money for ideas and experimentation, incentivizing learning, and valuing feedback over efficiency and conformity. Maximize transparency and the free flow of information to help with alignment. Google's famous 20 percent policy, which allows employees to work on whatever they like for roughly one day per week, is a great example of a policy that has led to experimentation and innovation. Google News, Gmail, and AdSense all began their lives via this experiment. When it comes to innovation and experimentation, how many places really put their money where their mouths are? This culture type is the polar opposite of Control culture, so removing as many rules and controls as possible will help the shift in this direction. In fact, Create cultures are renowned for breaking the odd rule. The topic of experimentation will be covered further in chapter 8.

Dialing Up Collaborate Culture Traits

In a 2019 presentation,[12] Simon Sinek speaks of working with the US Navy SEALs. If any outfit knows what it takes to build great teams, it's the Navy SEALs. What they told Sinek was that they look at two factors when deciding whether to take someone onto their team: performance and trustworthiness. Of course, everyone wants the high performer who is also highly trustworthy, and no one wants the low performer who is also untrustworthy. That's the easy bit. The interesting thing was that the SEALs would rather have the medium performer who is highly trustworthy than the high performer who is untrustworthy. The former makes a far better team player and, although he may not appear to be a high performer individually, he can make the *team* significantly more effective. Individual performance is great if you're an individual worker, working purely in a silo. When you're part of a team, however, this stops making sense.

Many organizations measure individual performance, but how many measure trustworthiness? As I mentioned earlier, things that are hard to measure often don't get measured. This leads to organizations placing great value on things that can easily lead to toxicity. Reed Hastings, CEO of Netflix, puts it this way: "Do not tolerate brilliant jerks. The cost to teamwork is too high."[13] To dial up the Collaborate culture, invest time and resources in developing people, relationships, trust, teamwork, and connections. Move from individual incentives to team-based incentives to increase cooperation and collaboration. Get teams to spend time together in person. There is no substitute for face-to-face, personal interactions when it comes to building social capital. Focus on engagement and participation. These things are easy to ignore, especially as ignoring them keeps costs down—but the cost of *not* doing them is far higher in the long run. Managing for high engagement will be covered further in chapter 7.

> ### Reflection
>
> Does your organization have a clear picture of which traits it would like to decrease and which it would like to increase? What type of structural and policy changes could lead to that? Are there some easy wins that would safely be introduced and would lead to behavioral change? How might leadership need to change their behavior to exemplify the new behaviors?

Chapter Summary

- An organization's culture can have a powerful positive or negative impact on its business performance.

- Current and desired cultures can be identified using the Competing Values Framework.

- Many organizations struggle to adapt and innovate because they predominantly sit in the exploit domain–friendly Control and Compete cultures.

- Mastering the explore domain is likely to require a shift toward a Create and Collaborate culture.

- Culture cannot be changed directly. It is a product of people's collective behaviors. These behaviors can only be influenced by changes in structures, policies, incentives, metrics, and leadership behaviors. For maximum effect, these changes should span all six enablers.

- As the levers to shift culture are almost always under the control of senior leaders, they should be the main drivers of culture change.

Key Practices for Business Agility

- Understand, and communicate the underlying values of the organization. Build these values into behaviors at all levels.

- Consciously focus on creating the culture that will deliver the best outcomes. Dedicate time and effort to maintain, and improve, culture on an ongoing basis.

- Map the current, and desired, culture of an organization before beginning to plan changes. Select structures and policies that are in alignment with the desired culture.

- To increase business agility, favor cultures that encourage flexibility, experimentation, and customer focus.

- Start with small policy changes to incentivize, and reinforce, the desired behaviors.

- Exemplify the desired behaviors with leaders and managers leading by example and walking the talk.

Further Reading and Resources

Books

- Kim S. Cameron, Robert E. Quinn, and Jeff DeGraff, *Competing Values Leadership: Creating Value in Organizations*, 2nd ed. (Cheltenham, UK: Edward Elgar, 2014)

- Kim S. Cameron and Robert E. Quinn, *Diagnosing and Changing Organizational Culture: Based on the Competing Values Framework*, 3rd ed. (San Francisco: Jossey-Bass, 2011)

- Daniel Coyle, *The Culture Code: The Secrets of Highly Successful Groups* (London: Random House Business Books, 2018)

- Frederic Laloux and Ken Wilber, *Reinventing Organizations: A Guide to Creating Organizations Inspired by the Next Stage in Human Consciousness* (Brussels: Nelson Parker, 2014)

- Edgar Schein, *Organizational Culture and Leadership*, 5th ed. (Hoboken, NJ: Wiley, 2016)

- Ben Horowitz, *What You Do Is Who You Are: How to Create Your Business Culture* (New York: HarperBusiness, 2019)

Websites, Articles, and Videos

- Please see www.6enablers.com/resources for more on this topic, including a downloadable reading list.

CHAPTER 6

Organizational Structure

A hierarchy isn't responsive enough to change.

—JEFF BEZOS

IN THIS CHAPTER, WE WILL EXPLORE

- the increasing importance of customer-centricity in organizational design
- the challenges of organizational silos and the benefits of cross-functional teams
- why the network model is more adaptive than traditional hierarchies
- how to design ambidextrous organizations that can excel at both exploring and exploiting.

The Importance of Structure: Adopting Electricity

Walking through almost any factory in the eighteenth century must have been quite an experience. Before the use of electric motors that were small enough to be connected to individual machines, mechanical power came from water flowing through rivers. The water turned waterwheels, which, in turn, rotated a central steel line shaft that ran the full length of the factory. A complicated system of belts and gears, known as millwork, connected subsidiary shafts that drove looms, hammers, presses, and all manner of other machines. Drip oilers were required throughout the factory to keep the system well lubricated.

During the mid-nineteenth century, the development of coal-powered steam engines led many factories to switch their power source from water to coal. In this model, a single, huge steam engine turned the central line shaft instead of water. There were many benefits to transitioning to this model, including greater availability of energy and the freedom to build factories in any location, not just on fast-flowing rivers.

Despite the change of power source, factory design remained unchanged throughout the nineteenth century. A central power source was still required, albeit coal rather than water. A central line shaft still ran the length of the factory. And the complicated millwork was still needed to supply mechanical power to the factory's various machines. In effect, very little changed, other than the power source, and the changes were therefore not at all disruptive. The line shaft design was highly inefficient. If just a single machine in the factory needed to operate, the coal fires were required to be fully operational to create the power to drive the line shaft. This meant that, in practice, workers were continuously required to feed the coal fires and keep the factory lubricated, with much of that energy going to waste. This had long been a source of frustration for factory owners, as it drove up operating costs.

The year 1882 saw the dawn of another great leap forward in powering factories: the world's first coal-fired power station opened in London. Owned by Thomas Edison and known as Edison Electric Light Station, it provided electricity as a commodity to the public for the first time. Later that year, Edison opened a second station, the Pearl Street Station in New York City.

It wasn't long before some forward-thinking factory owners saw the potential of electricity and began experimenting by replacing steam engines with electric motors. After all, many had previously switched their power source from water to coal with minimal disruption and great benefit. They knew how to do it. By 1899, however, some 17 years after Edison opened his first power stations, less than 5 percent of mechanical drive power in factories was coming from electricity.[1] Most were still using coal. Those who had invested in installing electric motors to replace coal-powered steam engines had faced large capital investment costs and were disappointed with the returns. They saw few of the promised productivity increases or cost savings. This revolutionary new technology, which dawned with so much promise, was failing to live up to the hype.

Why? It turns out that the problem lay with *how* the technology was implemented. Factory owners who did experiment with electricity did so by following the same playbook as when they had transitioned from water power to steam power. They merely ripped out the existing steam engines and replaced them with electric motors. New factories were built using the standard blueprint of the time. This left factory design unchanged, with only the power source switched. Hence, none of the changes needed to unlock the benefits of electricity had been made. Cost savings and productivity gains did not materialize, and disillusionment about electricity grew.

What was not understood at the time was that getting real results would require far greater structural changes than simply replacing one power source with another. Electricity had the potential to deliver power exactly where and when it was required. Small steam engines were hopelessly inefficient, but small electric motors were perfectly viable. This meant that factories could contain large numbers of small power sources each driving a smaller line shaft, rather than a single giant source driving a single monolithic one. In theory, every workbench could even have a machine with its own electric motor, something that would allow the operation of individual machines as and when they were required—a far more efficient setup. Power would not be transmitted through a single spinning line shaft, but through thin wires. This would mean factories could be arranged far more efficiently around a production line rather than the central shaft. The whole design of the factory, along with production processes, needed to be fundamentally rethought. Even the way workers were recruited, trained, and paid needed overhauling to account for their newfound control. In short, there was very little that would *not* need to be adapted to the new way of working. Most factory owners were reluctant to make such wide-ranging, disruptive changes—and investments. This meant they merely tinkered at the edges and failed to reap the benefits.

In the end, electricity became cheaper, workers became more expensive, and manufacturers finally figured out how to use a technology that was, by then, over four decades old. By 1920, 55 percent of factory machines were powered by electricity,[2] and productivity in America was soaring. Businesspeople finally understood that there was no easy way to reap the benefits. They finally accepted that using electricity efficiently meant changes to architecture, logistics, and personnel—changes that would fundamentally shift operations. Change on that scale takes time, vision, and no small amount of courage.

This story will likely sound familiar to anyone who has been involved with organizational change. I have seen many places train a few team members, encourage them to work differently, then expect the magic to happen without any significant changes to team structures. When that magic fails to materialize, one can hear claims of "We tried that," and "That does not work here." Nor will it, unless the associated structural and operational changes also happen. As we have seen, many organizations are designed around Industrial Revolution principles of efficiency and optimizing for the exploit domain. But as I said in chapter 3, an oil tanker will never be as nimble as a flotilla of speedboats. Regardless of how much training its crew receives, a tanker is just not designed for speed. When it comes to business agility and mastering the explore domain, changing organizational structure is unavoidable. It requires far more than a quick lick of paint. It requires deep organizational change. Like redesigning an entire factory, that can be hard, and it can be disruptive. To survive in an increasingly complex and volatile world, however, it is necessary.

It is worth noting that organizational structure is a large contributor to organizational agility. It is also a rare enabler over which leaders have direct control. Unlike culture, which emerges as a result of behaviors, values, and mindsets, team structures can be deliberately designed for a given property. For that reason, they tend to be of particular interest to leaders.

With the importance of teamwork on the rise, it is vital for leaders to understand their role in setting teams up for success. Below are some "pillars" that support high-performing, collaborative, self-managing teams (figure 14):

- *A foundation of trust, transparency, and psychological safety.* The sense that teammates can be relied upon, and a feeling that it is OK to ask for help, make mistakes, and be vulnerable. This underpins all relationships, collaboration, and teamwork.

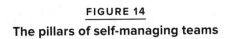

FIGURE 14

The pillars of self-managing teams

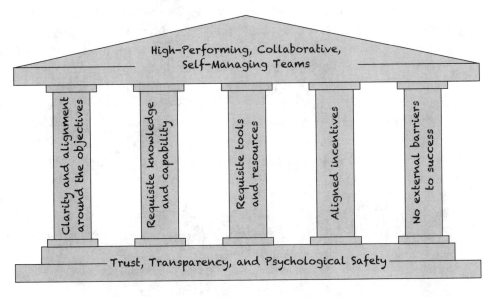

- *Clarity and alignment around the objectives.* An unambiguous mutual understanding of what is to be achieved. This is the sense of direction.

- *Requisite knowledge and capability.* The correct skillset on the team to achieve the objective. This ensures the team is able to travel in the desired direction.

- *Requisite tools and resources.* Access to everything the team will need to achieve the objective. This allows the team to travel more quickly in the desired direction.

- *Aligned incentives.* No conflict between individual, team, and organizational interests. This ensures that the desired direction of travel is the same for all.

- *No external barriers to success.* Nothing outside the control of the team that will be an impediment to delivery. This ensures that there are no roadblocks.

What is clear is that organizational structure can have a disproportionate effect on team performance and should therefore be at the forefront of leaders' thoughts. While teams should be accountable for delivering results, the absence of any of the aforementioned pillars will likely have a detrimental effect, and it's the responsibility of leaders to ensure these are in place. I rarely encounter truly bad teams, just teams operating under bad leadership. With that in mind, next, I will outline four key principles for organizational structures that support business agility and innovation. If organizations fail to embrace these, and to learn lessons from the story of electricity, many will incur the same 40-year lag between the emergence of agile approaches and the achievement of true business agility. This will see them figure it out sometime around 2041. Assuming, of course, that they survive that long.

Reflection

Is your organization considering the structural changes as part of its transformation journey or merely focusing on the team-level practices? If it is not considering the structural changes, could this be a reason why it feels like agility might not be applicable in your organization?

Principle One: Customer-Centricity

Jeff Bezos, founder and CEO of Amazon, once said, "If we can keep our competitors focused on us while we stay focused on the customer, ultimately we'll turn out all right."[3] But businesses did not always have to be customer focused. Rewind 100 years and a lack of competition meant that there was little incentive to innovate or to delight customers. There was a widespread mentality of "We make it, you take it." If customers did not like one business's product, their options for seeking out a better one were limited. Thus, power lay in the hands of whoever was making the product. The customer had no choice but to revolve around the organization.

Today, the picture looks very different. With lower barriers to entry, deregulation, widely accessible new technology, and lower switching costs, new entrants have sprung up in every market to challenge the thrones of the established players. This has driven up competition, and the battle for customers is a fierce one that must be fought on a daily basis. A dissatisfied customer can easily find another place with which to do business. Innovation and providing great service have, therefore, become vital tools in keeping hold of customers. In 1954, Peter Drucker said, "There is only one valid definition of business purpose: to create a customer."[4] Thus, organizations now have no choice but to revolve around the customer. In his book *The Age of Agile*, Steve Denning calls this shift the Copernican Revolution in Management,[5] after the original Copernican Revolution, which saw humans' view of the universe shift from the geocentric model, in which the earth is at the center of the universe, to the heliocentric model, in which the sun is at the center of the solar system, with planets revolving around it. Denning's revolution represents a fundamental shift in the relationship between business and customer, with power having flowed away from organizations and into the hands of customers.

While we undertake creative work and search for new products and services, there is no substitute for understanding the customer. When innovating, design and construction are so tightly interwoven that they are almost indistinguishable from each other. When moving away from traditional bureaucratic management practices, there must be a clear understanding of which problems are being solved, and for whom. Only then will it be possible for teams at the coal face to make the best decisions. People are not inspired or motivated by being mere cogs in a machine, and the "cog effect" is exacerbated when there is no clear sense of that machine's end product.

In their book *Strategy from the Outside In*, George Day and Christine Moorman define two approaches to strategy.[6] The *inside-out* approach is guided by an inward focus and the belief that internal capabilities, company resources, and greater efficiencies will create success. An organization that is inward-looking and focused on competitors over customers, however, will only ever be a follower, never an innovator. The cultures that fit this approach are those found in the two left quadrants of the Competing Values Framework, Control and Collaborate (see chapter 5). The *outside-in* approach values collaboration with customers, seeing it as a way to provide value and to solve their problems. This approach begins with the market, not an organization's capabilities. Outside-in tends to be favored by cultures on the right side of the CVF, Compete and Create. Business agility is far more aligned with the latter approach, with the *Manifesto for Agile Software Development* strongly emphasizing the fast, and frequent, delivery of customer value. Bezos put it this way: "Companies get skill-focused. When they think about extending their business into some new area, the first question they ask is 'Why should we do that? We don't have skills in that area.' That puts a finite lifetime on a company because the world changes, and what used to be cutting-edge skills have turned into something your customers may not need anymore. A much more stable strategy is to start with 'What do my customers need?' Then do an inventory of the gaps in your skills."[7]

Few would argue against focusing on the customer, and many organizations profess to espouse it. And yet, take a look at most organization charts and what you will see is a hierarchical pyramid with no obvious way to map to the customer. Jack Welch once defined hierarchical organizations as those in which "everyone has their face toward the CEO and their ass toward the customer."[8] Often, all but a few people are completely abstracted away from the purpose of the organization and the problems it seeks to solve for the customer. As we will see in chapter 7, this is often a key reason why employee motivation and engagement are so low. Many organizations are still designed around specialized job roles. This is a hangover from the days when innovations were few and far between and there was little need for collaboration, either internally or with customers.

In a high-VUCA environment, internal and external collaboration is core to creating value. Organizations must reflect this reality in their design. It must be less concerned with efficient execution of individual tasks, and more concerned with cooperation and the quick and effective delivery of value. Once design reflects that change, the organization chart begins to look very different, and the entity looks less like a machine and more like a living organism.

Reflection

Are the teams in your organization based on function, or customer outcomes? What is the reason for that? What are the benefits? What are the downsides?

Principle Two: Small, Cross-Functional Teams

Imagine this scene: A family is awakened in the dead of night by the deafening siren of a smoke alarm. The parents instantly detect a strong smell of smoke. The father frantically runs to check on the kids while the mother quickly calls the fire department. On her first few attempts, the line is busy and she cannot get through. On the fifth attempt, she is successful, but is told that everyone is busy, and that a team of firefighters can't be there for about five hours—because they first have to complete the other jobs on that night's list. The family is able to get out of the house and to safety, but by the time the team arrives, the house has been razed to the ground by the flames.

Later that month, Dean, the manager of the fire station, receives a bonus for increasing efficiency at the station for the sixth month in a row. The utilization rate (i.e., the percentage of available time that his firefighters are productive) has jumped from 10 to 80 percent. The team's idle time has been significantly reduced, meaning they spend more time being productive than ever before. This has resulted in huge cost savings for the station, as fewer firefighters are required to carry out the work. Dean is now in line for a promotion through which he will oversee the implementation of his cost-saving measure across multiple fire stations. This is despite the incident that saw the family just mentioned lose their home.

Let's think about this situation for a minute. It could be argued that Dean acted entirely reasonably given the outcome he was asked to deliver. Certainly I've seen many chief information officers take the same approach. More times than I care to remember, I have observed within product development a target to increase resource[9] utilization from, say, 85 to 98 percent. This is seen as efficient and a good way to deliver, while keeping staff costs as low as possible. Who wouldn't want their people to be busy? The whole system is subsequently designed to maximize the utilization of people as an indicator of effectiveness. This is known as *resource efficiency*, and intuitively, it makes sense. The logic is that the busier people are, the more work they will do each day. The more work people do each day, the more quickly value gets delivered. This is straight out of the Adam Smith and Henry Ford division-of-labor and specialization playbook. It is a hangover from early twentieth-century production-line thinking, and it mistakenly assumes that what is effective in the predictable exploit domain will also work well in the creative, unpredictable explore domain. Unfortunately, this thinking misses an important piece of the equation: line-ups, or queues.

The point that most miss, however, is that there is far more variability when searching (exploring) than there is when executing (exploiting), and where there is variability and high utilization, there will be line-ups—lots of them. While the Brits may be famous for loving a good queue, the truth is that line-ups and waiting lists in knowledge work are pernicious, silent killers of delivery and agility. When there is little excess capacity in the system, work ends up taking disproportionately longer to get done—often 10 to 20 times longer. This causes frustration at the inability to get things done, which in turn leads to further action designed to increase utilization in a futile attempt to speed things up. Thus the vicious cycle continues.

What most do not realize is that it's the high level of use that *causes* the problem. A fully utilized road is otherwise known as a traffic jam. It is worth noting at this point that not only do line-ups extend feedback loops and reduce agility, but they also have a major financial impact that may not be immediately seen. While the cost of delay is not always as obvious as when a house is on fire, delays are not free. Such expense is difficult to measure in organizations, and yet there is no question that delaying the delivery of value will have an economic cost. If structures are designed to maximize resource efficiency, traditionally tracked costs may look great on a spreadsheet, but they will belie the far bigger costs—those brought about by delays. When it comes to creative work, the biggest waste tends to be not idle workers but idle work. We must stop watching the runners and start watching the baton.

The interesting thing that I have found is that almost everyone already knows this. Ask anyone in an organization what she would do if she needed to solve a time-critical, complex problem and she will likely say that she would put together some variation of a tiger team. The term, popularized in 1970 by NASA after a cross-functional team of experts was brought together to ensure the safe return of Apollo 13, is now used to describe any small, dedicated team that collaborates to solve a complex problem. These teams are effective because of the diverse perspectives they contain and the (often temporary) removal of structural barriers to communication and collaboration that comes with them. They are designed to meet big challenges quickly and creatively.

To increase business agility then, organizations must leverage the same benefits. They must structure themselves in a way that maximizes collaboration, and that keeps work flowing rather than simply keeping people busy. It is the age-old trade-off of efficiency versus adaptability. As W. Edwards Deming once said, "Every system is perfectly designed to get the results it gets."[10] Only when leaders understand the result they are seeking can an appropriate organizational structure emerge. Trying to structure for agility *and* efficiency is akin to training for a marathon and a 100-meter sprint at the same time. They are just not compatible.

In their book *Lean Software Development*, Mary and Tom Poppendieck outline the seven wastes of software development, inspired by the seven wastes of manufacturing, which originated with the Toyota Production System.[11] The seven wastes of software development are hand-offs, waiting or delays, partially done work, task switching, extra processes, extra features, and defects. In my professional experience, the biggest source of these wastes is an inappropriate organizational structure. Organizational structures that are designed for resource efficiency—in particular, those structured into silos—are most prone to these kinds of waste.

A silo, from the Greek *siros*, meaning a pit for holding grain, is a large, vertical tower often used for agricultural storage of grain or feed. When it comes to organizations, silos tend to be functional units such as marketing, finance, or engineering. These siloed units tend to focus only on their own activity or function, and are not focused on outcomes. Much as in Henry Ford's production line of 1913, work flows sequentially through each silo until the final product emerges. As with the traditional production line, this approach can work when one is performing predictable, repeatable work. However, when it comes to creative work, collaboration *across* functions becomes vital. In their influential 1986 *Harvard Business Review* paper "The New New Product Development Game,"[12] Hirotaka Takeuchi and Ikujiro Nonaka note that the "relay race" approach, in which siloed groups of specialists pass the "baton" sequentially from one group to another, conflicts with the goals of speed and flexibility when it comes to new product development. The more holistic approach, by which multidisciplinary teams go the distance together, passing the "ball" back and forth much like a rugby team,[13] serves competitive requirements much more effectively.

When it comes to managing in the explore domain, there are two key things to understand. The first is that when performing collaborative, complex, creative work, the individual is no longer the fundamental building block of the organization—the team is. This has wide-ranging implications for how work is managed, performed, and incentivized and how organizations are structured. Today, work is often too complex to be performed by individuals, and passing work between departments becomes too onerous as organizations move away from neat, one-pass sequential processes to messy, iterative approaches with fast feedback and pivots. The use of tiger teams recognizes this fact.

The second thing to understand is that in a fast-paced, unpredictable world, the biggest problem teams face is knowing the right product to build. That requires experimentation and the ability to respond to feedback. It means different functions bouncing ideas off each other. It takes diverse perspectives from many disciplines working together to solve complex problems. Organizing for efficiency is no longer the answer. Teams need to organize for collaboration, creativity, and agility. This will, by definition, build some inefficiencies into the process. That should be welcomed by enlightened leaders who understand that building the wrong product efficiently is far more wasteful than building a great one less efficiently.

There is a second type of "efficiency" that I have, to this point, ignored: *flow efficiency*. What most people mean when they talk about efficiency is resource efficiency. This is the percentage of time a resource—often, but not always, a person—is busy. Divide busy time by total time and you get the proportion of time used. Flow efficiency is focused on the percentage of an item's lead time in which work is being performed on it versus the percentage of time it spends sitting in a queue. For example, say a picture needs to be sketched, painted, and framed. Those tasks may take 30, 70, and 10 minutes, respectively. The total *work time* is thus 110 minutes. But the sketcher may be busy working on other pictures for 105 minutes before he starts on this one. After that, the picture may then need to wait another 85 minutes for the painter, and 140 minutes before it can be framed. This means that the total *lead time* is 440 minutes. Flow efficiency, which represents the percentage of lead time during which work is actually being performed on the item, would thus be a mere 25 percent. The remaining 75 percent represents the proportion of time the item has spent *waiting* to be worked on.

It is not uncommon for traditional organizations engaging in creative work to find that work items typically spend between 80 and 95 percent of their total elapsed lead time sitting idle, waiting to be processed. This is a stunning amount of waste, and it is caused purely by the fact that the most popular form of organizational structure loves specialist silos and high utilization rates. Compounding this is the fact that queues in knowledge work, unlike in factories, are often invisible, and thus it is far harder to manage them.

With up to 95 percent of delays attributable to organizational structure, achieving business agility and the ability to innovate will mean remaking activity-based teams into *outcome-based* teams (figure 15). Activity-focused teams perform one function, such as marketing, design, or engineering. These tend to be specialist teams, which lead to the waste and delays just described. Outcome-based teams are the kinds of teams Takeuchi and Nonaka describe in "The New New Product Development Game." They focus on end-to-end delivery of customer outcomes. They are self-sufficient, containing all of the skills they need to deliver value without relying on other teams. They take ideas all the way from concept to cash.

Imagine that the sketcher, painter, and framer just referred to formed a small team responsible for an outcome—in this case, completed pictures. If they all focused on one picture at a time, there might

FIGURE 15

Activity-based versus outcome-based teams

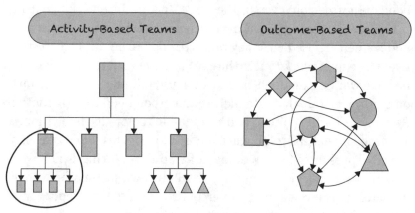

be, say, a 30-minute wait while they finished off an earlier picture, and they could then deliver a new picture in 110 minutes. That's a total of 150 minutes, rather than 440, despite the team members having a far lower utilization—that is, they each had more idle time. That's a significantly shorter time in which to gather feedback, course-correct, and deliver, making the organization far more responsive to change. In this model, team members can also collaborate throughout the process to ensure that the sketcher does not create something that would cause problems for the painter, thus avoiding costly rework.

There are many great examples of small, cross-functional teams focused on customer outcomes, from sports teams, to special forces teams, to medical teams, to tiger teams. In fact, think of any high-performing team, and you will almost certainly be thinking of a small, autonomous, cross-functional, outcome-based group. They are effective not just because they minimize hand-offs, queues, and delays. It is not only the fast feedback that counts. There is no way to create a shared goal within a group of people who just happen to be performing the same activity, each on different projects or products. With outcome-based teams, it is possible to create a customer-focused shared goal around which the team can organize. Shared goals are highly motivating. As well, it is possible to grant greater autonomy to such groups. Granting autonomy to a group responsible for a single activity will optimize it for *that* activity, often to the detriment of other activities. As discussed in chapter 4, autonomy within real teams allows for swift, contextual decision-making by those closest to the work. And as we will see in chapter 7, it is also highly motivating.

The final reason outcome-based teams are so effective is that they reduce interface failures. Many organizations farm out product components to separate departments, or even separate organizations. While each component can be efficiently produced in isolation, problems appear upon integration. It's rarely the components themselves that are the problem. It is the *interfaces among components*. These interface failures are caused by the siloed nature of development and add risk to development initiatives.

When Alan Mulally joined the Ford Motor Company as CEO in 2005, he set about breaking down the silos that had led to some of the company's high-profile failures. Having overseen the development of Boeing's 777 aircraft, he attributed its success to the collaboration among multiple previously separate groups. By integrating engineers and designers at Ford, he was attempting to do what Toyota had been doing for decades. He stated, "A designer who knew nothing about thermodynamics might create a great-looking grille only to discover that it did not allow enough air to flow into the engine compartment. An engineer with no knowledge of ergonomics might develop an exhaust system that worked perfectly but was impossible to install."[14] When integrating functions, Mulally strongly emphasized a shared purpose to keep everyone aligned on customer outcomes. It proved an incredibly successful approach—as it has at places like Apple, Google, and Amazon.

When transitioning to cross-functional, outcome-based teams, to ensure that people do not lose touch with others performing the same role, informal communities of practice can be helpful to share knowledge, define standards, and build connections across teams.

> ### Reflection
>
> Are the teams in your organization designed for efficiency or agility? Do people with different skills operate in silos, or collaborate? Do teams have shared goals? What are the pros and cons of that structure?

Principle Three: The Network of Interconnected Teams

It is generally accepted that modern humans have been around, in their current anatomical form, for about 200,000 years. For roughly the first 95 percent of that time, we lived as hunter-gatherers in small bands of a few dozen at most. The evidence suggests that these were largely egalitarian groups with no hierarchy and effortless cooperation. Anyone who tried to become the alpha of the group would be collectively suppressed by the rest.[15] These bands were highly connected, highly collaborative, and small enough that everyone could have a personal relationship with everyone else. Trust was high and people looked out for one another. While conflict did still occur, on the whole, these were highly effective societies. Over that 190,000 years, the human brain evolved perfectly for this kind of existence.

Then, initiated by the shift from foraging to agriculture around 10,000 years ago, the first farming villages began to appear. These villages consisted of a few hundred people at most. As the population expanded, filling up the land, groups came into conflict with each other. In his book *Ultrasociety: How 10,000 Years of War Made Humans the Greatest Cooperators on Earth*, Peter Turchin argues that the main driver for the advent of coordinated hierarchies and the rapid growth of societies was warfare. There is a French military saying: "God is on the side of big battalions." Larger, more hierarchical societies were able to outcompete smaller ones in battle. This led to ever-larger and ever more centralized hierarchical societies, able to produce weapons, create strategies, and organize themselves in battle effectively. In this new landscape, these more hierarchical societies thrived at the expense of smaller, flatter ones. The first formally centralized societies, simple chiefdoms, emerged a mere 7,500 years ago in Mesopotamia and consisted of a few thousand people. This growth of societies accelerated, culminating in nation-states of hundreds of millions of people today.

Whether it's the first small farming villages, the Catholic Church, the Roman Empire, or Max Weber's bureaucratic management system, as soon as groups surpass a certain size, hierarchical pyramids are seen as the only viable construct. How else can organizations mobilize large numbers of people toward a common goal? Most don't even consider that there could be another way—but, in fact, many entities *have* found another way. In evolutionary terms, 10,000 years is the mere blink of an eye. We are still evolutionarily primed for far smaller, far flatter, and far more cooperative societies. Hierarchical structures and functional silos tend to work against the ways in which our brains have evolved. They prevent collaboration, stifle innovation, and inhibit the ability to be responsive to change. They are a hallmark of Control and Compete cultures (see chapter 5) and, while effective for certain types of exploit work, are inappropriate for the more creative explore domain.

What's more, management consultant Gary Hamel and Michele Zanini estimate that the extra middle managers and coordinators necessary to maintain the hierarchical model account for one-third of an organization's payroll.[16] These excess layers of management cost the OECD countries $9 trillion annually in lost economic output.[17] Whichever way you look at it, managing a hierarchy is eye-wateringly expensive, requires an army of coordinating managers, and slows down decision-making. The issue to date has been finding a viable alternative that does not precede the descent into chaos.

Small, cross-functional teams, if set up well, can be incredibly effective. People can build trust, create a shared vision, maintain relationships, and easily collaborate and self-organize in quest of an outcome. This is how humans are designed to work. In early 2002, Jeff Bezos, CEO of Amazon, took some time off to read and think about his company. Upon his return to work, he restructured Amazon to be built around "two-pizza teams." These are teams small enough to be sufficiently fed by two large pizzas if, say, they're working late. In practice, that meant they would be composed of fewer than 10 people. Bezos wanted teams to be independent and entrepreneurial. As Neil Roseman, an Amazon executive, puts it, "Autonomous working units are good. Things to manage working units are bad."[18] At the time, Bezos was responding to technology giants like Microsoft. Such companies had multiple layers of managers arranged in a top-down hierarchy, which slowed decision-making, stifled innovation, and destroyed employee engagement.

Consider what makes for great teams, and a few attributes will likely stand out: trust, shared goals or purpose, autonomy, frequent interaction and communication. If this is true for teams, could it also be true for multiple teams collaborating on a bigger goal? What if organizations could achieve similar benefits with large teams to those seen with teams of fewer than 10? Life would be rather simple if every product or endeavor could be tackled effectively by a single two-pizza team. Unfortunately, some things—putting a human on the moon, for example—require more people. Bigger endeavors often require multiple teams to collaborate in the service of a bigger goal.

In the 1990s, British anthropologist Robin Dunbar suggested that there was a limit to the number of people any person can trust. His range was 100 to 230,[19] but many use 150 as the magic number. This is often referred to as "Dunbar's number." Because of this, there is a temptation to reorganize larger groups only at the lowest level, and to keep the standard hierarchy in place for anything more highly ranked. In this way, teams are rearranged to be cross-functional, but all the higher levels of the classic hierarchy are retained. There are thus high levels of communication and collaboration *within* teams, but little *among* teams. When cross-team coordination is required, that still remains a top-down endeavor, with all of the delays and extra processes that incurs. This is what Stanley McChrystal, a retired US Army general and former head of the US Joint Special Operations Command, calls a command of teams.[20] Teams are treated as silos, albeit autonomous, outcome-based silos, but managers largely coordinate among them. There will be some benefit to this approach, but the complex coordination structures, program management, and go-betweens will remain. Overall agility will be drastically limited.

To create a structure in which true business agility can be achieved, organizations need to go a step further. They must move away from the hierarchical pyramid and embrace the network model (figure 16). In a network of interconnected teams—a team of teams, if you will—multiple autonomous teams collaborate with one another, with leadership, and with customers to reach an overall goal (figure 17). Communication among teams is informal and done as necessary by those within the team, rather than by external coordinators such as project or program managers. As discussed in chapter 4, in order for

FIGURE 16

Command versus network of teams

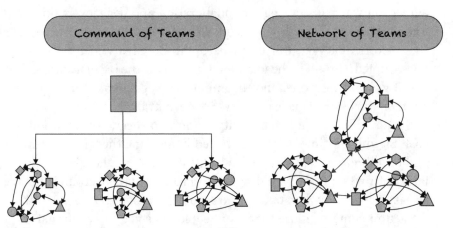

Source: Stanley McChrystal, *Team of Teams: New Rules of Engagement for a Complex World* (New York: Penguin, 2015), 224.

FIGURE 17

The wider network

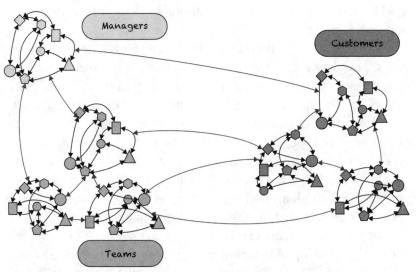

Source: Steve Denning, "Explaining Agile," *Forbes,* September 8, 2016, https://www.forbes.com/sites/stevedenning/2016/09/08/explaining-agile.

control to be vested in this way, there must be crystal-clear alignment regarding larger goals, the requisite technical competence, and agreed-on ways of working for collaboration and decision-making. These networks are highly resilient. As control is distributed across the network, it is very difficult to disrupt it. Cut off a spider's leg and it is crippled. Cut off its head and it dies. Cut off the leg of a starfish, and it grows a new one, and the amputated leg can also grow into another starfish.[21] This is the power of decentralized control.

Such resilience and adaptability do not, however, come without cost. Significant time must be invested in aligning the whole group and building trust. With a little attention, trust is relatively easily built within teams, but building trust across the larger group is not so easy, especially when taking into account Dunbar's number. What if the unit contains more than 150 people? The good news is that it is not necessary for *everyone* to have a deep connection to everyone else. There is simply no way that that many close, trusting relationships can be developed. Our brains are just not wired for it. Fortunately, all that is required is for *someone* on each team to have a connection with *at least one* person on each of the other teams. That way, all teams will be mutually connected. These connections may take the form of single relationships or multiple ones. Thus, there is trust both *within* and *among* teams, which makes interteam collaboration far easier.

Many of the most progressive and adaptive organizations structure themselves according to the principle of a network of autonomous, cross-functional teams rather than the traditional hierarchical pyramid. Take the supremely innovative W. L. Gore, the makers of Gore-Tex, which generated over $3 billion in revenue in 2017 and employs over 8,000 people in more than 45 plants across the world.[22] W. L. Gore has no hierarchy and no bureaucracy. It is a company in which anyone can talk to anyone, a company with no bosses or supervisors. It is built around self-managing teams, arranged in a lattice, all of which strive to make money, and to have fun.

Dutch health care provider Buurtzorg employs over 14,000 nurses and carers working in teams of up to 12. Supporting around 1,000 self-organizing teams, Buurtzorg has a total of 50 support staff, 18 coaches—and zero managers.[23] Teams take care of the whole process, from recruitment, to new clients, to planning and delivering the work. Buurtzorg's care costs are the lowest in the Netherlands, its health care professionals spend more time with clients, and employee engagement is the highest among any Dutch company of over 1,000 people.

Multinational home appliances and consumer goods giant Haier, based in Qingdao, China, is another prime example of the power of organizational structure. Founded in 1984, Haier (pronounced *higher*) only began its transition to self-management in 2009. Led by founder and CEO Zhang Ruimin and cofounder Yang Mian, and inspired by Morning Star's self-managing model, Haier set to work dismantling the traditional hierarchical pyramid. The company removed around 4,000 middle managers, a move that has led over 4,000 cross-functional, self-organizing teams to flourish. Instead of answering to bosses, teams now answer to the customer, and are responsible for all aspects of a product or service. Armed with detailed customer information, entrepreneurial workers are free to build teams around their ideas, sharing in the profits and functioning as autonomous micro-enterprises. They stay connected to customers and other internal units via sophisticated technology platforms. If there is any doubt that the self-organization model can scale far beyond single teams through the use of the network model, Haier's success should put paid to it. Haier is one of the few companies that initially operated as a bureaucratic hierarchy—that is, it was not born agile. Today, it is the world's largest manufacturer of home appliances, with revenues of $32 billion and $2.4 billion in profit. It has 70,000 employees and features on Boston Consulting Group's list of the top 10 most innovative companies in the world.[24]

The final example, and another that has made the difficult transition from hierarchy to network, is Swedish multinational bank Handelsbanken. Founded in 1871, the bank named Jan Wallander CEO in 1970, and he found an organization in crisis. A strong, centralized hierarchical structure and top-down decision-making led to delays of months for even low-level decisions. Centralized departments and bureaucracy were getting in the way of serving customers. There was frustration on the front line as employees' detailed knowledge of customers was not matched by the authority to make decisions.

In response, Wallander implemented a model of radical decentralization. He point-blank refused to make major decisions, instead referring clients to local branches. Those branches were run with genuine autonomy, by networks of small teams comprising up to 10 people. Wallander removed centralized groups and centralized budgets. Branches now controlled their own visions, strategic planning, and marketing, as well as what products were offered, including pricing. They controlled the hiring and firing process, and the head office assumed a supporting role with next to no control. Branches were measured on their cost-to-income ratio, among other indicators, which was made transparent and drove branches to improve. Handelsbanken now has a minimum return on investment of 12 percent and annual growth of 15 percent, outperforming most banks.[25]

Reflection

When teams collaborate on a bigger goal, are there external coordination structures or do they collaborate between themselves? Is there a shared goal across teams? Is there trust across teams? What barriers are in place to communication and collaboration? How could these be addressed?

Principle Four: Ambidextrous Organizations

What we have discussed in this chapter thus far is how to think differently about organizational structure. We've explored how to harness the evolution of the human brain by organizing to maximize cooperation. Creativity rarely happens in a silo. There is a magic that happens when people from diverse disciplines, fields, and cultures are brought together. In his book *The Medici Effect*, Frans Johansson[26] describes how the Medicis, a wealthy Florentine banking family, sparked an extraordinary explosion of creativity in fifteenth-century Italy, contributing significantly to the Renaissance. They did so by bringing to the city of Florence an array of painters, sculptors, poets, financiers, architects, and scientists. The coming together of such diverse skills and the breaking down of traditional boundaries led to a flurry of creativity, new ideas, and innovation.

The same is true in organizations. Steve Jobs was obsessive in his attention to detail when designing the headquarters of both Apple and Pixar. He shared the view that innovation is sparked by "serendipitous interactions" between people with diverse perspectives and experiences, once stating, "If a building doesn't encourage [collaboration], you'll lose a lot of innovation and the magic that's sparked by serendipity. So we designed the building to make people get out of their offices and mingle in the central atrium with people they might not otherwise see."[27] David Radcliffe, the man who created Google's work environment, echoed that perspective: "Casual collisions are what we try and create in the work environment. You can't schedule innovation, you can't schedule idea generation and so when we think about our facilities around the world we're really looking for little opportunities for engineers or for creative people to come together."[28] This thinking supports the imperative to tear down structural boundaries and create networks of small, customer-focused, multidisciplinary teams. It's simply the most effective way to carry out creative work. It is often the case, however, that organizations must look both forward and backward, working simultaneously in the exploit and explore domains. That takes a little more thought.

Running parallel structures, cultures, leadership models, and policies within the same organization is extremely challenging. The natures of searching and executing are diametrically opposed. It is for this reason that many choose to create separate organizations, each with its own operating model. Innovation tsar Clayton Christensen himself has advised as much, stating, "When confronted with a disruptive change, organizations cannot simultaneously explore and exploit but must spin out the exploratory subunit."[29] While the appeal here is clear, this is not always the most effective approach. When working in the explore domain, the desired level of integration with the wider organization can often be determined by considering the level of strategic importance of the potential new product and its alignment with the wider organizational strategy, and the extent to which the new product, service, or business would benefit from leveraging core business assets and competencies such as talent,

FIGURE 18
When to structure for ambidexterity

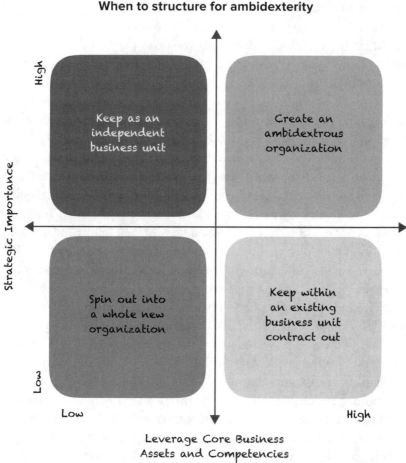

Source: Charles A. O'Reilly and Michael L. Tushman, *Lead and Disrupt: How to Solve the Innovator's Dilemma* (Stanford, CA: Stanford Business Books, 2016), 175.

marketing, manufacturing, technology, or brand. In their book *Lead and Disrupt: How to Solve the Innovator's Dilemma*, Charles A. O'Reilly and Michael L. Tushman use a two-by-two matrix to show four scenarios (figure 18).[30]

Considering only the cases of high alignment with the strategy of the wider organization, we can see two clear scenarios. When there is little opportunity to leverage organizational assets, it makes sense to create an entirely separate, autonomous business unit. This can

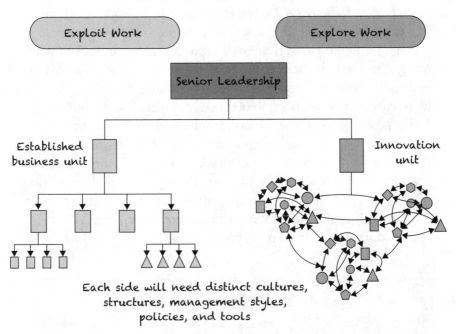

FIGURE 19

An ambidextrous organizational structure

Each side will need distinct cultures,
structures, management styles,
policies, and tools

work well, but often, when an organization innovates, the lack of immediate returns means that they are, during their initial years at least, often starved of resources. The ability to leverage assets, resources, and capabilities from a mature organization and to have senior leadership provide light-touch oversight can yield a significant advantage. This must be achieved with sufficient distancing to allow the exploiting and the exploring sides of the organization to form their own visions, values, cultures, structures, and policies. In this way, they will operate largely as separate organizations, each with its own distinct operating model, but with a level of leadership that spans both sides (figure 19). This will allow for cross-fertilization of ideas and give the exploring unit access to the recourses and capabilities of the wider organization. The units need to be simultaneously *separated* and *integrated*. A fine balancing act is required from leaders to enable enough integration not to starve the exploring unit of resources, while also not overburdening it with unnecessary processes and policies from the established business. This cannot be overstated.

3M is one of the most innovative businesses in the world. It constantly strives to increase revenue through new products, defined as products less than five years old. Upon its introduction of Six Sigma, an exploit-friendly tool employed to boost productivity in manufacturing, 3M found that productivity did indeed increase. Unfortunately, Six Sigma had the opposite effect on innovation and agility, and the proportion of revenues from new products fell.[31] What works in execution of the status quo often stifles creativity and the search for the new. Over time, the exploring unit may demonstrate a product-market fit, scale up, and become an established business. It may then be appropriate to integrate it back into the wider organization.

Using this approach, and separating the exploiting activities from the exploring with minimal integration, organizations can truly excel at both exploiting and exploring, become truly ambidextrous, and maximize the chance of enduring success.

Reflection

In your organization, is the uncertain, creative work treated the same as, or differently from, the more predictable, execution work? Do the cultures, structures, and policies that work for one side work for the other? If not, how could the different types of work be separated while still allowing access to shared assets and capabilities? What might ambidexterity look like for your organization?

The Importance of Structure: Fighting Terrorism in Iraq

In 2004, General Stanley McChrystal was leading one of the world's most elite counterterrorist forces, the Joint Special Operations Command (JSOC). Its mission was a daunting one: to defeat al-Qaeda in Iraq (AQI), a terrorist group led by Abu Musab al-Zarqawi, which had flourished in the wake of the fall of Saddam Hussein.

JSOC was ready for the job. Its members were highly trained, were well funded, and had access to the most sophisticated equipment available. By contrast, AQI seemed like no more than a ragtag band of local Iraqi radicals with little training and only makeshift weapons. There should have been no contest. On paper, JSOC should have wiped the floor with its enemy.

But as we saw in chapter 4, when I recounted the story of the disorganized, untrained French army taking on the mighty Prussian army, things do not always play out as expected. A few months into the JSOC mission, attacks by AQI were increasing, not diminishing. By any measure, the elite force found itself losing the battle to an enemy that it should have been dominating. Over time it became clear that, far more than the enemy, JSOC's biggest challenge was an environment that was fundamentally different from anything it had planned or trained for. The speed at which events unfolded, and the interdependence of those same events, had produced a landscape for which JSOC's structures, processes, and leadership models were not designed. To begin to compete, JSOC would have to transform itself into a whole new type of organization. McChrystal details this transformation in his book *Team of Teams: New Rules of Engagement for a Complex World.*[32]

McChrystal soon saw why JSOC was failing to have an impact. It was structured, like many other organizations, into a formal, rigid hierarchy. Orders flowed down, and information flowed up. This setup was based on the work and thought of men like Frederick Taylor, Max Weber, and Henri Fayol, whom I discussed in chapter 4. It was about achieving maximum efficiency through division of labor and separating "thinking" from "doing." By contrast, AQI had very little structure or hierarchy. Instead, it took the form of a dispersed network of independent cells that proved devastatingly effective. It seemed able to shape-shift at will, continually reinventing itself and changing its tactics based on what worked and what did not. Every time JSOC made a gain, AQI would quickly adapt and regain the advantage. It did this without seeking permission from those higher up in the AQI chain. Thus, its members were able to operate effectively in an environment of high interconnectivity, rapid change, and very little predictability. In short, they were extremely agile.

It soon became clear that JSOC's revered efficiency was far from sufficient for the battle. McChrystal soon came to the realization that what was needed to keep up with, and ultimately defeat, AQI was not efficiency at all, but adaptability—the ability to move more quickly and change approach consistently as new challenges unfolded. To achieve this, decades of institutional thinking would need to be unpacked.

The first step was to address JSOC's traditional, hierarchical structure and create great teams. AQI's fluidity and adaptability were reminiscent of some of the finest teams in the military, including US Army Special Forces and Rangers teams, and Navy SEAL teams. McChrystal saw that these teams were effective at operating in the most complex, unpredictable environments. They had evolved to cope with supreme levels of VUCA. In a situation like this, a single leader cannot possibly make unfailingly accurate predictions and stay on top of developments. There are far too many moving parts. The only way to stay ahead is if team members learn to trust each other and are able to make decisions on the ground. That requires transparency and clarity around a shared purpose. JSOC began to focus heavily on building trust and shared purpose within teams. It realized that while these activities were not traditionally seen as an efficient use of time and resources, they helped build capacity to respond far more quickly in the fog of war.

The second step was to take this concept further. Creating this "command of teams" had yielded some improvement in responsiveness at the team level, and it was definitely more effective than the previous, fully hierarchical approach, but JSOC was still not able to keep up with AQI. The latter's ability to melt away and reform using different tactics meant that JSOC was constantly playing catch-up. Each squad had become an effective team, but cooperation *among* teams was almost nonexistent. Front-line Special Forces or SEAL teams would often capture valuable intelligence during a raid, then bag it up and ship it off. It might then be days before analysts received the material, and even then, they had little context in which to exercise effective decision-making. With the vast amounts of information spread across so many teams, and each team only seeing a small part, there was no way for teams to join the dots. With so many interconnecting parts, a team-level approach meant that no one could ever see enough of the picture to be effective. The teams were operating well within their silos, but they needed to find a way for the whole of

JSOC, not just individual teams, to achieve the necessary agility. To do that, they would have to structure themselves like their enemy.

McChrystal needed to find a way to reproduce the conditions for great teams across the whole organization. This included various front-line units as well as many intelligence agencies and politicians in Washington. Trust, and a sense of shared purpose, needed to be built across all teams, but with thousands of people involved, that was no small task. Either way, JSOC needed to move beyond the current "command of teams" and toward the network model, or "team-of-teams," as McChrystal called it. Achieving this would take a big investment, and yet more painful reorganization. Building trust across hundreds of teams would prove a challenge. The approach JSOC took was to create "embedded liaisons." These were people who would spend time working as part of entirely different teams. During that time, they would both build trust with that team and gain a better appreciation for what they did and how they operated. This proved useful not just in terms of making it easier to know when to involve that team in something but also because it allowed people on different teams to get to know each other, which made collaboration far easier. People are far more likely to cooperate with a person they know and with whom they have built trust.

Using this method, each team built at least one connection with each other team. Trust between teams began to grow as relationships blossomed. To ensure all teams were pulling in the same direction, radical decentralization was matched by equally radical transparency. The risk of sensitive information being leaked was dwarfed by the risk of missing opportunities because people did not have the information they needed. In the bunker that held the JSOC command center, partitions were torn down, screens containing information and video feeds were placed on walls for all to see, and all calls were held on speaker. Silos and secrecy were out, and openness across all ranks was in. As long as each team saw only a few dots, there would be no ability to make connections between them. Everyone needed to see the bigger picture in order to connect those dots, to learn to whom to escalate matters in a timely fashion, and to understand the whole. A daily operation and intelligence briefing was opened up to all for the same reason.

These changes made a huge difference to JSOC's effectiveness. Its members were finally able to match the speed of the enemy—and even, for the first time, get one step ahead. It was acknowledged that investing time and money in building trust and shared understanding could be seen as wasteful, but McChrystal believed that it was precisely the overlap and so-called inefficiencies that allowed JSOC to become sufficiently nimble to win. The ability to respond and execute nimbly in such a complex and fast-changing environment proved to be the deciding factor.

And yet there was one final step to complete this transformation. JSOC had become vastly more integrated, collaborative, and responsive, but it was still not quite fast enough. There were too many instances of tardy response, even by a few seconds. Targets were still getting away. For exactly the same reasons Field Marshal Helmuth von Moltke the Elder had identified over 130 years before, JSOC was still unable to act quickly enough. For certain things, like launching a strike, there was still a chain of command, which cost valuable time. AQI could act in the moment, but gaining approval cost JSOC valuable minutes. Often those minutes were the difference between success and failure. McChrystal realized that he was often merely green-lighting solutions created by those with the information. The risks of acting too slowly and missing opportunities outweighed the risks of letting competent people make judgment calls. The final step was to empower teams fully to act in accordance with the "shared consciousness" created by all the information sharing and alignment sessions.

In June 2006 an airstrike was launched in which Abu Musab al-Zarqawi was killed. AQI began to retreat, and JSOC was able to make advances in its mission. By 2007, JSOC was finally winning the fight against AQI. JSOC's members had become smarter and far nimbler in their execution. They were learning and evolving more quickly than the enemy. Targets were hit with increasing frequency, and for the first time, they were even being hit during the day. That would not have been possible without the deep trust and collaboration between intelligence operators and analysts that had emerged through the network model. JSOC had ceased to be an efficient machine and had become an effective organism.

The similarities between this story and those of many organizations are stark. While lives tend not to be on the line in most business environments, an inability to respond quickly enough to complex, fast-paced environments is common to many entities. Organizations that find themselves encountering these challenges must recognize a rigid, hierarchical organizational structure as a key cause of difficulties. Merely attempting to tinker around the edges will yield little or no benefit. To compete truly, those neat hierarchical organization charts must begin to look far more like messy, interconnected networks of autonomous teams collaborating closely with customers, and each other, in the service of larger goals.

Reflection

Are there elements of these stories that are applicable in your organization? If so, how could you go about making similar structural changes? What would need to be in place before you did?

Chapter Summary

- Human beings have evolved to exist in units of up to 50 with no formal hierarchy and high levels of cooperation.

- Many organizations structure themselves according to ideas that emerged from the Industrial Revolution, featuring division of labor, hierarchy, and silos meant to increase efficiency. This efficiency focus greatly inhibits their business agility.

- When in the explore domain, small, cross-functional teams operating in a network are far more effective and adaptive than rigid hierarchies consisting of groups of specialists.

- Truly ambidextrous organizations leverage the benefits of both models, allowing for separate culture, structures, and policies to emerge.

Key Practices for Business Agility

- Move away from functional silos that are responsible for specialized activities and toward cross-functional teams that are responsible for customer-focused outcomes.

- Create and communicate an inspiring, shared goal for teams to create alignment and guide decision-making.

- Invest in building trust, connection, and cooperation within teams through proximity, first-class collaboration tools, and the removal of barriers to communication.

- Grant teams the autonomy to work toward their desired outcomes within guardrails.

- When multiple teams are required to work together toward an outcome, structure them in a loosely connected network over a traditional hierarchy.

- Invest time, and resources, creating alignment and shared goals across the teams and in building links and trust between teams through embedded liaisons.

- Create ambidextrous organizations that can simultaneously exploit and explore by leveraging the power of both hierarchies and networks of interconnected cross-functional, self-managing teams. Create with a layer of senior leadership, spanning both sides for high-level integration without interference.

- Allow each side to create the distinct structures, cultures, and policies to best support its work.

Further Reading and Resources

Books

- Stanley McChrystal, *Team of Teams: New Rules of Engagement for a Complex World,* with Tantum Collins, David Silverman, and Chris Fussell (New York: Penguin Portfolio, 2015)

- Charles A. O'Reilly and Michael L. Tushman, *Lead and Disrupt: How to Solve the Innovator's Dilemma* (Stanford, CA: Stanford Business Books, 2016)

- Scott D. Anthony, Clark G. Gilbert, and Mark W. Johnson, *Dual Transformation: How to Reposition Today's Business While Creating the Future* (Boston: Harvard Business Review Press, 2017)
- Arthur Yeung and Dave Ulrich, *Reinventing the Organization: How Companies Can Deliver Radically Greater Value in Fast-Changing Markets* (Boston: Harvard Business Review Press, 2019)

Websites, Articles, and Videos

- Please see www.6enablers.com/resources for more on this topic, including a downloadable reading list.

CHAPTER 7

People and Engagement

It's easy to say you want talented people, and you do, but the
way those people interact with each other is the real key.

ED CATMULL, FOUNDER AND CEO OF PIXAR

IN THIS CHAPTER, WE WILL EXPLORE

- the importance of employee engagement and why the majority of people are disengaged at work
- how to create an environment for thinking and collaboration
- some key drivers of employee engagement and intrinsic motivation
- some modern HR practices for creative knowledge work.

The Case for Employee Engagement: Wake Up and Smell the Success

In 2002, the CEO of a small, four-year-old company pinned a note to the wall in the office kitchen. The note read, "These ads suck."[1]

This was not the act of a typical CEO—but then, this was not a typical company. The CEO in question was Larry Page, and the company was Google. Page had been playing around with the Google site, typing in search terms and reviewing the ads that subsequently appeared in relation to those terms. He was displeased with many of the paid ads in particular. They seemed unrelated to the search terms. For example, a search for a term like "Kawasaki H1B," a model of motorcycle, would display results for lawyers offering help with H1B visas and other unrelated services. This was in the early days for the project called AdWords, and it was not going all that well.

Page printed out the questionable ads, highlighted them, and posted them on the wall with his note. He then went home for the weekend, saying nothing to anyone about the issue. Later that night, an engineer called Jeff Dean saw the note. Working in a different area of the company, Dean had no particular reason to pay attention to this or do anything about it. But he went back to his desk and, without informing anyone, began playing around with the problem. Ignoring his own work, he continued to grapple with this complex problem, a problem that the best minds at Google had yet to resolve despite months of effort. He then returned to the office on Saturday to continue working on the problem. He returned again late Sunday and proceeded to work through the night. At 5:05 on Monday morning he sent an email outlining a detailed fix, then disappeared off home to bed.

The fix resolved the problem, and dramatically boosted the accuracy of the AdWords engine. This subsequently led to AdWords' becoming the dominant pay-per-click engine. The following year, Google's profits went from $6 million to $99 million. By 2014, AdWords was generating revenues of $120 million per *day*. Today, Google is among the most valuable companies on the planet.

When I look at most organizations today, I see places where this could never have happened. Why would people fix a problem for another department without being asked? Why would they work through the night and over the weekend to get it done with no obvious incentive? Would they even be allowed to do so without permission? The answer is a thing called *engagement*, and it's a rare thing indeed.

Along with finance, human resources (HR) departments are, with a few rare exceptions, ignored by most organizations seeking to increase their agility. I have always found this astounding—especially given that the first (and, for me, most important) value of the *Manifesto for Agile Software Development*, written back in 2001, is "Individuals and interactions over processes and tools." Organizations can only ever be as effective as their people. Becoming a high-performing agile organization is a process that starts and ends with people, yet for many entities it begins without first ensuring that the department that looks after people is safely on board the bus, or at least heading in the same direction. If we need people to behave, think, and work in different ways to achieve agility, does it not make sense to involve those who set the policies and incentives in that area?

With that in mind, here we take a look at one of the most important parts of an organization: its people. We will also cover one of the most important leading indicators of a successful organization, employee engagement.

When I was 16 years old, I undertook two weeks of "work experience" at a local community center. My duties included stocking shelves, cleaning, answering phones, and performing various other mind-numbing tasks that didn't excite me in the slightest. I found myself bored, demotivated, and moving as slowly as I could get away with. This does not mean I was unhappy. I wasn't. I just wasn't putting my heart and soul into the work. I didn't really care about it— that is, until day 9 of 10, when I was asked to clear out the basement. I was given all day and just told to "sort it out."

When I got down there, I spent some time planning what I would do, then I set about my work. I worked solidly all day, clearing out boxes, removing rubbish, and organizing things into an easy-to-find system of boxes on shelves. By the end of that one day, I had done more work, and added more value, than I had in the entirety of the previous eight days. It was my job, I owned it, and I wanted to go above and beyond. My supervisors were delighted, and more than a little surprised, with the result. I felt energized and satisfied with my day's work. I did not have a word for it back then, but in fact, I was, for the first time, *engaged* in my work.

Every few years, Gallup publishes a wealth of data regarding employee engagement across the globe in the *State of the Global Workplace* report. The 2017 edition covered 155 countries and almost all industries. The report represents the most comprehensive source of employee-engagement findings around right now. Gallup uses 12 questions, commonly known as the Gallup Q^{12}, to identify the level of engagement of each respondent. The results place employees into one of three groups that underline their emotional attachment to their organization. Gallup defines the groups as follows:

- *Engaged:* "Employees are highly involved in and enthusiastic about their work and workplace. They are psychological 'owners,' they drive performance and innovation, and they move the organization forward."

■ *Not engaged:* "Employees are psychologically unattached to their work and company. Because their engagement needs are not being fully met, they're putting time—but not energy or passion—into their work."

■ *Actively disengaged:* "Employees aren't just unhappy at work—they are resentful that their needs aren't being met and are acting out their unhappiness. Every day, these workers potentially undermine what their engaged coworkers accomplish."[2]

Given these definitions, I believe most would agree that maximizing the percentage of employees who are engaged would yield significant performance improvements. Engaged employees care about their place of employment and will move mountains to ensure that it succeeds. They are more productive, make far better decisions, and are far more likely to innovate and to find creative solutions than a disengaged workforce. These are precisely the kind of employees who excel at "explore" work.

If anyone is in doubt about the economic value of high engagement, there is much hard data out there to back this up. Gallup, Best Companies, Great Place to Work, and Glassdoor have all found that high engagement is correlated with better stock market performance. Gallup found that business units in the top quartile for engagement outperform those in the bottom quartile in many key areas:

■ 21 percent *higher* profitability

■ 20 percent *more* sales

■ 17 percent *higher* productivity

■ 10 percent *higher* customer metrics

■ 70 percent *fewer* safety incidents

■ 59 percent *less* employee turnover for low-turnover organizations

■ 24 percent *less* employee turnover for high-turnover organizations

■ 41 percent *less* absenteeism

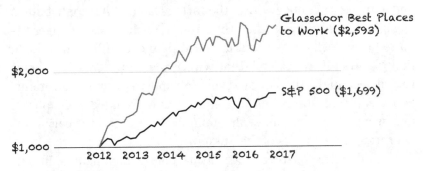

FIGURE 20

Stock price, based on $1,000 investment in 2012

Glassdoor Best Places to Work ($2,593)

$2,000

S&P 500 ($1,699)

$1,000

2012 2013 2014 2015 2016 2017

Source: Jacob Morgan, *The Employee Experience Advantage: How to Win the War for Talent by Giving Employees the Workspaces They Want, the Tools They Need, and a Culture They Can Celebrate* (Hoboken, NJ: Wiley, 2017), 160.

- 40 percent *fewer* quality incidents (defects)
- 28 percent *less* shrinkage[3]

In his 2017 book *The Employee Experience Advantage*, Jacob Morgan shows the difference in value on $1,000 invested in the standard S&P 500 Index ($1,699) and in the Glassdoor Best Places to Work ($2,593) between January 2012 and October 2016[4] (figure 20). According to the Engagement Institute, disengagement costs up to $550 billion each year in lost productivity.[5]

Given the real impact of employee engagement on the bottom line, one could be forgiven for thinking that it would be high on any leader's agenda as an issue to address. Unfortunately, I have found that, time and again, that does not seem to be the case. Much lip service is paid to it, but little real action is taken beyond token gestures and annual engagement surveys. Ultimately, despite all the platitudes, very little tends to change.

I believe there are two main reasons for this. The first is that it is extremely difficult to demonstrate a causal link between high engagement and an increased bottom line. These things do not show up on spreadsheets next to costs. Would Jeff Dean have worked on the Ad-Words problem if Google had taken a traditional approach to management? Would Google be the organization it is today?

The second reason engagement often isn't taken seriously is that it is particularly difficult both to measure and to shift. Most leaders and managers are not aware of the various factors that contribute to engagement. And even when they are, the behavioral changes required to unlock engagement are hard to anchor in organizational policy and culture. Couple that with leadership and HR policies rooted deep in the Industrial Revolution and, in most organizations, we observe widespread disengagement. As I discussed in chapter 3, management innovation, while of immense impact, is a scary wander through the forests of the unknown.

This all makes for some pretty dismal engagement figures. In Gallup's 2017 report, just 15 percent of employees were engaged in their work globally (figure 21). That means only a tiny proportion are innovating, being creative, and driving the performance of their places of employment. Given the imperative for these things in the new, high-VUCA world in which we operate, that represents a monumental waste of human potential. It's little wonder that the impact on the bottom line is so extreme. Now more than ever, to gain a competi-

FIGURE 21

Global employee engagement figures

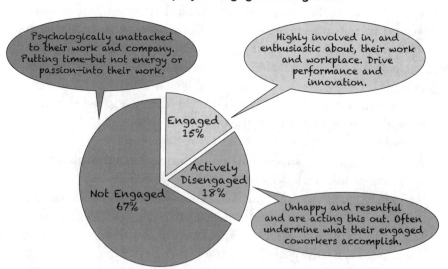

Source: Gallup, *State of the Global Workplace*, 2017, p. 3, https://www.gallup.com
/workplace/238079/state-global-workplace-2017.aspx.

tive advantage, organizations need people to go beyond the mindless following of orders. They must be committed to bringing their whole selves into work and to working tirelessly to deliver value to customers—not because they are forced to, but because they *want* to. The most effective organizations—which are rare—are jam-packed with people like this.

The second level in the Gallup report is "not engaged," and Gallup found that 67 percent of respondents fell into this category. These are people who show up, but only in body. They bring no energy or passion with them and will do the least possible to remain in their role. You will often find these people celebrating at lunchtime on Wednesday that they are halfway to the weekend. I have been that person. It is not a particularly fulfilling existence.

Then, after that, there are the "actively disengaged." These people are downright dangerous and are working against the interests of the organizations in which they are employed. We explored some rather extreme examples of this in chapter 5 with the NUMMI story, but it happens to a lesser degree in organizations everywhere. Amazingly, at 18 percent, there are more of these people, on average, than there are engaged employees. Is it any wonder that many places are struggling to compete?

I find these figures particularly difficult reading. Important though the financial impact is, the real cost here is the human one. This process began in the late nineteenth century, during the early days of management and the work of Frederick Winslow Taylor. Once-proud craftsmen were reduced to mere cogs in a machine—utterly disempowered and disconnected from the decision-making process and the end goal of the employer. They became fungible, faceless "resources" who were no longer required to think for themselves. This is why Taylor's methods are frequently thought of as inhumane. And in today's world of creative knowledge work, this is only exacerbated. I have experienced life in all three of the categories of engagement and I can say unconditionally that people deserve nothing less than to be fully engaged in their work and passionate about what they do. The thought of large numbers of the population spending the vast majority of their careers unfulfilled is a sad one indeed. This is especially concerning given that most people spend around one-third of their lives at work. The thought of my children, and millions of others, growing up bound to decades of unfulfilling drudgery is almost enough to bring tears to my eyes. It is a large part of the reason why I do what I do—it's so that, someday, engagement will be the norm and people will be excited about heading into work on a Monday morning. If that sounds unrealistic, I can tell you that I go to work with a spring in my step every day. And I do so because the conditions for off-the-chart engagement *exist*. If I weren't that highly engaged, I might not have spent a Saturday night writing this chapter. Right now, my desire to have an impact is greater than my desire to relax.

Before we explore the conditions that lead to increased employee engagement, and how to put them into place, we must first understand how the human brain works. Once leaders understand that, they can design policies and structures that work in harmony with our evolution and maximize the effectiveness of knowledge workers, rather than inadvertently sabotaging it.

Reflection

Are employees in your organization engaged? Is employee engagement something that is actively tracked? What would be the benefit of improving engagement for the organization, and for people?

The Neuroscience of Knowledge Work: Priming the Brain for Thinking

Most people have been in a situation in which their minds have gone completely blank. Whether in an exam, an interview, or a presentation, try as you might, that information you've recalled a thousand times before is suddenly and inexplicably out of reach. Simple tasks that, only minutes before, were as easy as tying a shoelace become utterly mind-boggling. When this happens, it is not that we have forgotten how to do these things—it is that the brain, while trying to protect us, can often end up working against us. Understanding how and why this happens has become increasingly important for leaders in the modern workplace, where the main activity is no longer following orders, but thinking creatively. For that to happen, leaders need to understand two important parts of the brain and how they work.

The Prefrontal Cortex (PFC)

The last major region of the brain to evolve, the PFC makes up around 5 percent of the brain's volume. Don't be fooled, however; like a shot of good bourbon, what it lacks in size, it makes up for in impact. The PFC controls what is often referred to as "executive function," and it is thus in use when you are thinking consciously as opposed to being on autopilot. In his book *Your Brain at Work*, David Rock identifies five key functions of the PFC: deciding, recalling, understanding, memorizing, and inhibiting.[6] These functions represent the majority of conscious thought. Without these, we would be unable to set and pursue goals, make plans, solve problems, prioritize, make decisions, think creatively, grasp abstract concepts, or control impulses. It thus won't surprise you to learn that in humans, the PFC is not fully developed until the age of 25. Maybe we should give teenagers a break, then, after all. Kids aside, upon reading a job description for almost *any* knowledge work position, we will generally see that it consists almost exclusively of some combination of the activities just mentioned. Knowledge work is performed almost entirely in the PFC. Keeping it functioning smoothly is thus essential.

Unfortunately, as with all good things, there are significant downsides to the PFC. The first is that it burns through metabolic fuel, such as glucose and oxygen, way faster than any other part of the brain. Like a 600 horsepower SUV, it is powerful, but expensive to run. The more we engage the PFC, the less energy there is to power it later in the day. That's why willpower tends to evaporate in the evening, and you find yourself reaching for that glass of wine. It is also why prioritizing and making tough decisions should be done in the morning.

The second downside is that the PFC is a bit temperamental. Conditions must be just right for it to function properly. Amy Arnsten, professor of neuroscience at Yale University, has playfully dubbed it the "Goldilocks of the brain."[7] Too much stress or fatigue, which can easily happen over the course of a day, and there will be a sharp decline in PFC function. This is precisely what happens when a person's mind goes blank. The PFC, the executive function part of the brain, has become impaired. This is far from ideal if you are standing in front of a hundred people, about to deliver an important presentation. This is why rehearsing relentlessly is so important. Once a task becomes ingrained, it is no longer handled by the PFC. The basal ganglia, a separate part of the brain, takes over routine tasks, given that they no longer require conscious thought. This process is significantly more energy efficient than the way the PFC works. It is also why Navy SEAL lore states that "under pressure, you don't rise to the occasion, you sink to the level of your training. That's why we train so hard." Unfortunately, for most knowledge work, training and rehearsing will not help, as the same situation is rarely encountered twice, and thus the PFC is continually called into action to solve new problems.

The Limbic System

Sitting on top of the brain stem (which is often referred to as the lizard brain) is the limbic system, composed of a set of structures that includes the hypothalamus, amygdala, thalamus, and hippocampus, among others. One of the limbic system's jobs is the regulation of emotions. Reptiles do not have a limbic system, which is why, unlike your cat or dog, lizards and snakes never look pleased to see you. As well as emotion, the limbic system is also responsible for what Evian Gordon describes as the overarching principle of the brain: to minimize danger and maximize rewards.[8] The brain will tag each stimulus as either good (approach) or bad (avoid). Rather interestingly, the limbic system fires up far more quickly, far more intensely, and for far longer when it senses a threat than when it senses a reward. It seems that, as humans, we *walk* toward, and *run* away. This is why humans often avoid highly beneficial opportunities in which there is potential for failure. Whether in business or at the high school prom, it's far safer to avoid the potential threat and live to fight another day than it is to chase the reward. This makes sense, given that only the most hypervigilant of our ancestors survived.

When we do perceive a threat, it is down to a pair of almond-shaped structures in the brain called the amygdala to trigger a fight, flight, or freeze response. When this happens, stress hormones like cortisol and adrenaline are released into our veins to prepare us for physical exertion. An active amygdala, however, does something else as well. It inhibits the neural pathways to our PCF, causing significantly impaired cognitive function. This is not a problem in a truly life-threatening situation—if you're in the woods trying to flee from a bear, you have few abstract problems to solve or goals to set. In that instance, running fast would likely be your best bet (that, and the good fortune to encounter a bear that's not hungry). Given the PFC's energy-hungry nature, your body could ill afford to run it at full power at such a time.

The problem is that there is significant evidence that the brain cannot distinguish *social threats* (situations that may cause embarrassment) from *primary threats* (those that threaten life).[9] The result is that the amygdala is maladapted to its environment, and like a smoke alarm bellowing out its deafening squawk at the merest hint of burnt toast, its overeagerness can become problematic. While trying to keep us alive, it can end up doing damage to our careers and relationships. Daniel Goleman, in his best-selling book *Emotional Intelligence*, refers to this as "amygdala hijack."[10]

Key for any leader, or indeed team member, seeking to drive engagement and collaboration is understanding the types of interactions that could send people into stress mode. In his 2008 paper "SCARF: A Brain-Based Model for Collaborating With and Influencing Others,"[11] David Rock outlines five domains of human social experience. These domains activate the same threat-and-reward circuits in our brain as any primary threat to life and rewards. The implications of this are profound. Any perceived reduction in one or more of these domains will lead to a fight, flight, or freeze response and corresponding massive impairment of a person's executive function—and, consequently, job performance. Conversely, any perceived increase in these domains will activate the brain's reward center, resulting in increased job performance.

The five domains go by the acronym SCARF. They are as follows:

- *Status:* One's importance relative to others. Keeping people out of the loop, offering them "feedback," or criticizing them publicly can result in a decrease in their sense of status. If they learn, improve, or hit goals, their perceived status will usually increase.
- *Certainty:* The ability to predict the future in a particular context. Lack of clarity about a boss's expectations or not

knowing whether one's job is safe can lead to a reduction
in certainty. Upon sensing gaps in information, the brain fills
in those gaps, often with the worst-case scenario. Open and
honest communication can help increase a sense of certainty,
at least to some extent.

- *Autonomy:* A sense of having choices and control over events.
  Being micromanaged and consistently overruled can reduce
  perceived autonomy. Having choices and degrees of freedom
  to achieve an outcome will increase it.

- *Relatedness:* A sense of safety and connection to others.
  Working in silos or remote locations can make us feeling left
  out of the "tribe," as can being excluded from social interaction. Socializing together and sharing personal aspects of
  ourselves can increase the sense of relatedness.

- *Fairness:* The perception of equal treatment by and fair
  exchange with others. This can be reduced by nepotism,
  special perks for a select few, or a lack of transparency about
  pay. Clear and transparent decision-making and meritocracy
  can increase this.

It should now be crystal-clear why all of this matters. In the modern workplace, dominated by creative, complex knowledge work, employees' main tasks now consist largely of thinking creatively and
problem-solving. For those things to take place, leaders must create
an environment in which people can think effectively, and then they
must grant enough autonomy to allow fast and effective decision-
making by those with the most information—those *doing* the work.
The ease with which leaders and colleagues can unintentionally trigger a threat response means that we must always be mindful of the
effects of our actions.

Reflection

Does the environment in your organization encourage creative
thinking? How do the policies and leadership behaviors affect people's
ability to think? Are there opportunities to revise them to avoid excess
stress and the likelihood of people entering threat mode?

Managing for Engagement: From Compliance to Creativity

Gary Hamel, in his book *The Future of Management*,[12] outlines a hierarchy of human capabilities and their contribution to competitive success. At the bottom of the hierarchy is *obedience*, the ability to follow orders. The next level up is *diligence*, the ability to be accountable and conscientious. The next level is *intellect*, having knowledge and skills. Then comes *initiative*, the ability to discover new ways to add value without being asked. Second from the top is *creativity*, trying things and having ideas without fear of failure. And finally, right at the top sits *passion*. Passionate people will move mountains to make things happen. Passion is infectious and can turn ideas into mass movements.

If it were possible to measure the relative contribution of each capability in the hierarchy, we'd see something like the numbers in figure 22.[13] It's not that those capabilities at the bottom are not useful. They are. It is just that they can be bought anywhere in the world easily and cheaply. The secret sauce for succeeding in today's fast-paced, creative knowledge-worker economy, however, consists of things for which we rarely manage in organizations. In fact, what I observe in most organizations is that the vast majority of management processes and practices in place are focused on diligence and obedience. From expense policies, to core hours, to governance processes, to dress codes, it's about following the rules.

When it comes to what really matters, particularly in the explore domain—initiative, creativity, and passion—there is not only precious little thought given to how to achieve those things, but, all too often, existing policies actively stifle them. People are, in effect, encouraged to leave their most valuable capacities at the door. Google recognized this back in 2002, but for many, Industrial Revolution–style management designed for the exploit domain is stymying exploratory, innovative work. There is no business agility or effective knowledge work without passionate, creative, engaged humans working together. There is no Jeff Dean working on AdWords through the night if we focus only on compliance. So how can we manage for what matters?

FIGURE 22

The hierarchy of human capability

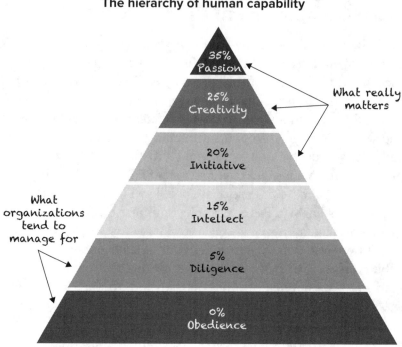

There's a fable called "The North Wind and the Sun." In it, the North Wind and the Sun argue over which could get a man traveling along the road to take off his warm winter coat more quickly. The North Wind boasts of great strength and declares that the task is quite simple. It then blows so hard that leaves fly around and birds cling to the trees. Yet the harder the wind blows, the tighter the man hangs on to his coat. Then it is the turn of the Sun, which comes out from behind a cloud and shines warmly on the man, who begins to unbutton his coat. The Sun shines brighter and brighter until the man is too warm and takes his coat off entirely.

Engagement, like motivation, innovation, creativity, and many other things, is not something that can be commanded. Like the North Wind blowing with all its might, trying to force these things will almost certainly result in the opposite of the desired effect. In my experience, every single one of us has all of the capabilities outlined earlier within us all the time. They are as natural as breathing and playing. The trick for managers and organizations is simply *not* to knock them out of people. Not to cause them to be left at the door. Not to turn people into machines programmed for obedience.

Of course, achieving compliance was *exactly* what the early management pioneers were seeking to do. They were certainly not doing all they could to maximize people's creativity, initiative, and passion. They were not seeking to create just the right environment for complex problem-solving and deep thinking. They were not doing their best to maximize ideas and to keep people operating in the prefrontal cortex. Instead, they lived during a time when organizational effectiveness meant mastering the art of exploiting with efficiency—and they really solved that problem.

We, however, have a different problem to solve. We are seeking also to master the domain of exploring. To do that, we must become adept at creating the new. Our competitive advantage comes not from the efficient execution of known solutions but from the creation of novel ones. It comes not from individuals working mindlessly in silos but from people working together as teams—incubating ideas, solving problems, and innovating. We do this naturally as humans. All managers need do is not get in the way. They must avoid knocking out of people the very ingredients for success. Once we understand that, we realize that we are not working *against* human nature, like the early management pioneers—we are working *with* it. We are sailing *with* the wind, not into it. After this realization, life gets a little easier. The following are some guidelines for moving from managing for compliance to managing for engagement.

Get the Hygiene Factors Right

As with the first two levels on Maslow's hierarchy of needs (figure 23), physiological needs and safety needs, fundamentals must be in place from the start, or nothing else will matter. It is true that these things on their own are not enough to create engagement. Their absence, however, will lead to a sharp drop in engagement, as they lay the foundation for everything else. These fundamentals include pay and benefits, workspace, and physical and mental well-being. Daniel Pink, in his book *Drive: The Surprising Truth about What Motivates Us*,[14] outlines decades of research that debunks the myth that knowledge workers are motivated primarily by money. He shows

FIGURE 23

Maslow's hierarchy of needs

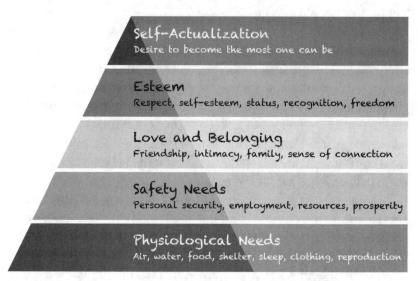

Data source: A. H. Maslow, "A Theory of Human Motivation," *Psychological Review*, 50, reprinted at Classics in the History of Psychology, http://psychclassics.yorku.ca/Maslow/motivation.htm.

that, in fact, the larger the cash incentive, the poorer the performance. Money and a nice office environment do not, in and of themselves, motivate people or lead to engagement. Neither does supporting a person's physical and mental well-being. All of that, however, is vital to get right, or efforts at initiatives higher up the hierarchy will fail. Most organizations are doing reasonably well at these things.

Communicate a Shared Purpose and Values

In 1666, the Great Fire tore through London, destroying some of the most iconic buildings of the time. Not long afterward, Sir Christopher Wren was commissioned to rebuild St. Paul's Cathedral. The story goes that he visited the site in 1671 and spoke with three bricklayers, asking what they did. The first answered that he was "a bricklayer, laying bricks to feed my family." The second said simply that he was "a wall builder, building a wall." And the third, standing tall, replied that he was "a cathedral builder, building a wonderful cathedral." There is no way of knowing whether the story is true, but it demonstrates the power of a shared purpose. The first man had a job, the second a career, and the third a calling. Only the third was passionate about and deeply connected to the organization's purpose. A well-communicated vision or purpose can be a powerful multiplier of engagement. Pink describes purpose as one of the three pillars of intrinsic motivation (alongside autonomy and mastery). You can see it in Tesla's espoused vision to "accelerate the world's transition to sustainable energy." If anything is going to get you up each morning, it's helping to preserve the planet for future generations.

Not every organization is going to have such lofty ambitions, but understanding the *why* behind an organization is a powerful motivator. Even a focus on creating a great user experience and making your customers' lives better in some way is far better than simply seeking to maximize shareholder value. That will get no one up in the morning. People will never be passionate and enthusiastic about their work if they don't know why they are doing it. Values support the purpose in terms of desired behaviors. Leaders must be careful to embed these values into the HR process intentionally, so they are truly incentivizing and not just platitudes written on the walls in head office lobbies.

Build Trust and Transparency

According to the Edelman Trust Barometer (2016),[15] 64 percent of executives, 51 percent of managers, and only 48 percent of rank-and-file employees trust their organization. That means that the farther you travel down the hierarchy, the lower the levels of trust. Trust is the foundation of all relationships. An absence of trust is the source of almost all team dysfunctions.[16] Transparency and trust are vital to knowledge workers because without them, our brains perceive a threat to our safety. A lack of transparency triggers a reduction in our sense of certainty, which means that we cannot predict what will happen next. This is a survival threat, and our amygdalae will thus spring into action. In the absence of information, people fill in gaps, and they tend to do so with the worst possible scenarios. That is exactly how we have evolved, and why transparency is key to building trust. As Buffer CEO Joel Gascoigne puts it, "Transparency breeds trust, and trust is the foundation of great teamwork."[17]

Overcommunicating is key, even when the news is not good. Default to transparency and only keep things opaque when there's a valid reason. Buffer publicly publishes its salaries, customer pricing model, revenues, equity grants, and money spent on retreats and perks. "Default to transparency" is one of its core values. Its leaders don't just talk about it, they live and breathe it every day. This has led to Buffer's becoming one of the highest-trust organizations in the world. Upon publishing its salary formula, Buffer received a 50 percent increase in applications for employment. There are far fewer things to gossip and speculate about when information is freely available. Bottom line: people do not give their discretionary effort to organizations they do not trust.

Foster Belonging and Connection

As I discussed in chapter 5, a sense of belonging is vital to humans. As tribal creatures, we need to feel like we belong. We need to feel like we are among friends. The alternative is feeling that we are around foes, and that will trigger a strong fight, flight, or freeze response. Any perceived decrease in relatedness will severely impair employees' ability to think creatively or to collaborate, to say nothing of destroying all feelings of engagement. The third level of Maslow's hierarchy of needs is love and belonging. This is about friendship, intimacy, and a sense of connection. All high-performance teams have this in bucket loads. In a world where remote work is on the rise, there is no substitute for physical proximity when it comes to building a sense of cohesion, safety, and connection. Get this right, and teams will be far more than the sum of their parts, and engagement will go through the roof. Encouraging team members to spend social time together is a powerful technique for this. In the next section, I will outline some HR policies that can accelerate—or, indeed, destroy—this process.

Treat People Like Adults

Henry L. Stimson, a famous American lawyer and politician, once said, "The only way to make a man trustworthy is to trust him." Despite the rather gender-biased nature of the sentiment, it rings true. If we treat people like adults, they will generally act as such. One of the key concerns from managers about the removal of behavioral controls is that without them, people won't work hard and will seek to fiddle the system. But the truth is that that is not the case. There are many underlying assumptions here, but one theory sums it up nicely. Published in 1960, Douglas McGregor's influential management book *The Human Side of Enterprise* was something of a step change in the way some managers regarded workers. In it, McGregor described two theories of human nature. The Theory X perspective assumes that people dislike work, avoid responsibility, need constant direction and coercion to get work done, have no ambition, and therefore need to be bribed or threatened to get them to work. This is fairly well aligned with the perspective of the early management pioneers. When I ask clients whether they recognize themselves in that description, very few do, yet they accept that many of their organizational policies seem to be based on Theory X assumptions. From requiring senior sign-off for small expenses, to tracking holidays, to enforcing strict dress codes, the underlying assumption seems to be that much control is needed.

There is, however, an opposing set of assumptions. These form the Theory Y perspective. This assumes that people are happy to work on their own initiative, will take responsibility and be self-motivated, enjoy decision-making, and can solve problems creatively and imaginatively. Many people identify with this description—and it is, in fact, far more reflective of human nature. While people can, and sometimes do, exhibit Theory X behaviors, those tend to be produced by the organization in which they are working. If a business believes that its people are demotivated, that business is either hiring demotivated people or hiring motivated people and demotivating them. Neither reflects well on the business. If people are treated like children, they may indeed behave as such.

A change in circumstances can lead to a dramatic change in behavior, as I found out during the two weeks of adolescent work experience that I discussed earlier. In my case, as in many, being given complete ownership and autonomy over the outcome changed everything. As Dee Hock, founder and CEO of Visa, once stated, "Simple, clear purpose and principles give rise to complex and intelligent behavior. Complex rules and regulations give rise to simple and stupid behavior."[18] Great examples here are Mary Berra, CEO of General Motors, replacing a 10-page dress code with two words: "Dress appropriately." Or Netflix's expense policy, which states simply, "Act in

Netflix's best interest." Many organizations are also doing things like scrapping holiday limits and instead trusting their employees to do the right thing. This is the difference between rules-based and values-based management. One is an engagement killer, and the other a powerful driver. The benefits of the latter far outweigh the small risks.

Maximize Autonomy

The second of the three pillars of intrinsic motivation mentioned by Daniel Pink is autonomy. Traditional management policies can be effective if you require compliance, but when aiming for engagement, creativity, passion, initiative, and all the other capacities that drive entities forward, autonomy and self-direction are the way. In chapter 4, we covered how distributing authority so that it resides with the information allows for faster and better decisions. Such distribution is also a powerful driver of engagement and motivation. No adult enjoys being micromanaged and told what to do all day. Some may appear to enjoy this, but I have found that in that kind of scenario, people tend to feel unsafe making decisions because of a culture of fear and blame. Once that problem of culture is removed, people will step up and start to take control. As anyone who has tried to control a child will know, a reduced sense of choice and control over one's life drives a powerful threat response in the brain. As we saw earlier with the SCARF model, autonomy is vital to keeping people operating in their prefrontal cortex, and therefore thinking. Freedom and respect are key aspects of the esteem level of Maslow's hierarchy—the second level from the top. Seeking to maximize people's choices at every opportunity will drive excellent engagement. Managers should continually ask the question, "How can those performing the work be given more control and flexibility over how outcomes are achieved?"

Support Learning and Growth

The third and final pillar of intrinsic motivation is mastery. This plays to our feeling of status and is part of the SCARF model. Improvement in this area provides a powerful, and addictive, dopamine hit. Humans receive a reward response from their brains whenever they win—even, it seems, when competing against an earlier version of themselves. Learning, growth, and moving toward a goal are powerful drivers of engagement and reward responses. An inability to progress will likely cause a threat response and increase stress. Self-actualization, the desire to become the best one can be, also happens to be at the very top of Maslow's hierarchy. The most effective leaders recognize this and focus on developing the capabilities of those around them through coaching and mentoring. Keys to success in this area are giving people autonomy over their growth goals, supporting growth with time and resources, and accepting failure as a necessary precursor to success. These things must be built into the HR process. More on that in the next section.

Practice Recognition and Gratitude

Recognition is one of the most significant things people can receive, and it's surprisingly easy to give. Recognition and gratitude are both ranked high in Maslow's hierarchy—second from the top, under esteem—and play to the brain's desire for status and relatedness. When we are recognized, it shows that someone has noticed what we have done, and cares. How likely are you to bring discretionary effort to a task when no one will notice? And saying "Thank you" or "Great job!" is not just about gratitude; it reinforces a sense of belonging that leads to safety, connection, and motivation that is quite contagious. Recognition and gratitude should not come simply in the form of a gold watch given for long service. They should be about encouraging people to live and breathe the values of the organization and encouraging the behaviors that lead to great teamwork, products, services, and customer metrics.

There are three points to note when implementing a recognition and gratitude process. (1) Recognition needs to be timely and continuous. It should be an everyday occurrence. (2) It's not about money. A thank-you will activate the same reward circuits in the brain as a cash reward. It needn't be an expensive thing to do. (3) Focus on manager and peer recognition. Peer recognition is 35 percent more likely to lead to increased retention and financial results than manager recognition.[19] Both are valuable, but it seems we value being appreciated by our tribe over our line manager.

While important for all kinds of work, the items just mentioned are absolutely essential when working in the explore domain and for seeking business agility. This demands the kind of work in which teams of people collaborate to create, experiment, and innovate around knowledge work. Mapping these areas back to the Competing Values Framework as covered in chapter 5, we see that many are hallmarks of a Collaborate culture and, to a certain extent, a Create culture. Catalyst Leaders, as described in chapter 4, are likely to focus on creating an environment for high engagement, as are leaders who follow the Intent-Based Leadership model. The one thing that could be considered missing here is psychological safety. But if the items just mentioned are in place, particularly belonging and connection, people will feel psychologically safe. It is the *result* of the things discussed here. People will then feel secure enough to admit mistakes, ask for help, or suggest that crazy, but possibly brilliant, idea.

Now that we have covered some generic principles, let's dive into some specific HR practices.

Reflection

In your organization, how much focus is there on managing for engagement versus compliance? What opportunities are there to make policy changes to increase engagement levels? Which of the areas discussed in this section are done well? Which might need more attention?

Reinventing HR:
A Twenty-First-Century Approach

As with many management areas covered in this book, HR has been operating in a certain way for some time. And as with many of those other areas, there was a time when the approaches covered here were, to a certain extent, effective. With the dramatic increase in VUCA over the past few decades, the context in which work is done has changed dramatically; HR, however, has not been so quick to change on the whole. What worked in terms of getting large numbers of people to show up and be compliant does not appear effective at inspiring twenty-first-century knowledge workers engaging in creative, complex exploratory work. In short, many HR policies appear geared to achieving obedience, diligence, and operational efficiency rather than to unleashing people's initiative, creativity, and passion so that they can explore and innovate. The question then becomes, "How can we reinvent HR systems and processes to ensure that people bring their most effective, creative, engaged selves to work every single day?" Focusing on the guidelines discussed earlier would be a great start, but I will now discuss some different approaches to more traditional HR / line-management processes.

Performance Management

I have yet to meet anyone on either side of the discussion who enjoys the process of the annual performance review. They are backward-looking; no one remembers further back than 3 months; goals that were set 12 months ago tend to be out of date; and these reviews provide very little value overall. According to Gallup, a mere 14 percent of employees strongly agree that performance reviews inspire them to improve.[20] They are expensive and often do more harm than good. It's no wonder many have ditched the process. Organizations such as Microsoft, IBM, Deloitte, Adobe, Accenture, GE, and PWC, to name but a few, have all scrapped this outdated approach. Whenever I speak with leaders about HR, I ask the same question: "Why is it important that we align the cadence at which we review employee performance with the cadence at which the earth moves around the sun?" This normally elicits a small smirk, and the realization that there is absolutely no reason for it at all other than "it's always been done that way," a phrase that tends to mean, "It's time to explore some different approaches." There's every reason to suggest that the annual performance review was once appropriate. In a time when the world moved at a less frenetic pace, it was probably sufficient. Today, however, 12 months between reviews is far too long—too much can change in just a few short weeks for any annual discussions to remain relevant.

The companies that do this well tend to have a couple of things in common. (1) Reviews and feedback happen all the time. One-on-ones every week or two are far more proactive, and focus on helping employees to grow and receive timely feedback in the moment. This turns the process into less of a review and more of an ongoing conversation. (2) These reviews involve more than just managers. As work becomes more complex, interconnected, and creative, it is no longer possible for managers truly to understand what is being done. This is especially so when they may not even be in the same location as the teams they manage. In that case, it is reasonable to question whether managers are the best people to judge performance. Netflix moved to a frequent 360 evaluation process that, rather than focusing on managers, involves each team member answering three questions: *What should you stop? What should you start? What should you continue?* This kind of timely, relevant, forward-looking feedback can allow for fast-changing circumstances and easy course-correction.

Pay and Incentives

It has long been known that extrinsic motivators, carrots and sticks, tend to destroy intrinsic motivation, our internal drive. Researcher Edward L. Deci notes that "paychecks and pink slips might be powerful reasons to get out of bed each day, but they turn out to be surprisingly ineffective—and even counterproductive—in getting people to perform at their best."[21] All the research in this area suggests that paychecks do not lead to passion. And yet organizations persist in offering bonuses and other rewards as the main means of getting more and better work out of people.

No one would question that good pay and benefits are important things, but the idea that they function as the ultimate incentives is based on a Theory X view of the world. That's a view in which we believe that people will not work unless they are somehow lured or coerced. The irony is that in placing all the emphasis on money, you take away the sense of autonomy from those doing the work. The work now becomes solely about doing what someone else wants, and that reduces intrinsic motivation. When the three pillars—autonomy, mastery, and purpose—are in place, there is no need for this outdated approach.

The other thing to note about incentives is that organizations should think carefully about *what* they incentivize. The biggest challenge I encounter in this area is individual incentives given with the expectation that people will, in return, put the team first. One of the hallmarks of great teams is a sense of mutual accountability. If organizations wish to see teamwork, cooperation, collaboration, broader learning, and a team-first mentality, they should think about how to incentivize *those* things rather than focusing narrowly on developing one specialized skill and how each person performs work individually.

Policies such as stack ranking, which sees managers rank employees on a curve based on their performance, can prove particularly pernicious. With the top 10–15 percent rewarded and the bottom 10–15 percent placed on performance review, and sometimes even fired, the result tends to be competition and knowledge hoarding. When Microsoft abolished its stack-ranking approach, it saw a huge uplift in collaboration, cooperation, and teamwork, which many believe has contributed to the company's resurgence and renewed innovative spirit. Rewarding people for putting their interests ahead of the interests of the team almost always leads to dysfunctional competition and a dearth of cooperation. We saw a similar response in my company when we brought in team-based commission for our sales team. It suddenly made far more sense for team members to collaborate than to compete. As in the case of the famous paradox of the prisoner's dilemma, the best outcomes are a result of working together.

The final thing to say about pay and incentives is that it is wise to make the process as transparent as possible. Everyone has a different idea of what "fair" means, but as long as people know why things happen, that tends to mitigate any sense of unfairness. Certainty and fairness are key social domains that can drive a threat response, and organizations must get in front of that. Transparent pay formulas like those at Buffer leave no room for allegations of nepotism or unfairness.

Learning and Development

We saw earlier why learning and growth are so important. It's a big driver of engagement, motivation, and, of course, organizational performance. Most people tend to want to work in a place where they can grow. A lack of opportunity for growth is a common reason why people leave their jobs. Organizations are only as good as the teams within them, and those teams are made up of people. Investing in learning and development is likely to be the best investment you will make. Agile organizations are made up of great people who can respond quickly and creatively to whatever strategic challenge comes hurtling around the corner.

Other than committing to investing in people's growth, there are a couple of points to take into account. The first is to encourage people to own their own growth and to set their own development goals. This has a powerful effect on their sense of autonomy. Also, set goals for a shorter term than 12 months. Quarterly personal objectives and key results (OKRs) work well, with a weekly check-in on progress and to get some coaching. The key to OKRs is to detach pay and performance conversations from growth. Putting them together encourages gaming of the process and the setting of smaller, easier goals, as they will be easier to hit. This process should not be about performance, but about growth.

Feedback

Having covered feedback in both the performance management and learning and development sections, I would like to highlight things that can cause feedback to be ineffective. *Feedback* is one of those words that invoke the same sense of dread as hearing footsteps behind you on a dark night. The reason it does so is that it touches on all five of the social domains that our brains treat as social threats. It threatens our sense of status, as feedback can often come from superiors in a very parent-child dynamic. It threatens our sense of certainty, as we tend not to know what to expect. It threatens our sense of autonomy, as we rarely have any control over the process. It threatens our sense of relatedness, especially if the feedback is negative. And it threatens our sense of fairness, as feedback is so often subjective. It is no surprise, then, that research by Avraham N. Kluger and Angelo DeNisi suggests that after feedback is delivered, performance improves 21 percent of the time, while 38 percent of the time it gets worse.[22] This is because once we shut down the prefrontal cortex, our cognitive function is dramatically impaired. Anyone delivering feedback should bear that in mind, and seek to mitigate the challenges outlined.

Job Descriptions

The traditional job description, with its rigid activities and role definition, may have served a purpose during the Industrial Revolution, but today, the fundamental building blocks of organizations are *teams*, not individuals. Teams need overlapping skills, they need to collaborate, and they need someone to step in when there's a bottleneck. In short, we need the people with a broad base of skills, and a deep knowledge of one or two. These people are often referred to as *T-shaped*, with the *T* reflecting the breadth and depth of their skills. That means moving away from job descriptions and toward hiring for culture fit, and cultivating a wide range of soft and hard skills. Ultimately, people should be allowed to grow into whichever area makes their hearts sing. That is an engagement supercharger.

As you can see, all of this is not about a new intent for HR. Many of its goals remain unchanged. It is instead ultimately about getting the best out of the people in the organization. For the modern, creative economy, that means managing for high engagement, autonomy, and growth. It means creating the environment in which people can form deep connections and trust, and then work together to innovate, to explore new ideas, and to solve complex problems, all underpinned by psychological safety. This means finding new tools and processes to support that.

Reflection

How aligned are the HR policies in your organization with creative knowledge work? Are your HR policies enabling or inhibiting agility? Which of the areas discussed here might be opportunities to evolve your HR policies to be more aligned with high-performing, innovative teams?

Chapter Summary

- Employee engagement is a key leading indicator of business results and yet is often overlooked by organizations, leading to widespread disengagement and poor performance.

- In order for people to think, collaborate, and be creative, they require just the right conditions for effective functioning of the prefrontal cortex of the brain. Leaders must work hard to create those conditions.

- Engagement cannot be commanded. It is the product of organizational policies that strengthen certain behaviors and connections among people.

- Traditional HR policies are designed to achieve compliance. They must be reinvented to maximize engagement, growth, and collaboration.

Key Practices for Business Agility

- Systematically track employee engagement and take steps to continuously improve it over time. Treat engagement levels as a key leading indicator of organizational effectiveness.

- Where possible, remove policies designed to achieve compliance, and focus more on those that unlock creativity thinking, passion, and the ability to take initiative.

- Place a strong, shared purpose and values at the heart of communications and decision-making. Reinforce these with organizational policies.

- Practice a Theory Y perspective by trusting people and treating them like responsible adults. Build trust through radical transparency and open, honest communication.

- Create an environment whereby teams can form strong connections and feel a deep sense of belonging with frequent acts of recognition and gratitude from peers and managers.

- Maximize people's choices over their work and career. Consistently ask the question, "How can more control be safely delegated?"

- Encourage and support people's growth and learning with time and resources. Invest in the creation of multiskilled, collaborative people (specializing generalists) over single-function specialists who operate in silos.

- Move from annual, backward-looking performance reviews to frequent, forward-looking coaching conversations about goals and growth. Provide constructive feedback in the moment and in a manner that does not elicit a threat response.

- As much as possible, create the environment for intrinsic motivation over relying on the carrot-and-stick approach. To maximize cooperation, incentivize at the team, rather than individual, level.

Further Reading and Resources

Books

- Glenn Elliot and Debra Corey, *Build It: The Rebel Playbook for World Class Employee Engagement* (Hoboken, NJ: John Wiley and Sons, 2018)

- Pia-Maria Thoren, *Agile People: A Radical Approach for HR and Managers* (Austin: Lioncrest, 2017)

- Reed Hastings and Erin Meyer, *No Rules Rules: Netflix and the Culture of Reinvention* (London: W. H. Allen, 2020)

- David Rock, *Your Brain at Work: Strategies for Overcoming Distraction, Regaining Focus, and Working Smarter All Day Long* (New York: Harper Business, 2009)

- Marcus Buckingham, *First, Break All the Rules: What the World's Greatest Managers Do Differently* (Washington, DC: Gallup Press, 2016)

- Daniel Pink, *Drive: The Surprising Truth about What Motivates Us,* main ed. (Edinburgh: Canongate Books, 2018)

■ Patrick M. Lencioni, *The Truth about Employee Engagement: A Fable about Addressing the Three Root Causes of Job Misery* (San Francisco: Jossey-Bass, 2007)

■ Tony Hsieh, *Delivering Happiness: A Path to Profits, Passion and Purpose* (New York: Business Plus, 2010)

■ Ricardo Semler, *Maverick! The Success Story behind the World's Most Unusual Workplace,* reissue ed. (London: Random House Business, 2001)

Websites, Articles, and Videos

■ Please see www.6enablers.com/resources for more on this topic, including a downloadable reading list.

CHAPTER 8

Governance and Funding

To blindly conform to the original plan when it no longer
represents the best economic choice is the act of a fool.

—DONALD REINERTSEN

IN THIS CHAPTER, WE WILL EXPLORE

- how many traditional organizations approach funding work
  and the challenges those approaches bring
- how to reinvent investment and governance processes to
  enable innovation and agility
- some tools and techniques for providing effective governance
  at each stage of a product life cycle.

Budgets, Projects, and Outputs: Building the House of Cards

Founded in 2007, Better Place had dreams of revolutionizing the car
industry in Israel. Its bold vision was to provide a battery-charging
and battery-switching service for electric cars that it sold. These cars
would be sold cheaply, and a pay-by-the-mile model would be used
for battery services. Customers would be able to overcome the cars'
relatively short battery range by charging at one of a network of stations, or by switching out a flat battery for a fully charged one at a
station and simply driving off. The latter approach would eliminate
the need to wait while the battery charged, with robots removing
a flat battery and replacing it with a fully charged one in under
five minutes.[1] Backed by venture capital, Better Place raised around
$850 million, allowing it to invest in building 37 switching and charg-
ing stations.[2] Retaining ownership of the batteries meant that Better

Place could keep the cost of the cars themselves low and simply charge a monthly fee for the batteries.

The business case and projections looked rosy for Better Place. Given the high cost of oil in Israel and a desire to transition away from an energy source that funded many countries hostile to it, there was much optimism about the venture. The prevailing view was that it was poised for success. Sadly, as with so many ventures, the results did not match the initial optimism. In 2013, after selling only 750 cars, Better Place filed for bankruptcy. Despite the hype, the business case, and the optimism, it had forgotten one important thing: to test the assumptions on which it relied.

Countless examples of similar scenarios play out with varying degrees of impact across organizations every day. Research by Simon Kutcher shows that 72 percent of all new products flop.[3] It is little wonder that in a McKinsey poll, 94 percent of managers said that they were dissatisfied with their companies' innovation performance.[4] While there's no question that weak spots in any of the other five enablers of business agility can contribute to poor innovation performance, I have observed a consistent failure in organizations to address perhaps the most vital enabler in this context: the methods by which money is invested in initiatives, and how those initiatives are run. The inescapable reality is that I have never observed, or heard of, an organization successfully increasing its business agility while retaining traditional governance approaches. The Business Agility Institute supported this observation in its 2020 *Global Business Agility Report*,[5] in which it identified adaptive, outcome-based funding models as one of three key predictors of business agility.

It's long been a cornerstone of management that, unless it is somebody's birthday, surprises tend to be a bad thing. Gary Hamel describes management as an "unending quest to regularize the irregular."[6] Regularity is achieved through various traditional management practices such as standardization, plans, and controls. In theory, regularity and predictability make it easier to hit milestones and forecasts as well as to demonstrate a level of control over proceedings—whether that control is real or imagined. These traditional management practices include detailed business cases, plans, strict governance processes, and an army of controllers. Yet it is that very drive for regularity, predictability, and control that hamstrings teams when exploring new horizons. There is nothing regular and predictable about the emergence of great ideas.

Despite this, I once got promoted off the back of a "failed" project. The reason? I ensured the delivery of the product on time, on budget, and within the agreed scope. Job done, backslaps all around. The only problem was that few people used the product, and those who did didn't like it. While traditional cost accounting reflected that we had been efficient in our delivery, in reality the project represented a monumental waste of the business's money, about $5 million. There was no transparency about this, and there were no repercussions. From a delivery perspective, all success criteria were satisfied and, as a project, we remained on time throughout, a feat rarely seen in that company. I would love to say that this was due to my amazing skills as a project manager, but in reality, a team of A players made my life significantly easier. There was much accountability around building the product predictably and to the plan, but there was no accountability over building the *right* product.

Over the years, through conversations with managers and observation of processes, I have distilled what I believe to be the underlying assumptions behind most governance and funding models—models like the one that rewarded me for delivering a bad product. These assumptions lead to a whole range of controlling measures. These measures make perfect sense when viewed through the lens of the assumptions. They are as follows:

1. It is possible to know up front the solutions that will delight our customers and bring the highest return.

2. It is possible to know up front how long it will take and how much it will cost to develop an initial solution.

3. Centralized bureaucracies removed from the customer are best placed to pick winning ideas.

4. Very little will change as the plan progresses.

For managers whose worldview is well articulated by these four assumptions, it makes perfect sense to approach the governing of

The key assumptions underpinning traditional governance and funding models

Underlying Assumption   Associated Policy

1 It is possible to know up front the solutions which will delight our customers and bring the highest return	A small number of large bets should be made based on business cases and return-on-investment
2 It is possible to know up front how long it will take and how much it will cost to develop an initial solution	Detailed plans should be made and followed
3 Centralized bureaucracies removed from the customer are best placed to pick winning ideas	Investment boards consisting of managers decide which initiatives go ahead
4 Very little will change as the plan progresses	Conformance to the agreed plan becomes the main metric of effectiveness

investments via a small number of large bets, based on return-on-investment figures presented in business cases created after months of detailed analysis. It then makes perfect sense to track the progress of the development based on conformity to the agreed-on plan. And it makes perfect sense to seek to deliver the known solution at the minimum possible cost using cost accounting techniques to maximize operational efficiency and output-based productivity (figure 24). If a small number of high-value initiatives can be correctly identified, why continue to explore anything else? If the best solutions can be predetermined, why waste time seeking feedback throughout the process? It's far better to lock the scope down and execute it efficiently, highlighting and correcting any variances along the way. With that, a few management approaches begin to feel appropriate, including the following.

Projects and Outputs

In many ways, the concept of projects has been around for centuries, yet it was only toward the mid-twentieth century that project management as a formal discipline emerged.[7] Projects are now so ubiquitous in organizations of all sorts that people rarely question why almost all non–business-as-usual work is wrapped up in them. Projects bring a sense of order, control, and predictability to work. They tend to be green-lighted, or not, in annual cycles based on annual budgets. Detailed business cases and plans are compared and the most promising are selected. Locking in scope, budget, and timescales means that people know what they are going to get, when they will get it, and what it will cost. This affords a great deal of comfort to decision makers. Projects are then tracked against the baselined plan to ensure minimal variance until the agreed outputs are delivered.

Cost Focus

Budget comes from the old French *bougette*, meaning a little bag or pouch used to hold coins. The word entered the English language during the period of Norman rule in England. It went on to refer to the pouch that carried documents from the monarch requesting money from Parliament.[8] Budgets represent a constraint on what can be spent in any given time period. As with project management, a world in which business budgeting did not exist is hard to imagine. In fact, it was in 1922 that accountant James O. McKinsey, founder of the consultancy that still bears his name, popularized the concept in his book *Budgetary Control*. With cost accounting come cost-focused metrics by which the performance of departments is judged. The challenge is to deliver the agreed-on outputs at the lowest possible cost in order to be as efficient as possible.

The intentions behind these and myriad other measures are good. In implementing them, leaders are rightly seeking answers to four key questions:

1. Are the organization's precious resources being allocated to the highest-impact initiatives?

2. Are current and future initiatives aligned with the strategy of the organization?

3. Are the proposed solutions being approached in an acceptable way?

4. Are the proposed solutions compliant and unlikely to put the organization at risk?

These questions represent the key areas of risk in searching out a new product, service, or business model. The issue lies not with seeking to mitigate these risks—it would be negligent not to do so—but rather with the underlying assumptions behind *how* organizations choose to go about that risk mitigation. Once again, knowing how to approach risk mitigation involves understanding the true nature of the work.

Reflection

What are the assumptions that underpin the governance model in your organization? Do they recognize the inherent uncertainty of developing new products and services? Are the subsequent policies an enabler or inhibiter to agility?

Customers, Value, and Outcomes: Taming Uncertainty

In 2002, Caterina Fake and Stewart Butterfield created an online game called *Game Neverending*. With chat room messaging a key part of the game, Fake and Butterfield decided to develop a live photo-sharing feature as part of it. The game was too complicated for most people, however, and was unable to attract enough players. Failing to generate enough revenue to be viable, the game was ultimately shut down. Butterfield, however, had noticed that the photo-sharing aspect was proving popular. In 2004, he and Fake decided to put a prototype on their website that would allow the sharing and managing of photos online. A year later, their platform, known as Flickr, was sold to Yahoo for a reported $40 million.[9]

Undeterred by the failure of *Game Neverending*, in 2009 Butterfield decided to try again to realize his dream of creating a successful online, multiplayer game. This time it was called *Glitch*, an updated version of his previous game. Despite raising around $17 million from investors,[10] *Glitch* failed to attract enough players and, in 2013, it too ran out of money and was shut down. Butterfield once again managed to rescue some valuable elements from the ashes. Having found all communication tools available at the time unsatisfactory, the team developed its own for internal communication and collaboration. When *Glitch* was shut down, the team once again reinvented itself—this time as creator of a chat tool. After its initial public offering, Slack was valued at over $24 billion.[11]

In the vast majority of organizations, Butterfield's endeavors would have resulted in failure and that would have been the end of it. So how was he twice able to snatch success from the snapping jaws of failure? As we have seen throughout the previous chapters, it is vital that organizations recognize that different types of work require different approaches. To highlight that, we shall now explore a concept that I have used to good effect with leadership over the years: the difference between *designing* and *building*.

The construction industry has traditionally separated these two activities, often with a middle step of *bidding*, in which different contractors bid for the building work. First, design is carried out with architects, structural engineers, and similar highly trained, expensive teams. This is a creative, iterative, and extremely unpredictable process. It involves a search for the right design, which must go through many rounds of feedback. Teams rarely end up where they expect they will. It is a disordered process in which great things emerge from what seems like a chaotic mess. Once an acceptable design is finalized, plans are made for its construction, and the blueprints are handed over to a different team, or company, to execute.

Once into the build phase, the nature of the work is entirely different. While the most important aspect of design is to get it right and to create value, what matters in building is effective execution.

The work is tracked entirely differently; it stops being driven primarily by value creation, and starts being driven by conformance to the plan. Just as I was rewarded for delivering a bad product on time and on budget, contractors are graded based on how closely they stick to the plan. When it comes to building rather than designing, the planning approach is different, techniques for managing the work are different, and key performance metrics are different. There is a clear journey from *searching* for the right design, a creative process, to *executing* that design, a predictable, plannable process. The majority of the time is spent on the latter.

As I discussed in chapter 1, when work is *complicated*, we can still understand it well enough to make useful plans. This is often the case with construction work, where up-front analysis by experts is an effective risk-mitigation approach. The linear process of *design-bid-build* can thus be effective here. With *complex* work, however—and creating new things is often complex—this linear approach is not possible. The sheer number of moving parts and multiple interactions among those parts makes it all but impossible to model, and the number of leap-of-faith assumptions quickly escalates. Throw in sky-high volatility, uncertainty, and ambiguity, and seeking to know anything in advance through analysis and the creation of business plans is akin to whistling into the wind. This tends to be the nature of design work. One of the biggest mistakes in innovation is the belief that products, services, and business models can be designed up front, after analysis, in the same way a building can, and that the designing and building process can be separated and approached in the same sequential fashion. It is this mistake that underpins the assumptions I noted earlier. Peter Drucker once put it this way: "When a new venture does succeed, more often than not it is in a market other than the one it was originally intended to serve, with products and services not quite those with which it had set out, bought in large part by customers it did not even think of when it started, and used for a host of purposes besides the ones for which the product was first designed."[12]

If innovating were mostly *building*, then the assumptions would hold true, and the tracking of outputs and conformance to the plan would be an appropriate performance metric. In reality, what is needed when innovating is the total integration of design and build activities. It stops being a linear, sequential process, and becomes one process—design and build going hand in hand. Like yin and yang, they are interconnected, interdependent, and complementary. The design influences the build and the build influences the design to the point where it becomes all but impossible to distinguish between them. Searching and executing become one. Among the most effective organizations with which I have worked, every single one approached new knowledge creation as a *design* process, a process of searching, with feedback tightly integrated (figure 25).

FIGURE 25

The integration of design and build

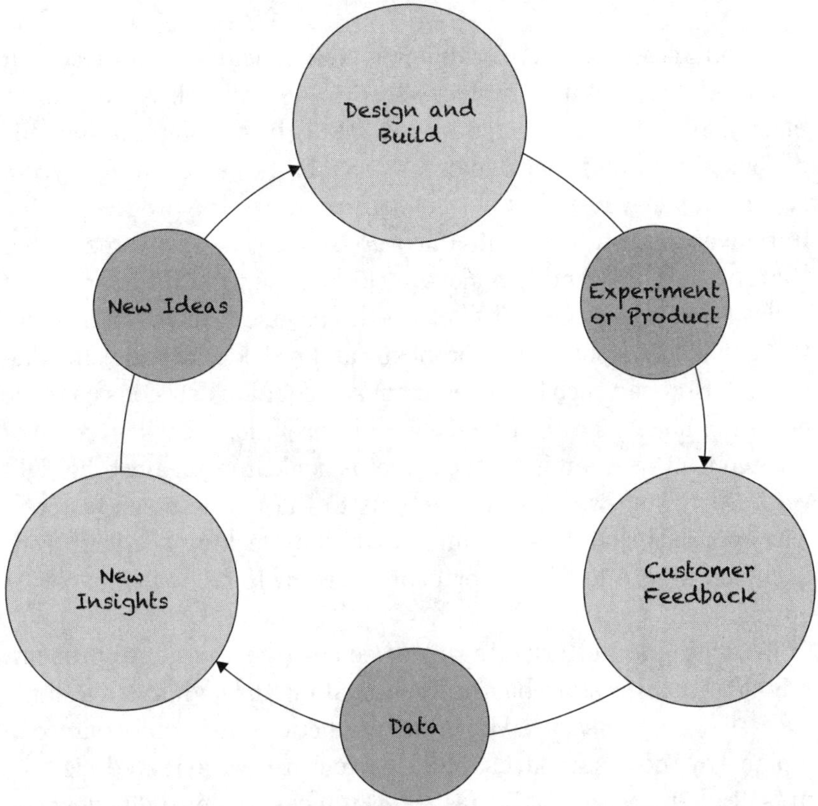

Source: Adapted from Eric Ries, *The Lean Startup: How Constant Innovation Creates Radically Successful Businesses* (London: Portfolio Penguin, 2011). COPYRIGHT: © Eric Ries, reprinted by permission of the author.

It is unworkable to separate design from build. They must happen in parallel. People who view the work through this lens end up with four very different underlying assumptions about how work should be approached. These assumptions are the following:

1. There is no way to know up front the solutions that will delight our customers and bring the highest return.

2. There is no way to know up front how long it will take and how much it will cost to develop an initial solution.

3. The best innovations come at the intersection of the customer and those doing the work.

4. Things will change a lot as we learn through feedback—we will need to respond accordingly.

For managers whose worldview is well articulated by these four assumptions, it makes perfect sense to approach investments by placing many small bets and incrementally increasing funding only of those initiatives that demonstrate viability based on *data from real customers*. It makes perfect sense to track the progress of the initiatives based on insights uncovered and value delivered rather than by outputs. And it makes perfect sense to build in frequent inspect-and-adapt points to ensure the product evolves into something that solves customers' problems and provides actual value (figure 26). How can such big investment and solution decisions be made at the point at which we have the least information we will ever have? As Stephen Covey put it, "If the ladder is not leaning against the right wall, every step we take just gets us to the wrong place faster."[13] Any approach that does not mitigate risk by seeking frequent feedback, learning, and course correction is going to fail in a high-VUCA environment.

Returning to Butterfield's roller-coaster ride as an entrepreneur, it is clear that his story has a thread running through it. It's that his success was not measured by initial predictions and conformance to a plan—by those standards, both his ventures were incredible failures. Rather, success for Butterfield was measured by *outcomes*. The means by which those outcomes were achieved remained entirely flexible and allowed Butterfield to become a billionaire. Flickr and Slack would never have emerged in an environment of detailed busi-

FIGURE 26

The key assumptions underpinning modern governance and funding models

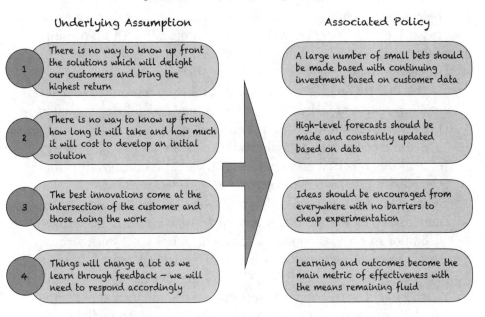

Underlying Assumption	Associated Policy
1 There is no way to know up front the solutions which will delight our customers and bring the highest return	A large number of small bets should be made based with continuing investment based on customer data
2 There is no way to know up front how long it will take and how much it will cost to develop an initial solution	High-level forecasts should be made and constantly updated based on data
3 The best innovations come at the intersection of the customer and those doing the work	Ideas should be encouraged from everywhere with no barriers to cheap experimentation
4 Things will change a lot as we learn through feedback — we will need to respond accordingly	Learning and outcomes become the main metric of effectiveness with the means remaining fluid

ness cases, rigid conformance to plans, milestones, and cost accounting. These are precisely the kinds of management approaches that kill innovation and adaptiveness, because so much new information emerges along the way and cannot be known in advance. Innovation is inherently unpredictable.

Management practices driven by cost accounting and the desire for predictability lead to approaches that stymie the creative design process, the search. They optimize for the predictable, plannable building process, the execution. Performance metrics include resource utilization (discussed in chapter 6), efficiency, and conformance to plans. These internal-facing measures completely ignore the customer and the chance to deliver value by searching for opportunities and designing great solutions. In short, cost accounting and projects belong largely in the exploit domain, not the explore domain.

A question I am often asked by those who are not in a position to influence governance policies is, "How can we work with agility when we cannot deviate from the scope once it is signed off?" This is a situation in which many find themselves. Rather unhelpfully, all I can do is reframe the question, as I believe they mean the following: "How can we respond to change and key lessons along the way if we're *not* responding to change?" It becomes clear at that point that their processes lock in business *rigidity*, the enemy of agility. This is presumably because predictability and efficiency are highly valued by leadership. One cannot be rigid and predictable and also be agile.

It is exactly this rigid approach that must be reinvented to make organizations fit for the twenty-first century and able to succeed in the explore domain. This reinvention involves helping those in finance and governance to understand and embrace a whole new way of working, one that accepts the realities of high uncertainty and complexity. Challenging though that may be, seeking to achieve business agility *without* reinventing mid-twentieth-century investment and governance approaches is akin to trying to stream a high-definition movie via a 1990s dial-up modem. It will not work because that is just not the job for which the old model is designed. Leaders will be left frustrated as the needle fails to move in any meaningful way. To achieve the desired results, a more modern approach is needed, an approach that recognizes the inherent unpredictability of innovation and product development. It is an approach that venture capitalists have been embracing for decades.

What is clear is that spending months creating an 80-page business plan supported by a web of spreadsheets and then asking for millions of dollars is just about the best way to throw away money. Inspired by Field Marshal Helmuth Von Moltke the Elder, entrepreneur and author Steve Blank once said, "No business plan survives first contact with a customer."[14] For organizations, life would be far easier if such certainty were achievable through up-front thinking and planning, if spreadsheets accurately predicted customer and market behaviors, and if the world stood still *just* long enough for products and services to be launched. I do understand the desire for certainty. It is human nature to seek certainty. For centuries, uncertainty meant potential danger to our ancestors, and we have evolved to be wary of it. During a leadership workshop I was leading at a large investment management firm, I was asked how people could be expected to make investment decisions, sometimes for eight-figure sums, in the absence of certainty about the outcome. The irony was not lost on them when I reminded them that their business was investing in the stock market, an inherently uncertain pursuit. It turned out that they already knew how to manage risk in highly uncertain environments—by placing multiple smaller bets, seeking continuous feedback, and then adapting to the data.

Reflection

In your organization, are investments project based or product based? What is the impact of this? Are there opportunities to evolve your governance model to be more aligned with the creative, uncertain nature of the work?

Managing the Portfolio: The Right Tool at the Right Time

It takes around 12 years and $1.4 billion to bring a new drug to market. Because of the high cost, pharmaceutical companies apply for patents to prevent other companies from manufacturing their drug for a period of time. While most patents last for 20 years from the date of filing, in reality, around half of that time consists of clinical trials aimed at getting approval for the drug, leaving, on average, only 10 years of protection for the product once it's on the market.[15] Drug prices remain high during the patent window, but once the patent expires and cheaper, generic versions hit the market, prices can fall by up to 90 percent[16] in what's known as a *patent cliff*. Unlike in most industries, pharmaceutical companies know the exact date when revenues for a particular product will drop precipitously. This means that unlike Kodak, Nokia, Borders, and many other businesses, they are fully aware that, to thrive in the medium and long term, they cannot rely on their current products. Patent cliffs constitute a daily reminder that pharmaceutical companies must continuously search for new drugs, drugs that will become the cash cows of the future. At any given time, thousands of compounds are being worked on to find the next blockbuster drug. Given the finite nature of their products, pharmaceutical companies are superbly set up both to exploit and to explore. They instinctively grasp the need to be ambidextrous.

While most organizations rarely have a hard date in the diary on which to expect a dramatic overnight drop in revenue, the reality is that every product, every service, and every business model has a shelf life, and owing to the accelerating pace of change, that shelf life is getting shorter every year. That is why organizations that wish to survive beyond the short and medium term need to think about their pipelines. There will always be a tension between allocating money, people, and resources to exploiting (maximizing the profits of current products) and to exploring (searching for the next product). They are in tension because the more an organization does of one, the less it does of the other. Resources are frustratingly finite. To think purely about the short term would be to focus on maximizing profits *today*, but this leaves organizations at increased risk of there being no *tomorrow*. Once the need to master both exploiting and exploring becomes apparent, there must be a coherent, strategic approach to allocating resources between the two. It is vital that this approach be designed with the whole picture in mind. There must be active product portfolio management and an investment and governance process that evolves with each life-cycle stage.

I often help organizations reinvent their approaches to making investment decisions and governing the work. My focus is on approaches that enable greater agility and innovation, the *explore* side of the organization. When explaining my approach, an analogy I often use is that of gold mining. Like the pharmaceutical industry, mining companies understand the notion of the finite well—they understand that in any given mine there is a finite amount of metal-rich ore. This means that finding *new* areas to mine is as important for long-term survival as extracting gold from *current* mines.

The high-level life cycle of gold mines has five distinct stages: exploration, development, operation, decommissioning, and postclosure.[17] *Exploration* involves searching for suitable sites on which to design and create a mine. It involves many disciplines, such as geography, geology, chemistry, and engineering. When it appears that the local geology indicates the presence of sufficient levels of gold, experiments are performed on samples to gather more information. Only

0.1 percent of prospected sites will lead to a productive mine,[18] so, at this stage, gathering maximum data at minimum cost is vital. Based on the data from the experiments at each prospective site, periodic decisions must be made regarding whether to discard the site, continue with further experimentation and data gathering, or progress to the next stage, development.

The *development stage* is not about validating whether to build a mine in a particular location—that has already happened. It is about building a site into a functioning mine as effectively as possible. There still may not be complete clarity about the most effective design for the site, or exactly how much gold it contains. Answers will emerge during this stage. As the mine is developed, decisions are made regarding the best way to extract the gold and how deep to excavate, based on the data collected throughout the process.

Once the mine is designed and built, it is time to move into the *operation stage.* During operation, the focus shifts from *exploring* to *exploiting* the mine, by extracting the ore and processing it into gold. At this point, things become far more predictable and repeatable. There is little learning, and a shift in approach from experimenting to efficiently executing. The more cheaply the gold can be extracted, the higher the profit margin. Finally, whether it is 2 or 100 years of operation, all good things must come to an end. Once the ore body is exhausted, or no longer economical to extract, the mine is safely decommissioned and closed.

Of course, at any given time, mining companies have many mines, operational and prospective, in their portfolios. These are spread across the life-cycle stages, with the highest number in exploration and very few making it further. The split of resources invested in each stage will greatly affect current and future success. The portfolio must be managed in alignment with the company's overall strategy. As we will see, the searching-building-operating model is one that carries over into product development.

Steve Blank, entrepreneur, and author of *The Startup Owner's Manual*, states that "a startup is an organization formed to search for a repeatable and scalable business model."[19] When doing this, start-ups tend to experiment frequently and course-correct as required. It is in their DNA. By contrast, established companies are often thought of as executing against existing products and services. This often manifests itself in statements such as, "We're not a start-up. We need to operate differently." This misses the point. The truth is that these days, few successful companies have a single business model. Most organizations have a portfolio of products at different stages of the life cycle. This means that all organizations must display the same traits as start-ups when operating in search mode. In that sense, established businesses must contain many start-ups that will transition into established business models in their own right.

Organizations, then, must engage in active product portfolio management, and need to use a similar process to that of drug and mining companies. Understanding the life cycles of products, services, and business models is vital when it comes to investing in and governing innovation. Whether it's gold mines or smartphone apps, coffee machines or cars, the high-level steps will be similar. Each organization will have its own version of the product life cycle, with slightly different activities, but most will have at least the following four high-level steps: *searching, developing, sustaining,* and *retiring.* Searching is about identifying, at a high level, new products, services, and business models. It involves identifying customer pain points and experimenting with many ideas to identify which solutions address them. This involves using highly experimental approaches like Design Thinking and Lean Startup and testing many ideas with customers. It involves searching for the right value proposition and a product-market fit.

Developing is about taking the validated value propositions and building out a scaled-up version that can be taken to market. This is by no means a pure *construction* process as, although product-market fit has been validated at a high level by this point, there is still no way of knowing how the exact solution or business model will look. Believing that the solution is both known and static at this point is a mistake many organizations make. This leads to outsourcing the development of their products and the view that the *design* is fixed, and the *build* must merely be executed cheaply. As we have seen, separating design and build is all but impossible. This is yet another by-product of the efficiency mentality caused by a belief that the work is merely complicated and not complex. While the vision of the solution is validated with customers and unlikely to change, the details will need to emerge through many rounds of design-build-feedback-insight throughout the process.

Sustaining is the act of running the product efficiently to extract as much value as possible. Improvements made at this stage are likely to be incremental. And finally, there will come a time when the product is no longer core to the organization and will go into a well-earned retirement. Any development is likely to stop, although there may be a longer tail of lightweight support and maintenance for remaining customers.

Designing an effective approach to portfolio management and governance is key to achieving business agility, and it is something on which leadership will have to spend some time. As part of that process, the following key topics will need to be considered for the portfolio as a whole:

■ *Resource allocation:* This is a highly strategic decision, and there is no universal ratio. Just as pharmaceutical and mining companies must make tough decisions on how much to spend on current cash cows versus the discovery and development of new ones, so must almost all organizations. A common starting point is a 70-20-10 split on current products, development, and discovery, and I have seen that work well. In this split, the lion's share of investment, 70 percent, is allocated to sustaining and incrementally improving existing products and services. This makes sense given that these products represent the primary revenue streams that fund everything else. The next-highest investment is 20 percent, which goes into developing new products and services. The final 10 percent is allocated to searching for and validating novel ideas to take forward. Each organization will have different innovation ambitions. Those in more competitive industries in which products have a shorter shelf life may want to focus less on existing products and more on finding new ones.

- *Decision-making:* Who are the key decision makers for each prospective product? Does a single person own it, or a committee? Does the same person own it throughout the life cycle, or is it various people, depending on the phase? Who can initiate experiments at the search stage? If anyone can, up to what value of investment?

- *Transparency:* Can the portfolio and all initiatives within it be viewed at a glance? Are the policies governing each stage understood and clear to all? Having a great portfolio is just the start. Everyone needs to understand how it works so they can make decisions in alignment with the policies governing it.

There are also vital topics for consideration for each individual life-cycle stage. As we have seen, the nature of the work is fundamentally different across different stages of the life cycle, and appropriate techniques must be in place for each. There exists no one-size-fits-all approach.

- *Goal:* What is the purpose of each stage? What are the activities designed to achieve? A financial return? Data? Learning? Understanding the purpose will shape the approach.

- *Investment approach:* What is the level of risk and uncertainty? Will many small bets be placed, or a few large ones? What will be the time horizon for investment decisions? Days, weeks, months, or years?

- *Measures of success:* What will be measured to determine whether the product is proving worthy of further investment? How will the metrics evolve across the life cycle of the product? Judging the search phase and the sustain phase in the same way is unlikely to yield an effective approach for both of them.

- *Strategy:* At what level will agility be required? Are you still validating that there is a product-market fit for the product, service, and business model (i.e., where to build the gold mine)? If so, could there still be pivots around the solution itself? If a fit has been demonstrated, will the pivots be confined to just design and feature set of the offering (i.e., what kind of mine is to be built)? This is highly dependent on the level of risk and uncertainty.

Gaining clarity on these areas will help to shape the tools and techniques used at each stage. We will now explore two of the four stages, *search* and *develop*. These are the two that fall under the explore domain (figure 27).

FIGURE 27
The product development life cycle

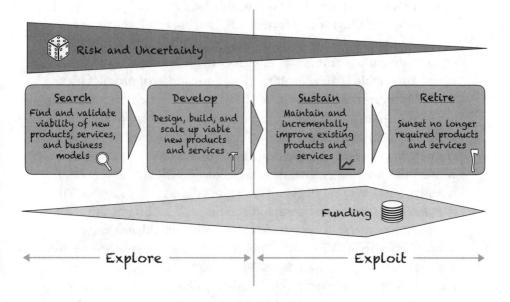

Reflection

Does your organization have a portfolio of projects or products? Is there a structured approach to taking experiments through to development? Is there a single view of the portfolio and how much is being invested at the various phases? Are there opportunities for greater transparency over the work in progress?

Searching: Casting the Net Wide

Out of the entire animal kingdom, seahorses (and their close relatives, sea dragons and pipefish) are the only species in which males give birth to offspring. Depending on the species, a seahorse can give birth to up to 2,000 eggs in one go. There is a good reason for this, and it is not that nature is intentionally wasteful. Survival is an uphill battle for a young seahorse, or fry, as they are known. From the moment they are born, they are left to fend for themselves. With predators on the loose, and a high risk of drifting away from the feeding grounds that are rich in the microscopic organisms on which seahorses feed, only around 10 of the original 2,000 fry will survive to adulthood.[20] In short, it is far too risky to place all hope in a small number of fry. When your survival rate is 0.5 percent, the most successful strategy is to play the numbers game. The failure to survive of 99.5 percent of seahorse fry is an inevitable part of the process. It is also inevitable that a similarly high percentage of product ideas will not survive the search phase.

During a period advising a large retail bank on innovation and agility, I encountered an innovation team that was charged with running experiments to uncover new, creative ideas. In the year in which the team had existed, it had produced little in the way of innovative ideas. A number of things inhibited the team's success. The first was that leadership had mandated that at least 80 percent of experiments must be successful—that is, they would need to show enough promise to progress. This was the key success metric by which they were measured. It would be wonderful if innovation were possible without failures. Unfortunately, failure is a necessary prerequisite of success. How leadership views failure will have a huge impact on the behavior of the teams that will ultimately form the culture. If failure is seen as bad and something to be prevented, then there will be fewer failures—not because the teams will come up with better ideas, but because they will never take risks. They will be less likely to fail, but almost certain not to create anything interesting. As Sir Ken Robinson said in, at the time of writing, the most viewed TED Talk of all time, "If you're not prepared to be wrong, you'll never come up with anything original."[21] Given the 80 percent policy, the so-called innovation team was never going to live up to its name.

The inconvenient truth for failure-averse organizations is that you cannot find a prince without first kissing hundreds of frogs. When searching for a new drug, for example, starting off with around 25,000 compounds in a laboratory will yield about 25 that can be tested on humans. Of those 25, a mere 5 will make it to market, and a single one will be counted on to recoup what was invested in finding it.[22] For every viable gold mine, there are over 1,000 that do not make the cut. In the innovation game, it is simply not possible to be right even half the time. Organizations must learn to view failure differently. Emphasis should be placed not on preventing failures but on reducing the money and time invested in those failures. After all, experiments are as much about learning what *not* to do as they are about learning what *to do*. As Jeff Bezos said of Amazon, "We've tried to reduce the costs of doing experiments so that we can do more of them. If you can increase the number of experiments you try from a hundred to a thousand, you dramatically increase the number of innovations you produce."[23] Few things affect the culture of an organization, and its ability to innovate, like leadership's attitude to failure.

The second big issue with innovation teams is that there are only so many ideas one team can have and experiments that team can run. If it's expected that these groups will be successful in coming up with great ideas, that rather assumes that good ideas are confined to a chosen few. In *What Matters Now*, Gary Hamel refers to this as innovation apartheid.[24] To innovate, good ideas must come from everywhere. They cannot be confined to a single team. When ideas strike, everyone must have the freedom to embark on small, safe-to-fail experiments to determine whether they are worthy of further experimentation. If the majority remain unable to innovate, most of the best ideas will remain just that—ideas.

New York Times columnist Thomas Friedman describes what he calls Carlson's Law: "In a world where so many people now have access to education and cheap tools of innovation, innovation that happens from the bottom up tends to be chaotic but smart. Innovation that happens from the top down tends to be orderly but dumb."[25] As such, organizations that encourage ideas and experimentation from everywhere will be more successful. For this to work, everyone must be trained in *how* to innovate. In most organizations I encounter, more time is spent training people on how to use timesheet systems than how to innovate. It is unreasonable to expect people to perform activities for which they are not properly equipped. I see very few organizations that consider innovation to be something that can happen anywhere, at any time, and come from anyone, and that arm everyone with the required skills.

Given that, the search phase should be characterized by many small, safe-to-fail experiments. This involves testing ideas quickly and cheaply. The idea is to determine whether there is a potential product-market fit. At this stage we want no assumption to go unvalidated; unvalidated assumptions represent risk. There is often a lack of awareness about what assumptions are being made. This leads to confusion over what is to be validated, and how. To help, I group what I believe to be the main areas to be validated into what I call the *Ladder of Validation,* which is an evolution of the desirability, viability, feasibility model. These validations will occur largely sequentially, although there will be an element of iterating across all levels, and some levels may be validated in the same experiment. The ladder consists of four levels (figure 28).

Level 1—Problem Validation: Do people have this issue or a particular job to do? First up is ensuring that, from a customer perspective, there is a job to be done, a pain point, or a potential gain. In short, it's about making sure that there is indeed a problem to be solved or opportunity to be exploited. If we have not validated this, then everything else is irrelevant. No one will buy a solution that does not help them to do a job or relieve some pain point. Maybe there are pain points, but they are not sufficiently painful to warrant a new solution. A common scenario is to start with a solution. But even if a solution forms part of the initial idea, it is always worth revisiting and validating the core assumption that there exists a problem to be solved. This is the foundation on which everything else will rest.

Level 2—Solution Validation: Does the proposed solution help with the issue or job? Once it is clear that there is indeed a problem to be solved or job to be done, the experiments can progress to vali-

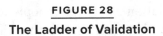

FIGURE 28

The Ladder of Validation

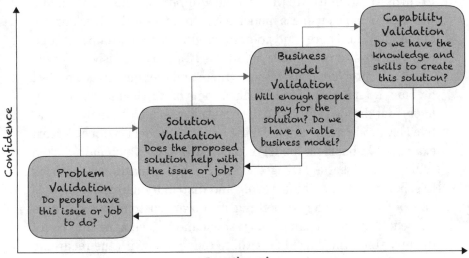

dating whether the proposed solution does indeed assist with the job or relieve some pain points. Many innovations involve solving existing problems in new ways. Uber provided an innovative solution to the existing job of getting from A to B. Airbnb did the same for accommodation, and digital cameras did the same for photography. People did not change the job to be done (taking photos); they merely shifted from one way of doing that job (printed images) to another (digital images), which eased more of their pain points around the process. It is at this point that there should be much iterating to find an appropriate solution. In 1999, Nick Swinmurn, founder of the online shoe store Zappos, set out to validate that people would buy shoes online without investing in a big infrastructure. He did it by taking pictures of shoes in local stores, posting them on a simple website, then running out to buy the shoes and shipping them once orders came in. Once he had validated that the solution did indeed relieve a pain point around buying shoes, and that enough orders were coming in, he invested in building out the business.

Level 3—Business Model Validation: Will enough people pay for the solution? Do we have a viable business model? Once it has been confirmed that a solution exists that people want and that allows them to get their jobs done more easily and with less pain, it's time to turn attention to whether people will *pay* for the solution, and whether a viable business model exists to warrant the development of the solution. There is no point in building a great product that already exists and is available at low cost. Take a spreadsheet, for example: the problem it addresses is there and the solution is a perfect fit, but with many options available, some of which are free, it is unlikely that the idea will give a return. And even a great, truly innovative new product can still fail if the business model is wrong. A great example of a business model pivot is Nespresso, which moved from selling businesses a packaged system of coffee machines and pods to separating the manufacturing and distribution of the machines and pods and largely switching its target customer segment to households. It also changed its revenue model, reducing the cost of the machines and subsidizing these reductions with the recurring revenues from the pods. While the business model evolved, the actual product, coffee machines and accompanying coffee pods, remained largely unchanged.

Level 4—Capability Validation: Do we have the knowledge and skills to create this solution? Once there is confidence that a good solution exists that solves a real customer problem, and that there is a viable business model around it, all that remains is to check whether the team has the capability to build it. Some high-level thinking will be required around the technologies needed to turn the concept into a product that customers will buy. If there are capability gaps in the organization, a decision will need to be made on how to address that.

The following are three principles to bear in mind when searching:

■ *Start cheaply and gradually increase funding.* Early explorations around whether the problem exists should cost a maximum of a few hundred dollars. Small, fast, cheap experiments increase the number that can be run, and reduce the barrier to entry. This means that experiments can be initiated from anywhere, by anyone, with very little risk. As the data from experiments indicates a need for further experimentation, investment can be made in increasing increments on a rolling basis. These more sophisticated and involved experiments should provide increasing confidence in the hypothesis.

- *Get out of the building and be data driven.* Steve Blank strongly advocates this approach. There is very little information about customer jobs, pains, and gain in the building, so getting out to talk and conduct experiments is vital. Asking customers what they want is a start; designing experiments and observing their behavior is better. When it comes to customer insights, what people *say* they will do and what they *actually* do are rarely the same. It is important to understand the measures that will indicate to us that our hypothesis is correct. Those measures must be defined as part of the experiment design.

- *Be prepared to pivot.* At various stages, decisions will need to be made to pivot, persevere, or stop. Being able to pivot to a different approach based on experimentation and data is vital in the early stages of a product. Pivots can be related to the problem being addressed, the customer segments being targeted, the solution itself, or the business model around the solution. It is better to end up with a great product that you were not expecting than a failed product that you were.

As I mentioned earlier, using the same measures of success across the entire portfolio is a common mistake in many organizations. Traditional management and financial accounting measures are designed for the exploit domain. They tend to rely on data about the performance of a product, which is not something that exists early in the life cycle. When it comes to the explore domain, and the search phase in particular, success can be defined as identifying and validating the problem to be addressed, the proposed solution, the proposed business model, and organizational capability as quickly and cheaply as possible in order to provide solid reasons to begin building a working version. In short, success here is learning about the market. It is about gaining new knowledge. This is knowledge we did not have before, and it is knowledge our competitors don't have. Early investments are made to acquire this knowledge, which, if used wisely, can turn out to be hugely valuable. That value will be realized down the road—so tools like financial return on investment are meaningless early on.

The process just described will be highly iterative. It will involve many rounds of defining hypotheses, designing experiments and measures to test the hypotheses, running the experiments and collecting data, analyzing the data, generating more insights—and then deciding whether to, in the words of Eric Ries in his book *The Lean Startup*, pivot, persevere, or stop.[26] Pivoting involves investigating new hypotheses. Persevering involves continuing down a path with increasingly sophisticated experiments and higher confidence levels. Stopping involves closing down the idea entirely. Initial investments will be small but will increase over time as confidence grows. Investments should always be inversely proportional to risk and uncertainty.

In the search phase, decisions are continually being made about whether to fund the next experiment, stop work entirely, or proceed to the develop phase. Once there is a reasonable level of confidence that the four areas have been addressed adequately, a decision may be made to invest a larger amount in building an initial version of the solution. This decision must be based not on detailed business cases and spreadsheets but on real data collected in the field from real customers that demonstrates a product-market fit and viability. It should include the total spend to date, and a request for time, money, and resources to progress into the develop phase.

Reflection

In your organization, is failure viewed as something to be avoided, or as a necessary step in the process of innovation? Is there an opportunity to run many safe-to-fail experiments in the search for new products? Who can initiate those experiments? Is there a structured process around identifying which to explore further and which to abandon? What other enablers would need to be addressed to allow for this way of working?

Developing: Bringing Ideas to Life

As with designing and building a gold mine, the develop phase is not about validating whether a product or service *should* be developed. That happens during the search phase. In the develop phase, we bring the idea to life. There is often a temptation at this point to assume that you have all the information necessary to build a great product, or at least that this information can be acquired up front by talking with customers. That is almost always a mistake.

In a 2004 TED Talk, Malcolm Gladwell discusses developments in the food industry.[27] In particular, he discusses how Howard Moskowitz went about helping Campbell's Soup to increase the market share for its Prego spaghetti sauce. Prego was struggling to compete with Ragu, which dominated the US spaghetti sauce market in the 1970s and 1980s. Moskowitz and the Campbell's Soup kitchen proceeded to create 45 varieties of spaghetti sauce, varying everything from levels of garlic to sweetness to spiciness. He then took his 45 varieties of tomato sauce on the road to test them with real customers. Upon trying multiple sauces, customers rated each sauce from 0 to 100. After many months and a mountain of data, it became clear that almost all Americans fall into one of three categories: those who like their sauce plain, those who like it spicy, and those who like it extra chunky. The final category, extra chunky, was the most interesting. In the early 1980s, there was no extra-chunky spaghetti sauce on the market. Prego introduced an extra-chunky line, and made over $600 million over the following 10 years.

What Moskowitz did with Prego challenged a fundamental view in the food industry at the time: that the way to make people happy is to *ask* them what they want. Indeed, for years, Ragu, Prego, and many other food companies in the industry had been doing just that. They had been holding focus groups in which people were asked what they wanted in a spaghetti sauce. In over two decades, no one ever said that they wanted an extra-chunky sauce. Despite the fact that the data showed that one-third of people preferred it, when they were actually *asked*, nobody *said* they wanted it.

This goes to the heart of the challenge with developing new products and services. People often do not know what they want *until they see it.* They know what jobs they need to do and they know what pains they're suffering in trying to get those jobs done, but they don't know exactly what they want. Because customers are knowledgeable about the *problem space*, organizations then expect them to be equally knowledgeable about the *solution space*. It turns out that they are not. It is not customers' job to design solutions. That's the job of product developers, of innovators working to create great new products and services. Henry Ford is often quoted as saying, "If I had asked people what they wanted, they'd have said faster horses."[28] Back in 1998, Steve Jobs said, "It's really hard to design products by focus groups. A lot of times, people don't know what they want until you show it to them."[29]

People do, however, know whether they like a solution when they see it. This is why the agile movement was born in the world of software development, and this is why the development process, even after many experiments have been performed, cannot be treated as a problem of execution, as purely a building process. Both build and design are involved, which means there is still a need for feedback on how the solution is emerging. This work still fits firmly into the explore domain (see figure 27). Most so-called agile frameworks are designed to build out products with flexibility, and the develop phase is generally where they begin to feature. These frameworks, such as Scrum, Large-Scale Scrum, and the Scaled Agile Framework, are designed to bring products to life in a way that recognizes the inherent uncertainty and complexity of the work.

It is, however, easy to forget that these frameworks only work well when combined with the changes we have discussed to this point. In this phase of the product life cycle, the problem to be solved and the high-level value proposition tend to have been decided on, but the exact design of the solution—the look and feel, say, or the exact features—will still need to be investigated. The frameworks address this issue by allowing for short feedback loops with real customers to solicit feedback. This leads to inevitable course corrections. This is to be welcomed as the product evolves into something that addresses real customer pain points. It is important to bear in mind that the best feedback comes from working versions of a product, so staying as close to that as possible is a prerequisite for getting feedback. After all, customers cannot rate the taste of a spaghetti sauce by merely reading the recipe.

If organizational governance processes require exact designs up front, then there will be little room for learning as the process progresses. That's why it's advisable to keep designs flexible and focus instead on business outcomes. Those outcomes replace outputs as the measure of effectiveness. Budgets cannot operate on an annual cycle because opportunities and threats do not operate on an annual cycle. The investment approach that best supports agility is rolling quarterly funding in a product-centric model. In this way, teams are funded for a quarter to deliver value against a particular product. Teams can be moved between products based on value delivered and the emerging business priorities. This leaves the organization in a position to respond to emerging market trends.

Managing the whole portfolio well is vital. A group will need to meet each quarter to assess the progress of each product that is in the develop phase. Whatever percentage of the overall budget is allocated to the develop phase, those scarce resources will need to be allocated across the various products to maximize impact. The easiest way to do that is by increasing, decreasing, or leaving unchanged the number of teams working on each product. Doing this roughly quarterly leaves space to respond to changes in the market or to promising new product ideas. Also, having a three-month maximum as an investment horizon effectively mitigates the risk of not investing in the right mix. If a product turns out not to be viable, it can be halted at any quarterly review point. Likewise, if a product shows more potential than anticipated, it can be scaled up more quickly. This is the essence of agility, and it can only happen with the product model rather than the project model.

Managing the portfolio properly requires accurate data on which to judge the performance of each product. Upon implementing this model at many large organizations, I have found that only by defining clear quarterly business objectives can teams really be judged on their effectiveness. Unlike in the search phase, where knowledge is the main outcome, the develop phase may see varying outcomes. This is because some products will already have launched into the market and be growing while others will still be at the prelaunch phase. Sometimes these outcomes are merely a forecast, based on roughly how long it will be until the product is ready to launch. Sometimes they concern customers acquired, revenue growth, or conversion. Understanding where teams are versus where they expected to be at each stage means having actionable metrics that can help with priority-setting. This is the kind of responsiveness that tends to be missing from annual project-based funding cycles. Moving resources from one project to another is not a trivial process, and the data that dictates when to do that is rarely available in annual funding cycles.

Once the product is successfully generating a return and the more creative side of product development has diminished, things may transition from the explore domain to the exploit domain. At that point, more traditional management and financial techniques may be applicable. This could involve longer investment horizons, perhaps of 6 to 12 months. It could mean making forecasts and projections in the same way an established business model would. There is, of course, always the option to transfer the more operational side of the product to the exploit domain, while keeping the more creative side firmly in explore, working within a system that enables creativity, innovation, and agility. This would allow the teams to continue to improve the product through smaller, more core innovations with the level of agility required to evolve the product in an uncertain climate. This is a highly contextual decision and is largely dependent on how much ongoing core innovation is required.

Reflection

When building out a product in your organization, how much flexibility is there around the design, feature set, and final solution? Are there governance models in place that could allow for more flexibility by tracking outcomes rather than outputs? How feasible is it to receive, and respond to, customer feedback throughout the development process?

Chapter Summary

- Traditional governance and investment approaches, involving detailed business cases, projects, and cost accounting, are rooted in the assumption that work is largely plannable and predictable, and are too constraining when applied in the explore domain.

- The nature of the work changes across the life cycle of the product, moving from highly uncertain and experimental when searching for a product-market fit to more stable and plannable as more is learned and uncertainty diminishes.

- When operating in high-VUCA environments, the most effective approach is the venture capitalist model of placing many small bets, doubling down on those that show promise, and stopping those that do not.

- Organizational governance policies must be reinvented to accommodate experimentation and allow teams to respond to customer feedback.

Key Practices for Business Agility

- Move from a project-based model with up-front business cases and large investments to a long-lived product-based model with frequent review points.

- Consider the search for and creation of new products and business models a process of creative design rather than of building and predictable execution.

- Switch focus from tracking outputs to tracking business outcomes.

- Create a portfolio management approach that incorporates different modes of operation at each phase—a mode for searching for a product-market fit, a mode for building out an idea with agility, and a mode for sustaining a well-understood product.

■ Make innovation everyone's job, and invest in helping people to learn how to test business ideas quickly and cheaply.

Further Reading and Resources

Books

■ David J. Bland and Alexander Osterwalder, *Testing Business Ideas: A Field Guide for Rapid Experimentation* (Hoboken, NJ: John Wiley and Sons, 2020)

■ Eric Ries, *The Lean Startup: How Constant Innovation Creates Radically Successful Businesses* (London: Portfolio Penguin, 2011)

■ Tendayi Viki, Craig Strong, and Sonja Kresojevic, *The Lean Product Lifecycle: A Playbook for Making Products People Want* (Harlow, UK: Pearson Education, 2018)

■ Evan Leybourn and Shane Hastie, *#noprojects: A Culture of Continuous Value* (n.p.: C4Media, 2018)

Websites, Articles, and Videos

■ Please see www.6enablers.com/resources for more on this topic, including a downloadable reading list.

CHAPTER 9

Ways of Working

The man who grasps principles can successfully select his own methods. The man who tries methods, ignoring principles, is sure to have trouble.

—HARRINGTON EMERSON

IN THIS CHAPTER, WE WILL EXPLORE

- some tools, techniques, and practices for effective teamwork
- how to foster a mindset of continuous improvement
- what to consider when measuring the performance of teams undertaking creative, explore-domain work.

Daily Team Practices: Patterns for Collaboration

Across chapters 4 to 8, we covered five of the six enablers of business agility. Those five can be considered a fundamental organizational operating system. They form the underlying platform on which everything else can be built. While each organization has a slightly different flavor, the key patterns across the five enablers covered thus far tend not to diverge wildly. The final enabler is a little different. It should not be viewed as a part of the underlying operating system, but rather as a set of applications that can be installed on the organizational operating system to meet the unique requirements of each organization. As is the case with computer operating systems, there is a wide range of potential applications from which to choose based on the nature of the work and the organization. With that being said, there is much commonality among them. I will now walk through some basic patterns that can increase the effectiveness of teams undertaking complex, explore-domain work.

High-Volume Communication

In the 1970s, the US government decided to look more closely into why some of their strategic engineering projects were successful while others were not. They wanted to understand what was causing the difference in performance. At the sharp end of this research was a young professor at MIT named Thomas Allen. His first port of call in understanding the differences was to focus on complex engineering challenges, like developing new weapons or satellite systems, that were being tackled by two or more separate organizations. These were either government agencies or private firms, and they were addressing exactly the same problems—problems no one had ever tackled before. With this, Allen was able to create a list of factors by which the success of each organization could be measured. These success factors would assess the quality of each entity's solution and the time taken to create it.

The results were startling. The most successful organizations were those in which people communicated best. These people seemed to solve complex problems far more quickly and effectively. Allen then set about trying to understand why those teams were better communicators. He could find no link connected to individual traits or education, but he did find a link that centered on where people sat—in particular, how far apart their desks were.

Allen determined that it was physical proximity that was the key to high-frequency, effective communication and collaboration. In fact, when Allen plotted the frequency of communications against distance, it showed a dramatic decline in the frequency of communication once a distance of just 8 meters was reached. At 30 meters, it approached zero.[1] This has become known as the Allen curve (figure 29). It seems that being in close proximity has a far bigger impact on team effectiveness than intelligence or experience.

The obvious question to ask at this point is whether a study performed over 40 years ago, a time when few digital collaboration tools existed, is still relevant today. The answer is a resounding yes. Scientist Ben Waber has demonstrated that digital communication follows the same pattern. He found that engineers who were colocated were 20 percent more likely to stay in touch via digital means than remote workers, being in virtual contact four times as frequently as

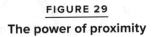

FIGURE 29

The power of proximity

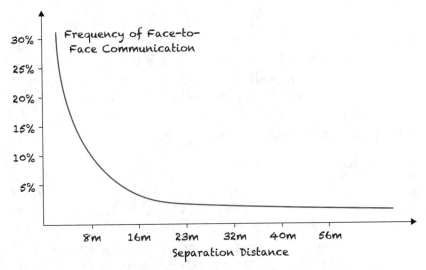

Source: Allen, Thomas J., *Managing the Flow of Technology*, Figure 8.3,
© 1977 Massachusetts Institute of Technology, by permission of The MIT Press.

those who were not. This more frequent communication led to projects being completed 32 percent faster.[2] With all the communication breakthroughs in the past 40 years, there still appears to be no substitute for proximity. It seems that being able to see people is more important than most realize. From an evolutionary perspective, this makes sense. We are programmed—from our species' early days in bands of up to 50 people who saw each other every day—for frequent, face-to-face communication. This is also how we continuously send and receive group "belonging" cues that are vital to a feeling of togetherness and safety.

While *personal productivity* can increase when we work on our own, innovation and the creation of the new do not come from individuals working alone. They come from teams working together and with other teams. For that, what is required is *collaborative productivity*. This, it seems, is severely impaired by any barriers to communication. Donald Reinertsen puts it this way in his book *Managing the Design Factory*: "Colocation is the closest thing to fairy dust that we have to improve communications on the development team."[3] There are, of course, good reasons for working remotely, as those who created makeshift offices in their homes during the COVID-19 pandemic can testify. These need to be taken into account. But with an increasing number of organizations moving in that direction, it pays to be aware of the data, and to work hard to mitigate consciously as many barriers as possible. This takes an investment of time, energy, and money. Think long and hard about how to foster an environment for frequent communications and the building of trust and belonging. Think doubly hard about it if teams are remote. It appears to be the secret sauce for creative teams.

Visualizing Work

On the factory floor, inventory and queues are easy to spot. In Lean terms, both of these things represent waste. Physical parts pile up in front of bottlenecked activities, providing a clear view into which operations require optimizing or increased capacity. It is then easy for workers and managers to understand priorities and how to improve processes.

This is not so easy, however, when it comes to *knowledge work*. There are no physical parts piling up, what is in progress is not always clear, and there is no clarity regarding where the bottlenecks lie. Queues, delays, excess inventory, and the lack of a clear understanding of what is going on can be killers of creativity and agility. The worst part is that they manage to kill agility both silently and invisibly.

Making work visible, even transparent, can have myriad benefits. The human brain has hundreds of millions of neurons devoted to visual processing. This accounts for about 30 percent of the cortex, with touch and hearing accounting for around 8 and 3 percent, respectively.[4] We are visual creatures. When teams visualize their work, it becomes significantly easier for them to manage themselves *and* their work. Transparency is the sunshine that illuminates priorities, what's in progress, who is working on it, and where there may be issues. Having the information displayed clearly on a wall or in a digital equivalent means that teams can easily know at a glance what they should work on next, who may need support, and which areas of the process should be improved. This is a key driver of engagement, collaboration, ownership, swift decision-making, and the reduction of external coordinators of work.

As with so many things, this visualization approach was pioneered at Toyota to support just-in-time production, although it took inspiration from the "two-bin system" developed in the United Kingdom when Spitfires were being manufactured during World War II. Today, so-called Kanban boards are ubiquitous among product development departments across the globe. Visualization is a great way for teams to understand just how much is in progress, and the same goes at the organizational level. Just visualizing the end-to-end value stream, how many things are in progress, and where things are getting stuck can be a real eye-opener.

Daily Alignment Meeting

Going by many names, including Daily Stand-up, Daily Huddle, and Daily Scrum, this is a simple but powerful practice that boosts collaboration, transparency, and communication among and between teams. When done well, it can dramatically reduce the need for other coordination activities and meetings.

This type of meeting provides a formal opportunity for those doing the work to synchronize and coordinate their activities and to plan the next 24 hours. Issues can be raised and collaboration opportunities can be discussed. Along with alignment on goals, the daily alignment meeting is a key contributor to the self-organization of teams, allowing them to check easily how they are progressing, who requires support, and whether they are working on the highest-value items possible.

It is, however, important not to fall into the trap of stopping conversations and coordination outside this meeting. The meeting is there to provide a formal opportunity for conversations, but it should not be the *only* time teams talk to each other, nor should people wait for the meeting before collaborating.

Where there is a network of interconnected teams collaborating on an outcome, it is not uncommon for there to be a team-of-teams–level daily alignment meeting to synchronize and coordinate *among* teams and to identify opportunities for interteam collaboration. This meeting should be attended by a subset of the teams doing the work, not professional coordinators. Those doing the work will have the greatest insight into where teams will need to cooperate.

These meetings are often held at the same place and time each day and are conducted standing up to keep things short and snappy, around 15 minutes at the most. For this, we can thank Queen Victoria, who in 1861 discovered that making people stand during meetings of the Privy Council of the United Kingdom ensured that the meetings would be over sooner.

Small Batches

In 1950, Ford and General Motors were making huge numbers of cars. The conventional thinking was that with a large fixed cost, the economics of large-batch production win out. With plenty of space in the United States to store that massive inventory, auto manufacturers didn't see much downside.

At the same time, Toyota was taking a different approach. Compared with the United States, Japan is a small country, and Toyota at the time could not afford comparable levels of storage. Holding too much stock would represent risk, as the cars might not sell, not to mention the capital tied up in all those unsold vehicles. The problem for Toyota was fixed costs—in particular, the cost of changing the dies on the large stamping machines, which took place each time a different model was to be made. The dies weighed many tons and needed to be installed with precision to within a millimeter, using large cranes. The process could take up to 24 hours, during which the production line stood idle. Toyota could afford neither the 24-hour shutdown of its factories to change dies (known as a transaction cost)[5] nor the lots on which to hold the large batches that made production economical by requiring fewer changes (known as a holding cost).

Advised by consultant Shigeo Shingo, Toyota did the only thing it could do in order to compete: it set out to reduce the transaction cost—which, in the West, was considered a fixed cost. It turned out that the cost was not as fixed as many imagined. By focusing on changeover process improvements, by 1960, 24 hours had become 15 minutes, and by 1970, a mere 3 minutes. This was a much more palatable period of time for which to stop the production line. When the transaction cost was reduced to the point where it became lower than the holding cost, smaller batches became more economical.

Toyota no longer needed to produce large batches before incurring the cost of changing the presses; it could produce cars as and when they were required, minimizing its held stock and therefore its holding costs, not to mention the risk of holding large amounts of stock. This allowed it to keep down the cost of production runs while keeping quality high. This became known as the single-minute exchange of die, and it was the key enabler for the just-in-time production method, which paved the way for Toyota to become the world's most profitable car company.

While there are crucial differences between manufacturing and product development—the former is very much in the realm of exploiting and the latter in exploring—there are many lessons to be learned from each. In any unpredictable process like innovation, large batches bring many disadvantages. Some organizations report up to a 95 percent decrease in testing time and a 33 percent decrease in defects merely by shrinking batch sizes.[6]

Large batches are an inhibiter of business agility. They increase cycle times, delay feedback, delay the delivery of value, increase variability, reduce transparency, and reduce quality. None of these things makes for a nimble, modern organization. The key to unlocking small batches is to drive down transaction costs. Back when I was a software developer, I observed some organizations whose manual regression test cycles of their software were up to 60 days long. That is a long, painful, and expensive process through which to go every time new value is to be released to eager customers. As such, releases were carried out twice annually. Holding on to that much value for months at a time is expensive—and risky. It destroys responsiveness and maximizes holding costs. Delaying value delivery turns out to be more expensive than most organizations realize. It also delays feedback, which increases the risk of not delivering the hoped-for value. As the old saying goes, it is best not to test the water with both feet.

This drawn-out process is a world away from how modern organizations work. They deliver value to customers multiple times per day. They do that by making it cheap to do so, by driving down the transaction costs of each release. In software, this is done by automating the test and deployment process until it is almost trivial. When a Tesla owner pointed out an issue with his car's "dog mode," a feature that keeps the temperature stable, allowing dogs to be left inside,

Tesla was able to resolve the issue and push the fix out over the airwaves within two days.[7] How long might a traditional, less responsive organization with high transaction costs have taken to resolve a similar issue? It takes a lot to live up to such levels of agility and customer focus. Other industries must take the approach that is right for them, but the benefit of small batches for agility is undeniable.

Slack Time

What do the wildly successful products Gmail, Post-It Notes, and Elixir guitar strings have in common? You guessed it—they were all created during so-called dabble time. That is, they were not officially sanctioned projects with business cases and return-on-investment projections. They were each created by an engineer who had an idea. Now, people in all organizations have ideas every day—great ones. That's not some rare trait, out of reach of all but a handful of innovative organizations. What *is* far less common, however, is the freedom to pursue those great ideas (and some not-so-great ones, too). Google, 3M, and W. L. Gore are companies that value innovation and entrepreneurship and, as such, create policies to encourage it.

The policy in question here is the time, and space, to pursue ideas without having to ask permission. This is more than the removal of the standard bureaucracy that gets in the way of creativity; it's a deliberate attempt to encourage experimentation during standard work hours. The way these organizations accomplished it was to encourage people to spend between 10 and 20 percent of their time working on their own ideas—no permission required. Providing this space has led to some incredibly creative and commercially successful products and services, but also to more subtle improvements. Great ideas rarely come when one is plowing through an overflowing inbox. Allow people the time and space to stop and think deeply. This will lead to some great ideas.

Slack time doesn't always have to be used for moon-shot innovations. It can also be used for smaller improvements and for learning. While working with an e-commerce organization, I observed a small group using the time to investigate more effective ways to collaborate as a team of teams. The impact of this, while intangible, was that the teams were better able to communicate and cooperate. After this change, teams were demonstrably more effective. I have also observed many cases of improvements to existing products in the form of fixes, or even new features for customers, that emerged from slack time. These are features that would never have come about through traditional means but can prove hugely valuable.

The final reason to build in slack time for teams is that it will lead them to deliver value to the customer more quickly. As discussed in chapter 6, loading up teams nearly to capacity appears to make sense but will lead to exponential delays. The time items spend on hold will double every time "excess" capacity is halved. As counterintuitive as it sounds, that means that taking a team from 75 percent utilization to 87.5 percent utilization will nearly double the time it takes for that team to deliver. This is because planners do not take into account the inherent variability of creative work. When such work is treated in the same way as the more predictable manufacturing, delays and queues begin to dominate customer lead times. As I said in chapter 6, who wants to be on a fully utilized road? Donald Reinertsen covers the theory behind this wonderfully in his book *The Principles of Product Development Flow*.[8]

Building in structured free time for people tends to work against the instinct of almost all managers of traditional organizations. Having people ostensibly idle or not contributing to the items deemed most valuable can feel wasteful and indulgent. It is not. The biggest wastes in organizations stem from queues, delays, and the squandering of human creativity. These wastes are underpinned by a lack of built-in slack time. Slack time boosts creativity, innovation, and engagement. It provides space to focus on learning and improving the system, and it almost always leads to value being delivered more quickly than would otherwise have been the case. In short, it increases organizational agility.

> ### Reflection
>
> How easy is it for teams in your organization to collaborate and communicate frequently? What are the structural barriers to communication? How can they be removed? Do your teams have dedicated time for experimenting? What could happen if they did?

Kaizen: A Mindset of Continuous Improvement

The Japanese word *kaizen* comes from the Japanese words "kai-" meaning "change" and "zen" meaning "good." It loosely translates to "change for the better." In the business world, particularly when it comes to agility, this tends to be referred to as "continuous improvement." First applied in post–World War II Japan, it was popularized across the globe as a key pillar of the Toyota Way. It has since subsequently been applied in almost every single industry. This mindset of always seeking to improve processes and practices is a key reason for the success of the Toyota Production System, from which the many flavors of the Lean movement were created.

Teams Own Their Own Process

When my elder daughter was around three years old, she had grown too big for her highchair, but she was still too small for an adult chair. The solution was an in-between chair aimed at toddlers. We bought just such a chair from Ikea and, in a rare feat of successful DIY, I assembled it without incident. Two years later, we went through the same process all over again for my younger daughter. Instead of simply buying a chair for her, however, we passed on the now two-year-old chair to her and bought a new chair for my elder girl. Once again, I prepared myself for assembly until my daughter, now five years old, decided that *she* wanted to assemble the chair. She did as decent a job as any five-year-old could do, then ran off to play. I tightened up the screws and placed the chair in position. At dinnertime that day, we heard about nothing but the greatness of the chair that *she* had "built." Indeed, this lasted for an entire week. It was as if it were the greatest chair ever assembled. The chair was, in fact, the same kind as the one that I had assembled two years earlier. That time, however, there was no praise for the chair.

So what was the difference? The answer is, of course, the fact that the second time around, she had put the chair together herself. She was under the sway of the Ikea Effect, a cognitive bias whereby people place disproportionate value on things they had a partial hand in creating.[9] I consoled myself with the knowledge that my daughter loved the chair not because it was superior to the one I'd assembled two years earlier but because she helped to create it. The same effect can be observed in teams when it comes to the processes and practices they use. Having teams own their ways of working is a huge driver of engagement, which leads them to be more likely to follow the process and more likely to improve it. Ownership also reinforces the feeling that they are indeed adults who can make decisions for themselves.

The improvement aspect is key here. The creators of the agile movement were deeply influenced by the Lean movement. Every single agile framework (for example, Scrum) has baked into it frequent formal opportunities to reflect on teams' effectiveness and improve it. This is even included in the final of 12 principles of the manifesto—such is the power of this mindset. Any approach taken by teams should include at least once per month the opportunity to inspect their own performance and how it can be improved. This event should be facilitated by someone with skills and techniques in this area. This is in addition to inspecting the performance of the product or service under creation.

Kaizen only works if it is performed at all levels of the organization, particularly by the teams doing the work. Time and resources must also be dedicated to this purpose. Indeed, in 2005 Toyota received more than 540,000 improvement items from its Japanese employees alone.[10] This stems from the belief that it is everyday workers who are best placed to solve complex problems. No matter how smart managers may be, there is just no way that they alone could come up with that much improvement—nor would teams be likely to listen if they did. No wonder few can keep up with the relentless pace of improvement happening at all levels at organizations that embrace this approach. It is often the case that it is faster, in the long run, to pause the felling of trees temporarily and spend a few minutes sharpening the ax before resuming. Slowing down can indeed speed you up.

Process Flexibility

I once worked with an organization that had recently implemented a new digital tool used by teams to manage their work more effectively. The decision to adopt this tool was made by department leadership, and all teams were required to use it. While I was observing a team, they held a kaizen event called a "retrospective." As just described, the purpose of this event was to reflect on the work of the previous two weeks and identify tangible improvements to how team members worked together so that they might be more effective over the coming two-week period and beyond. Out of this retrospective came a suggestion to alter their workflow steps slightly to enable more collaboration on activities in which there was often misunderstanding among team members. This was a sound idea and would almost certainly reduce the number of defects produced.

There was just one problem: the workflow management part of the new tool was locked. Only an administrator could alter workflow. The team duly sent a request for the change, only to be met with a blunt refusal from a distant floor. It became clear that all teams would be required to use the same workflow in order for management reporting to be uniform. This was incredibly frustrating but unfortunately not surprising. In my experience, that was the norm. Management would find the "one best way" and mandate that all teams use that one best tool in that one best way. No deviation. This was straight out of the playbook of Mr. Taylor himself.

Uniformity and standardization are hallmarks of Control-culture organizations. In some domains, particularly safety-critical ones, that can be highly effective—vital in fact. As with many things, the trouble comes when uniformity and standardization are applied out of context. When it comes to the explore domain, standardization will destroy creativity and engagement. It will also ensure that teams are working with processes and tools that are far less appropriate than those they might have chosen to use. Given that they understand the challenges they face better than anyone, this is a shame. Tools for managing work should always serve teams, not the other way around.

There are even reports of this practice going as far as the imposition of standardized desk layouts in a UK government department. One worker who dared to leave a banana on his desk was asked whether the banana was "active or inactive"—if the latter, that meant it was not to be eaten imminently and should therefore be hidden away in a drawer.[11] The doubtlessly well-meaning consultants responsible had almost certainly made a mistake similar to that of so many other questionable "Lean" consultants—they had misinter-preted a quotation from the father of the Toyota Production System himself, Taiichi Ohno. The offending quote is, "Where there is no standard, there can be no kaizen." Unfortunately for many out there, they have missed a crucial distinction. *Standards* are not *standardization*. The former documents the current process of a team; the latter ensures that all teams work in an identical way.

What Ohno is actually saying is that without first creating a baseline, there is no standard from which to improve. Standards should always be changing, and the changes must come from the teams that are encountering problems or opportunities. In fact, Ohno once berated a team on discovering that it had not updated its standard, and therefore its work practices for some time, snapping, "You have been doing it the same way, so you have been a salary thief for the last year. . . . What do you come to work to do each day? If you are observing every day you ought to be finding things you don't like and rewriting the standard immediately. Even if the document hanging here is from last month, this is wrong."[12] Some of the nuance may have been lost in translation, but the point is clear: work practices should never remain static. There are always improvements to be made.

What is true for tools and processes is also true for out-of-the-box frameworks and ways of working. Those that are more prescriptive can be easier to start with, but they soon become constraining. Never be a slave to a framework just because it has rules. Experiment and find a new way—a better way, a way that teams feel will best serve their needs. Avoid mandating processes, practices, and tools. Where synergy between teams is needed, those teams—never managers removed from the work—should come up with solutions within sensible constraints.

Cross-Pollination

In the 1960s, Rinus Michels was leading an innovation in soccer. Having managed Dutch team Ajax to league and cup success, he was pioneering an approach known as Total Football. This bold new approach was, at the time, in complete contrast to the rigid, fixed formations of the English, the Italian, and most European teams. In

Michels's approach, players moved fluidly across the pitch, effortlessly filling in spaces left by teammates. To do this well, every player with the exception of the goalkeeper needed to be able to play any other position as well as his own. This would allow the team maximum flexibility to respond instantly to events as they unfolded. This approach was extremely successful and led the Dutch national team to the final of the World Cup in 1974. A version of this system is still used today by arguably the world's most successful manager, Pep Guardiola.

This approach took a very different view of the role of players. Instead of being individual specialists with little need to stray from their positions, they became generalists who could quickly adapt to constantly changing circumstances. Players were jacks of all trades, masters of some.

There is a strong parallel here to creative teams in modern organizations. Gone are the days of brilliant individuals working in silos with headphones on to block out the world. Teamwork and collaboration are now far more important. Having an appreciation of all the work that is done on teams can give greater insight into the whole and avoid the local optimizations that can result from a Henry Ford production-line approach to specialization.

When two or three people working together on a problem bring multiple disciplines to the table, the cross-learning is powerful. Potential problems are spotted before they become issues, and each gets an improved understanding of other functions. Pair, or even group, work is the new normal. This fosters a learning culture and encourages the development of specializing generalists. An added advantage of this is the removal of the bottlenecks that occur with hyperspecialized team members. Complex problems are best solved by teams, not individuals within teams. It is far from wasteful to work in this way.

Reflection

How much time do teams spend on continuous improvement in your organization? Do teams own their own process? What prevents giving more control to teams to own and improve their processes and tools?

Measuring Performance: More Value with Less Work

The Pareto principle (often referred to as the 80-20 rule) states that 80 percent of your results are attributable to 20 percent of your efforts. With that in mind, it is a common scenario that teams can deliver a lot of output while delivering very little true value. This is akin to running very quickly in the wrong direction. Much effort is expended for minimal impact. This is a particularly hard to spot form of waste. It seems, then, that less can often be more.

Outcomes over Outputs

We touched on the benefits of tracking business outcomes over predefined outputs in chapter 8, but it is worth revisiting here. I am often asked how we can measure the effectiveness of teams. It's a fair question without a satisfactory answer. In his book *The Age of Diminishing Expectations*, economist Paul Krugman notes, "Productivity isn't everything, but in the long run it is almost everything. A country's ability to improve its standard of living over time depends almost entirely on its ability to raise its output per worker."[13]

Given the shift I have discussed from the individual to the team level, we can substitute the word "worker" for "team" here—but that still leaves us with a few issues. When the value being created is intangible, as it always is with innovation, output is a terrible proxy for value. If a worker picks 20 oranges per minute and that increases to 25 over time, that worker is clearly becoming more productive. If a knowledge worker has five ideas per day and that increases to six, is that person becoming more productive? What about teams building new software features? Is seven per week better than five? What if they implement one feature that is more valuable than all of the others? If outputs are measured, quantity is what will be delivered—probably at the expense of quality and impact.

As is no doubt now clear, when it comes to exploring, measuring productivity is not as easy as counting output over time, and thus output-based productivity is not useful. One can deliver huge output while delivering no value at all, and many organizations do just that. What is needed is some sort of *value-based* productivity measure—a way of measuring the value delivered over time. The trick, then, is actually to deliver the most value with the least output. The question thus becomes, what is value? Much of the work done by creative teams involves thinking and learning. How is this work measured? And what about risk reduction?

Far more effective than outputs are outcomes. Outcomes are quantitative measures that are meaningful to businesspeople and measurable by teams. Outcomes can rarely be gamed like other measures of team effectiveness, and they also drive end-to-end accountability and autonomy. They focus teams on problems to be solved rather than things to be built. Aiming for outcomes allows far more agility around how to achieve them than merely tracking outputs, which are often fixed, and may not even lead to desirable outcomes. This approach breeds a culture of experimentation and ownership of the whole problem. This is even more powerful if teams have had a hand in setting the outcomes. Techniques like objectives and key results can work extremely well. The type of outcomes and cadence at which they are set will vary throughout the life cycle of the product or service. See chapter 8 for more on managing the portfolio and the product development life cycle.

One thing to bear in mind is that if, for any reason, leaders are unhappy with the impact a team is having, there is a strong chance that the real issue is not the team. The vast majority of the time, there is some systemic issue at the organizational level that prevents teams from communicating and collaborating easily with each other or with customers. They may lack the right tools for the job, or be chafing under the unnecessary constraints that hold teams back. A bad team is often a reflection of a bad leader. Taking ownership of that is the first step toward improving the team. If a system does not yield the desired results, change the system, not the people within it. That's a leadership responsibility, and it requires the ability to see systemic issues.

Go See for Yourself

Staying with the Lean theme, Taiichi Ohno loved to make a young manager at Toyota stand inside a small chalk circle near a point of interest on the factory floor. He would be told to "watch" and not to leave the circle until Ohno collected him. Upon returning, Ohno would ask the disciple what he had seen. If the answer was unsatisfactory, he would be left in the circle, sometimes for hours at a time. Ohno had usually spotted some problem in the area and wanted the disciple to identify it and suggest an approach for fixing it.[14] It would then be the job of this manager to teach problem-solving to those doing the work, so that they could identify and resolve their own problems. If the problem was one that the team could not solve, the manager would get it resolved for them.

The Japanese word for the place where the real work is done is *genba* (sometimes spelled *gemba* in English). That is where the value is created by teams, and there is a growing tendency for managers and leaders to be removed from it. There is an equally growing tendency to substitute proximity to the work with reports and dashboards for keeping an eye on progress. What is clear is that, with that approach, leaders will only ever see the tiny subset of data for which they specifically ask. They will not see dysfunction, they will not see systemic blockers to effectiveness, and they will not see cultural and engagement issues. They will also never truly know how effectively teams are performing in the current system. These things rarely show up in dashboards, but they are issues that require constant leadership attention.

Taiichi Ohno is reported to have said, "Don't look with your eyes, look with your feet. Don't think with you head, think with your hands." And on a similar note: "People who can't understand numbers are useless. The gemba where numbers are not visible is also bad. However, people who only *look* at the numbers are the worst of all" (emphasis added).[15] With these two quotations, he makes clear that leaders who do not spend time where the value is created will have a hard time leading. This is very similar to Management by Wandering Around, developed in the 1970s at Hewlett-Packard. I believe that this is even more important when one is in a more creative space than manufacturing. For innovation, creating the right culture, structures, and policies is everything. So often, when I have encouraged leaders to venture out and really watch what is going on, talk to people, and get a feel for the mood and the challenges, it has been an eye-opening, significant experience that has led to significant policy changes and improvements.

Leadership in this new, high-VUCA world—agile leadership, if you will—is about understanding systems, understanding customers, understanding the subtle interactions among things, and acting to create an environment in which talented, creative teams can do extraordinary things—and then, of course, getting out of their way.

Reflection

How are teams assessed in your organization? Could there be some value in moving from tracking outputs to tracking outcomes? Do leaders spend time observing team interactions or rely on reports and dashboards to assess team performance? Could there be value in leaders getting closer to the value delivery system?

Chapter Summary

- While the other five enablers create the environment for agility by putting in place the fundamental organizational operating system, Ways of Working covers the specific processes, practices, and approaches used by teams.

- Think of these ways of working as apps installed atop the underlying operating system. There are many from which to choose, and every organization will have its own unique combination for its unique context.

- There are many frameworks and approaches to working with agility, and some underlying patterns that are all but universally applicable.

- High-volume communication, visualization of work, and daily alignment meetings catalyze collaboration and self-organization.

- Overprescriptive frameworks and tools can be restrictive and reduce team effectiveness, morale, and engagement.

- Teams must create and continuously improve their own processes based on what works best for them. This will inevitably lead to teams working in different ways and using different tools to support them.

Key Practices for Business Agility

- Design work environments with as few barriers to team communication and collaboration as possible. Close physical proximity is best; if that is not feasible, get teams together frequently and employ world-class digital collaboration tools while they are disbursed.

- Visualize the work to foster self-organization and transparency around the work and the bottlenecks to be addressed.

- Hold a team-level daily alignment meeting for no more than 15 minutes for synchronization and coordination of work among team members. When working with multiple, interdependent teams, hold a multiteam alignment meeting, with at least one member from each team, to coordinate among teams.

- Work in short cycles and small batches to reduce time to feedback, flow value to customers more quickly, and increase overall agility.

- Build in structured slack time for teams to increase the pace of delivery and to provide space for creativity, innovation, and learning. Great ideas rarely come up when people are continuously busy.

- Avoid the temptation to dictate practices and ways of working. Allow teams to figure out the best way to work for them. There is little benefit, beyond that to management reports, to teams working in a uniform way. Give teams ownership of and accountability for the effectiveness of their processes.

- Focus relentlessly on continuously improving every aspect of how teams work, as well as the products and services they create. Make time, and space, for teams to sharpen the ax.

- Managers and leaders must spend time in the place where the work is being done. There is no other way to observe interactions among teams, to get a feel for the mood, and to spot systemic issues that need leadership attention. Do not rely on dashboard reporting to provide this information. It will not.

Further Reading and Resources

Books

- David J. Anderson, *Kanban: Successful Evolutionary Change for Your Technology Business* (Sequim, WA: Blue Hole, 2010)

- Donald G. Reinertsen, *The Principles of Product Development Flow: Second Generation Lean Product Development* (Redondo Beach, CA: Celeritas, 2009)

- Jean Tabaka, *Collaboration Explained: Facilitation Skills for Software Project Leaders* (Upper Saddle River, NJ: Addison-Wesley, 2006)

Websites, Articles, and Videos

- Please see www.6enablers.com/resources for more on this topic, including a downloadable reading list.

CHAPTER 10

Leading the Change

If you dislike change, you're going to dislike irrelevance even more.

—GENERAL ERIC SHINSEKI

IN THIS CHAPTER, WE WILL EXPLORE

- the reasons behind failed business agility initiatives and how to prevent them
- some key principles that underpin successful change programs
- how to achieve alignment and transparency around a vision for success
- how to design a set of consciously coordinated, holistic actions that will result in true business agility
- how to use the Business Agility Canvas as a strategic tool for managing organizational transformations.

Why Most Change Fails: Avoiding the Pitfalls

The success achieved at General Motors' former Fremont plant upon its reopening as NUMMI (see chapter 5) demonstrates that large-scale change can indeed be successful. Once they'd achieved the primary goal of building a high-quality, profitably small car, it was time to focus on the secondary goal: to take the lessons learned through the joint venture with Toyota and implement them throughout the rest of GM. Given the number of plants across the United States, mastering this new approach across the whole organization would add billions to its bottom line. The first opportunity came about

400 miles south of NUMMI in the Van Nuys region of Los Angeles. With the Van Nuys plant facing closure, its manager had visited NUMMI and thought that the Toyota Production System might help to save his plant. This time, however, Toyota itself would not be a partner. The Van Nuys GM workers would be on their own.

Making Firebirds and Camaros, the Van Nuys plant had almost as bad a reputation as Fremont, with frequent union battles, defective cars rolling off the production line, and worker sabotage. Despite the fact that the plant was on the verge of being shut down, the workers did not feel an imminent threat to their jobs. Unlike at NUMMI, where people were being offered the chance to keep their jobs in return for a new way of working, workers at Van Nuys did not feel the imperative to cooperate with the new system—and with good reason. With more efficient ways of working, the Toyota system was seen as a threat to jobs. Indeed, were it to be successful, it would result in the loss of one-quarter of the jobs at Van Nuys, as output levels could be maintained at a higher quality but with fewer workers.

What's more, the whole concept of teamwork and job rotation eroded the current rule of seniority. Under the system prevailing at the time, the best jobs and special perks were awarded to workers based purely on length of service. Transitioning to a teamwork model would mean that people would rotate among jobs. Gone would be the right to years of a specific, cushy job, built up over long periods of service. Another issue was the collective responsibility of teams. In order to be effective, teams would need to eliminate anyone who was not pulling his or her weight. This was a big change from the workers-versus-management mentality. Considering all of this, unions were staunchly opposed to the change.

And they were not the only ones. Managers objected, too. They were equally reluctant to give up *their* privileges and perks. They did not want to share parking spaces and cafeterias with workers as part of one big team. Managers also resisted the introduction of Andon Cords and the idea of workers being able to stop the production line, because management bonuses were dependent on volume, not quality. Management actually threatened to quit en masse if the changes went ahead.

Perhaps an even bigger issue was the implementation of the continuous improvement (kaizen) principle. At NUMMI, the parts came from Japan and were of high quality. If there was a problem with the design of a part, Toyota engineers would rework it to resolve the problem. There was no such collaboration at GM. If a part needed to be reworked, the relevant department in Detroit was just not interested. The organization was completely siloed and departments did not collaborate with each other, nor was there any incentive to start doing so.

It seemed that change was being resisted on all sides. Despite being bad for the company, the status quo was serving the needs of workers and managers alike, as well as some at HQ. And this kind of change could never be successful in isolation. The whole organizational ecosystem would have to be included. Managers would have to concede that they were unable to resolve many of the issues faced on the factory floor. It soon became clear why Toyota was so willing to share its secret sauce: it knew that GM could not begin to reproduce Toyota's success without a complete overhaul of the whole organization. The upshot? In 1992, the Van Nuys plant was shut down for good, leaving 2,600 people without jobs.

Almost everywhere the former NUMMI managers showed up to turn around failing plants, they were met with resistance from entrenched bureaucracies and vested interests. Without high-level support from company executives, there was simply no way to turn around the battleship. Eventually, GM did begin to improve overall, but nowhere near quickly enough. In 2008, it became the largest bankruptcy in US corporate history, requiring a $50 billion taxpayer bailout. GM had failed not because of a lack of understanding of the Toyota Production System but because of a lack of willingness to make the painful changes required across the board to enable its benefits.

GM is by no means alone. True success in large-scale change initiatives is a rare thing indeed. Despite an eye-watering $10 billion being spent on change management consultancy alone,[1] research shows that that over 70 percent of organizations fail to achieve their stated change goals.[2] This means that of the $1.3 trillion spent on digital transformation alone, roughly $900 million was wasted.[3] My sense is that when it comes to so-called agile transformations, the picture is worse still. There is often little agreement about what it means to be agile, and even less about what it takes to achieve it.

Organizations are investing huge sums of money in coaches and consultants, with no clear approach in mind. Mike Beedle, one of the creators of the agile movement, used to say to me that it was "easier to grow a unicorn than to transform a dinosaur."[4] What Mike meant by this is that most of the truly adaptive organizations that are around today started off that way. New creative, nimble, and disruptive organizations emerge every year to challenge the established, and often flat-footed, old guard.

Unfortunately, there are precious few cases of established entities effectively transforming themselves to run with their younger competitors. Salesforce, Microsoft, and Dutch banking group ING are some of the few that can point to successful transformations after having made tough changes throughout their structures. For each success story, however, there are many failures. Those seeking to support such transformations can sometimes feel like Sisyphus, a figure from Greek mythology who was doomed for eternity to push a rock up a hill, only to watch it roll back down each time he reached the top. But it does not have to be this way. I have seen some wonderful successes over the years, both small and large, and I truly believe that application of the principles in this book could result in many more.

Having observed at close quarters dozens of agile transformations, I have a sound understanding of the key reasons so many organizations fail to achieve their desired outcomes. I will now detail the five biggest issues I tend to see, and how they contribute to failed change initiatives.

Lack of Commitment

In 1519, Hernán Cortés and his 500 soldiers and 100 sailors arrived in what is now Mexico after a treacherous voyage across the Atlantic. Their goal was to conquer the Aztec empire and to plunder its vast fortune of precious gems, silver, and gold. Outnumbered and undersupplied, Cortés's first move seemed bizarre. In order to eliminate any chance of a retreat, he ordered that his ships be destroyed. With this act, his men were in no doubt that there was no turning back. They knew that they would either succeed or die trying. With no plan B, succeed they did. As Euripides said, "Nothing has more strength than dire necessity." "Burning the boats" has since become a by-phrase for committing fully to a course of action.

The first step in trying to effect any change should always be understanding the problem or opportunity. Without this step, nothing else will be coherent, and few people will buy in. As Simon Sinek said in his hugely popular TED talk, "People don't buy what you do; they buy why you do it. And what you do simply proves what you believe."[5] Making the necessary changes to an organization to increase its agility is not a minor undertaking. As with anything of value, it is far from easy. People need to know why the change is important, or confusion and resistance will be rife.

While important, understanding the reasons for change is far from enough. To unlock the real benefit, leaders must also commit to driving through often-painful changes to their organizations. Failure to do so will result in shallow change and a veneer of agility, and little in the way of real benefits. Organizations will go through the motions in much the same way the cargo cults of Melanesia (see chapter 3) did during World War II. For real change to happen, a strong sense of urgency is necessary, a burning platform that compels action. In his book *Leading Change*, John Kotter states, "A majority of employees, perhaps 75 percent of management overall, and virtually all top executives need to believe that considerable change is absolutely essential."[6] This has rarely felt more relevant. As I complete this chapter of the book, I, along with millions across the world, am entering my tenth week of being unable to leave my home owing to the COVID-19 pandemic. Entities across the globe, many of which did not feel a sense of urgency to adapt, have suddenly been forced into a play for survival. I have seen more business agility in the past two months than in many years preceding.

The Wrong People Leading the Change

As I have discussed throughout this book, a shift to business agility represents a strategic decision to compete through innovation and responsiveness. Any successful transformation at that level will be initiated and driven by the most senior leadership in an organization. Too often I have observed change initiatives being led by middle managers. Yet it is almost unheard of for midlevel managers to possess the required authority to effect the key structural, policy, and cultural changes required to make this kind of initiative a success. They are just not empowered to update the organizational operating system.

I have lost count of how many times managers leading transformations have asked me the best way to "sell" the benefits of agility to senior leadership so that they buy into the change. While many of my activities, including this book, do focus on the case for business agility, I believe it is rare that books, keynote speeches, or consulting activities manage to convince leadership of very much at all. If the status quo is serving the needs, both personal and professional, of those in the highest positions, very little will change. The only successes I have witnessed have come about through senior leadership truly feeling a sense of urgency and committing to drive the necessary changes personally. In short, they must take personal responsibility for the success of the change and be actively involved in enabling it.

Considering what we have covered to this point, this should come as no surprise. Those who can shift the enablers discussed in previous chapters constitute no more than a handful of individuals in any given organization. The likelihood of middle managers driving through major changes to leadership styles, culture, structures, and policies is as slim as the likelihood of an organization becoming agile without those changes being made. This is why bottom-up change tends not to land. I believe that it is vital to have the support of everyone in a transforming organization; however, buying in and actively driving structural change are very different things.

Middle-Manager Resistance

How to overcome middle-manager resistance is the number one question I get asked by students and clients alike, and rightly so. Middle management can have a huge impact, both positive and negative, on a transformation effort. Modern organizations harness the power of teams, and much decision-making is made at the team level. This is because the vital information often resides among teams and customers. The people doing the work are thus far more empowered than ever before. We must always remember, however, that when one group of people is empowered, another tends to be disempowered. The disempowered group is mostly middle managers.

There will always be a need for a small number of leaders to cultivate the culture, decide on strategy, and set organizational objectives. Much of what middle managers once did, however, is now done by self-managing teams. While there will always be a need for coaching and mentoring, career guidance, and some level of administration, that need has dwindled. It is understandable that many members of this shrinking group will naturally resist the changes described in this book. People must be treated with empathy. Anyone whose position may be altered or eliminated by transformation must be supported with training into new roles where she or he can add value.

Having said that, the most significant change will involve a realignment of incentives. As discussed in chapter 5, the way to change culture is to change behaviors, and the way to change behaviors is to change policies. Misaligned incentives, such as those seen at GM's Van Nuys assembly plant, are the number one reason middle managers resist change initiatives. If people will be made worse off by changing, can we really expect a rational person to do so? Likewise, if people see they will be made better off by cooperating, resistance tends to melt away.

Too Narrow a Focus

As I have mentioned throughout this book, many organizations focus their changes mainly on processes, practices, and frameworks—what I call *ways of working* (see chapter 9). While these changes are important, many other areas must also be addressed but are often largely ignored. These neglected areas tend to correspond to the other five enablers discussed in this book. In many ways, the prevalence of this pattern led directly to the creation of the 6 Enablers model and the writing of this book.

This narrow focus tends to lead to talk of "hybrid models" and "pragmatic solutions." Loosely translated, this means doing largely what was done before, but with a veneer of agility that consists of a few new practices and processes. HR policies, governance, and success measures remain as they always were—and, unsurprisingly, so do results.

Lack of a Coherent Approach

Richard Rumelt, author of the best-selling book *Good Strategy/Bad Strategy: The Difference and Why It Matters*, describes strategy as something that "honestly acknowledges the challenges we face and provides an approach to overcoming them."[7] "Agile transformations" often involve a lack of understanding of the true problem to be addressed, and a complete absence of a coherent approach to overcoming it. This results in a lot of work but very little progress. It is worth acknowledging that agility must never be thought of as an organization's ultimate goal. It is, however, a strategic choice made by leaders to enable organizations to compete in environments marked by turbulence and unpredictability. Business agility will unlock improved organizational performance.

Once this is understood, it is vital to develop a coordinated approach to achieving the stated goals. In the same way that sending troops into battle without an overarching strategy is inviting defeat, hiring an army of business agility coaches and consultants to sit with teams in the hope that everything will come together is almost certain to yield little benefit. While many of the details will emerge along the way, the leaders driving the change *must* be crystal clear regarding the high-level steps to be taken and how they fit together to form a coherent whole. This almost always means involving a small number of deeply experienced, trusted advisers to help avoid common pitfalls and provide guidance on some high-level patterns that tend to lead to successful outcomes. Sadly, many so-called coaches have little experience with true business agility and the organizational patterns that will enable it. They focus purely on processes and frameworks over the organizational operating system, and often changes are conflicting. This also applies to many consulting firms that regularly reposition bright generalists as experienced coaches. In the absence of true expertise, they look to recipes and cookie-cutter approaches that do not take into account the unique nature of each organization's goals, culture, and products.

The pitfalls just described are challenging to overcome. Changing organizations is hard, messy, and painful. In business, as in life, very little of true value is achieved without a struggle. Not every organization is ready to embark on a journey toward business agility. Those that are not will continue to focus predominantly on exploiting what they have. This will serve them well in the short term. With very little capacity to innovate, however, they will seek to grow through acquisitions. While the cost of these purchases goes straight onto the balance sheet, and can initially boost share prices, many will overpay, and will struggle to integrate new organizations into their culture. If done well, creating a systematic approach to innovating from the inside will prove a far superior approach in the medium to long term. For those who are willing to embark on the true path to agility, we will now investigate some overarching principles to consider when beginning a complex change initiative.

> ### Reflection
>
> Which of the challenges described here have you observed in your transformation? Do you foresee any others becoming issues? What could be done to address those issues?

Seven Principles of Leading Change: Laying the Foundations

Every transformation effort needs to begin with the right mindset. The following seven principles form the foundation on which all else will rest. Along with the Business Agility Canvas, these principles are designed to sidestep the key causes of failure in change initiatives that are discussed earlier. Failing to follow these principles will endanger even the best-thought-through approach. They will both underpin the change and be woven into every aspect of how that change is approached. As such, they should be constantly forefront in the minds of those leading it.

Leadership Driven

Throughout this book, I have discussed real-life examples of organizations transforming themselves from one state to another with extraordinary results. From NUMMI (see chapter 5), to the USS *Santa*

Fe (see chapter 4), to Joint Special Operations Command (see chapter 6), there is a common factor that links them all. That is that the very top leadership were the *drivers* of the change. While there is always an element of bottom-up change in certain areas, setting the vision and objectives for the change cannot be done in this way. When it comes to the bigger picture—the organizational policies, structures, and culture—these are almost exclusively the domain of senior leadership. Buy-in will never be sufficient; leadership must own and drive the change.

That being said, organizational change cannot be something that is done *to* people. It is vital to bring people along, and to help everyone to feel ownership of moving toward the outcomes. It must be a balance of top-down and bottom-up change, with leadership removing large, structural barriers to enable teams to transform their work practices.

Embrace Experimentation

In the early 1950s, the Dayak people of Borneo were struck by a breakout of malaria. Acting on the advice of the World Health Organization, liberal quantities of dichlorodiphenyltrichloroethane (DDT) were sprayed in Dayak territory to control the mosquito population and halt the spread of the disease. While the malaria problem improved, other strange things began to occur. First, people's roofs began collapsing. Next, two more diseases, deadlier than malaria, emerged on the island—typhus and the sylvatic plague. It seems that the DDT killed not only the mosquitos but also a type of wasp that fed on the local population of thatch-eating caterpillars. No longer kept in check, the caterpillars began eating their way through roofs, causing them to collapse. Alongside this, local cats, which dined on local gecko lizards, which dined on the DDT-riddled insects, began dying. Without a natural predator to keep them in check, the rat population multiplied, which led to the spread of the new diseases. To mitigate the unintended consequences of its own advice, the World Health Organization organized the parachuting of 14,000 live cats into Borneo. Operation Cat Drop was undertaken by the United Kingdom's Royal Air Force and eventually stabilized the situation.

The lesson here is clear: the mindless application of out-of-the-box solutions can cause as many issues as it solves. Frederick Winslow Taylor espoused the virtues of finding the "one best way" and executing it. I have seen countless organizations and consultancies approach agility in the same way. The proliferation of playbooks, blueprints, and cookie-cutter approaches stems from the simple fact that few have deep experience advising on this type of change. As with any complex endeavor, there is no repeatable formula for success. There are too many moving parts and too much interconnectivity to make up-front predictions. As an unknown author once wrote, "The problem is not people being uneducated. The problem is that they are educated just enough to believe what they have been taught and not educated enough to question what they have been taught."

Organizations are complex ecosystems rather than complicated machines. Cause and effect can therefore not be predicted in advance. Do not copy and paste your change. Approach the change as if it were an innovation, or any explore-domain work. Take an experimental approach—an agile approach. Every organization is unique, and the right approach will only emerge over time. Make small changes, measure the impact, and course-correct as necessary. Be wary of those who present a detailed plan up front. While high-level patterns and plans, such as those described in this book, can help you steer, it is wise to leave as few assumptions unvalidated as possible. Data always trumps opinion.

Progress over Perfection

Desmond Tutu once said, "There is only one way to eat an elephant: a bite at a time."[8] Embarking on a transformation initiative of this kind can feel daunting. Few will achieve the kind of dramatic turnarounds we have seen inside 6 or even 12 months. It is likely to take far longer than that, with ups and downs along the way. The best way to begin is with a small step. Starting with just one product, engaging a handful of teams, and learning key lessons quickly and in one small area can ease the nerves of those who are reluctant to risk reinventing the organization.

Keeping in mind the importance of experimentation, note that there is no need to begin with a detailed plan and a fully mapped-out end state. There *is* no end state. All there can be is continuous progress toward the vision. As long as an organization is improving, then the changes will be making an impact. The process of change itself will never end. Evolution is the new normal.

Overcommunicate

Few things are as crucial as gaining alignment on the vision, the reasons behind the change, and what people can expect to come their way. Not supplying people with the context for change encourages disengagement and discourages buy-in. To excite, motivate, and inspire action, there must be little doubt as to what the organization is seeking to achieve.

As we have seen, openness and transparency breed trust and cooperation. Without clear and frequent communication, people will be in a constant state of alert, and will likely fill in information gaps with rumors, gossip, and speculation. By the time those leading the change have become bored of talking about the vision and next steps, others in the organization may just be starting to hear about it.

Measure and Reward What Matters

During British rule in India, the government became concerned about the large number of cobras in Delhi. A bounty was placed on dead cobras. Initially, the policy seemed to be working, as people killed the snakes for the reward. Soon, however, it became clear that some enterprising people were breeding cobras and cashing in. When the scheme was scrapped, the now-worthless bred snakes were released, and the overall population increased.

This, and the myriad other examples, shows us that metrics can be a thorny issue. On their own, they are neither good nor bad. They are in fact merely data. What *can* be either helpful or unhelpful is the policy that is wrapped around the metrics. Often, they can focus people on hitting a number at all costs, at the expense of doing the right thing. This can lead, as in the foregoing story, to some unintended consequences. There is also the reality that some things are measurable while others are not. It is all too easy to measure what is easy to measure at the expense of what is important. What is clear, though, is that incentives are a powerful driver of behavior and a key part of overcoming resistance and shifting culture. Choose your measures wisely and do not be a slave to them. Ideally, these will be product or business outcomes that are all but impossible to game.

Build Internal Capability

This may sound strange from someone who makes a living advising organizations on all matters of agility, but any coach or consultant who is not actively laying the groundwork for his or her client to be self-sufficient as soon as possible is doing that client a disservice. External guidance from a highly experienced partner will almost certainly accelerate progress, but part of the role of that supporting partner must be to develop an internal capability to the point where the change becomes self-sustaining sooner rather than later. I have seen many large consulting firms with hundreds of people on the ground for years, most of whom have little or no experience in the field. That is not only shockingly expensive, it will never yield a lasting change. Good partners will not want to be involved with a client for a single day longer than is entirely necessary. If a company is not highly skilled at capability building, be wary of engaging it. Never engage a firm without a clear plan to scale back its services.

The second reason why internal capability is important is that true agility requires people to fulfill different work roles. They will need to become multiskilled, and collaboration and communication will become increasingly valued skill sets. It is right that people be offered a formal pathway to develop these skills, and that they be reinforced. As more responsibilities are passed to teams, they must have opportunities to learn new skills. If innovation and testing ideas cheaply will be the responsibility of all team members, a plan must be put in place to upskill people.

Show Respect and Build Safety

As covered in chapter 7, if people do not feel safe, they will be in a constant state of stress and will be unlikely to do their best creative work, never mind support change. Periods of uncertainty and change can be difficult for people, especially where roles and career paths are concerned. Where possible, allay fears about job security, even if it is unlikely that there will be *role* security. Change programs tend to hit on almost all of the elements of the SCARF model (see chapter 7): status, certainty, autonomy, relatedness, and fairness. It is important to bear this in mind, and to consciously mitigate the effects of any reduction to these elements. Failure to do so will result in many people experiencing a threat response and strongly resisting the change.

As we have seen in previous chapters, when organizations are not achieving the desired results, the issue rarely lies with *people and teams*. It almost always lies with the *system*. People do not need to be changed—systems, structures, and policies do. Understand that people are doing the best they can in operating models that are no longer fit for purpose, and communicate your understanding to them. This will help reduce feelings of defensiveness and encourage people in your organization to move toward the vision.

Reflection

Are any of the principles described here missing in your transformation? If so, what would it take to put them in place? What is the impact of not having them in place?

The Business Agility Canvas: Your Transformation on a Page

No organization should embark on a transformation to business agility without first truly understanding the nature of what it seeks to achieve, the reasons behind the desired transformation, and, at a high level, the steps necessary to achieve it. I often encounter executives who have no comprehension of the depth and breadth of the changes they will need to make to achieve their goals. That is why, for me, education of the most senior leadership must be step one. Without a deep understanding of why most agile transformations fail, and of the types of changes a transformation will likely require, an informed decision on whether, or how, to proceed will be virtually impossible. Typically, a two-day workshop with leadership, to explore some of the topics discussed in this book, will suffice. That leadership team must then choose whether to embark on a difficult, risky, and uncertain process. And they must do so with their eyes wide open. That really is the only way to clear the path sufficiently for success. It is also a great way to help some organizations recognize when they are *not* prepared to undertake a true transformation. Continuing to do well what they currently do is favorable only to the appearance of change, not actual transformation.

While some will have solid reasons not to proceed, many will recognize the increasing necessity of doing so, and be prepared for the journey. At that point, it will be tempting to begin work on some or many of the enablers. Different individuals may even attempt to claim ownership of different pieces of the whole, driving change from their various perspectives. This can cause real issues, as changes need to be highly aligned and coordinated. Each area will affect and be affected by each other area, so treating them in isolation often leads to local optimizations that undermine the whole. Enter the Business Agility Canvas,[9] a tool I created to address the main causes of failure in most agile adoptions, such as those discussed in this chapter. It is designed to provide a framework for key conversations about the transformation approach, to create alignment, and to guide leaders through the thoughtful design of coordinated actions—actions that constitute a holistic approach to achieving their goals.

Before I introduce the canvas, I will provide some information on how it came to be and what inspired it. In many ways, the canvas is influenced by tools that have been around for some time. I have used them all in various combinations, and they have proved valuable. For over a decade, however, I have aspired to create something more holistic and more specific to the context of business agility. Those aspirations culminated in the Business Agility Canvas, but it is only right to recognize the tools that inspired its creation.

Kotter's 8-Step Change Model

First introduced in a 1995 *Harvard Business Review* article[10] and a year later in his book *Leading Change*, John Kotter's model has formed the basis for thousands of change programs across the globe. Having spent more than a decade observing over 100 change programs in some of the world's largest organizations, most of which failed, Kotter distilled the causes of failure down to eight key errors.

- not establishing a great enough sense of urgency
- not creating a powerful enough guiding coalition
- lacking a vision
- undercommunicating the vision by a factor of 10
- not removing obstacles to the new vision
- not systematically planning for and creating short-term wins
- declaring victory too soon
- not anchoring changes in the corporation's culture

Integrating points into agile transformation initiatives—particularly the vision, the powerful guiding coalition, and the active removal of obstacles—can be powerful. It takes a highly committed, continuously engaged team of senior leaders to work in this way. Without that, change rarely succeeds.

While this model is a good starting point, it lacks the creation of coordination actions that I feel are important to discuss along the way.

V2MOM

Created by Marc Benioff, cofounder and CEO of Salesforce, the V2MOM model was used annually at Salesforce, and subsequently many other organizations, to create awareness, alignment, and focus around how to operate. I have used this more tangible approach to great effect in transformations, in combination with Kotter's rather metalevel approach. Pronounced "vee-two-mom," it consists of five elements: vision, values, methods, obstacles, and measures. Getting into the details of the methods by which the vision will be realized and the current obstacles to it makes the change feel more tangible. Discussing success measures allows everyone to be clear on what success looks like and whether progress is being made.

When combined with Kotter's eight-step model, V2MOM can bring a clarity that is incredibly powerful. I have found, however, that the "methods" section becomes jam-packed with changes to be made, even if kept to a high level. Organizations need clarity about all the areas that must be addressed for success. The methods thus needed to be divided into multiple sections.

The 6 Enablers of Business Agility

My own model, I hope, needs little introduction at this point. A narrow approach, focusing purely on processes, practices, and frameworks, will not achieve true agility. When one splits the "methods" section of V2MOM into six separate sections, one for each enabler, the scope of the change becomes crystal clear. This provides a far greater understanding of the necessary focus areas, and ensures that nothing slips through the net. Leaving any key areas unaddressed must be a conscious choice made after deep discussion and consideration.

I found that a hybrid approach based on the three models just mentioned was bringing great success to the organizations with which I worked. But while discussions and alignment were greatly improved, the fact that things were largely tracked using spreadsheets meant that transparency was limited. I felt that something more visual, interactive, and tactile would better engage those responsible for leading change. To achieve that, I turned to a tool I have used many times.

The Business Model Canvas

I have long been amazed by the simplicity and brilliance of this tool developed by Alexander Osterwalder. Einstein is often quoted as saying words to the effect of, "Everything should be made as simple as possible, but not simpler." In creating the Business Model Canvas, Osterwalder elegantly captured on a single page the nine key elements of a business model and their interactions. This enabled start-ups and established companies alike to iterate ideas collaboratively and transparently. The alignment I have seen this create is incredible.

This inspired me to take what I had created over the years and make it visual. In doing so, I set out to create a tool that integrated the best elements of the models just mentioned and capture them on a single page. Its goal was to help make transformation strategy coherent, coordinated, and transparent to all who wandered past it and stopped to take a look. We will now explore the result of that creation—the Business Agility Canvas (figure 30).

FIGURE 30

The Business Agility Canvas

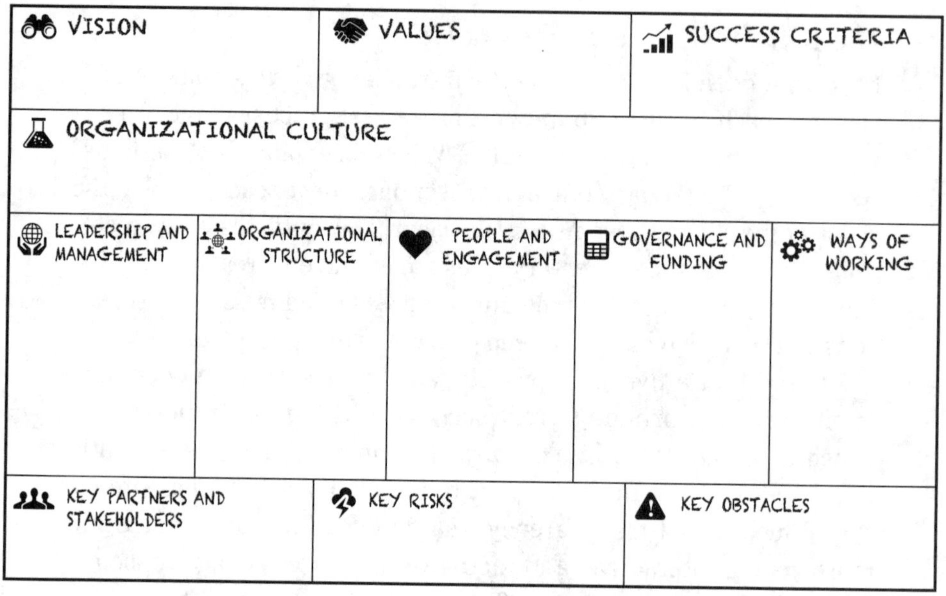

Source: Download the Business Agility Canvas + 20-page guidebook for free at https://www.agilecentre.com/the-business-agility-canvas/.

The canvas consists of three sections, each with multiple elements. The process of filling out the canvas is an iterative one, but there is definitely an initial flow to it (figure 31).

The Top Section (What and Why?)

The top section consists of three parts. The first is Vision—what exactly the organization is looking to achieve and why it is important. Without alignment on this point, people will pull in different directions and confusion will result. Vision should never stop being clearly communicated. Everyone involved in the initiative should be able to state clearly why the change is being undertaken.

Next is Values—the things that represent what is most important to people as the vision is pursued. These will underpin behaviors and must anchor all policies, incentives, and decision-making.

Finally, there is Success Criteria. These represent the key indicators of success or progress. What handful of key measures will indicate

The Business Agility Canvas flow

whether the organization is moving toward or away from the vision? Without such measures, it will all be guesswork. Getting this right is vital to putting the right policies in place. Failure to do so means you might hit the numbers, but miss the original intent of the change: increased agility and the ability to thrive in the face of uncertainty.

After there is clarity and agreement on the elements in the top section, it is time to move on to the *middle section*.

The Middle Section (How?)

The middle section consists of six elements, each of which can be mapped to one of the 6 Enablers of Business Agility covered in this book. Each element is a placeholder for a conversation about the concrete actions to be taken in that area. Filling out each element leaves no room for ambiguity. If an enabler is being overlooked, it will immediately be clear to all. The actions in each element may take many forms. They may represent tangible changes to be made, things to start doing, things to amplify, things to stop doing, or things to dampen. Some items are likely to involve extremely large changes. For example, creating an adaptive funding model based on incremental funding (as discussed in chapter 8) is a large piece of work. They can even be whole streams of work. It is important to state the intent, but the implementation will also require significant offline planning of multiple steps.

The reason organizational culture sits atop the other five enablers is that, more than any other, culture is a product of the other enablers. I have found it wise to begin this section with a lightweight culture assessment the likes of which I discussed in chapter 5. As we also saw there, the levers for culture change are structures, policies, incentives, metrics, and leadership behaviors. These changes will span the enablers that sit immediately under culture and will ultimately cause it to evolve in the desired direction. This will provide invaluable insight into the current and desired culture as well as the organization's attitude to change, be it incremental or transformational, fast or long term. An appropriate change approach can then be selected.

The canvas is ultimately about stating your intention to transform, and designing the coordinated, strategic changes required to achieve the vision. Seeing the high-level changes on a single page will make it far easier to check for alignment and coherence, while avoiding conflicting changes. What will *not* change is often as important to discuss as what will, so these should be made clear to all, along with any other constraints. Many of the high-level items are likely to include the patterns we have covered in this book, the exact implementation of which will depend on each unique context.

The Bottom Section (What Else?)

The final section represents some other important considerations. Key Partners and Stakeholders is the first of thing to consider here. Stakeholders are those to get on board and bring along on the journey. Some, like the heads of finance and HR, must be closely involved in designing changes in their areas, and others will merely have input, influence, and ideas. Some will be advocates, some will be more skeptical. This group must be actively managed and engaged. The partners will be those who support the change through coaching, training, and the supplying of key skills. Key Risks will track the events that could potentially affect the change. This is an opportunity to get out in front of them and mitigate them proactively. Finally, Key Obstacles is a list of things that, if not removed, will be a barrier to the transformation. As with risks, the leaders driving the change must be relentlessly proactive about removing these obstacles or the transformation will quickly stall.

The canvas is a tool for thinking through the transformation, for ensuring the changes are coherent, and for forging a path to the vision. It is also a great tool for collaboration, alignment, and communication, making clear at a glance what is to be achieved, the areas that must be addressed, and how the high-level changes within them complement each other. What is important is not creating the perfect canvas—no such thing exists—but instead having open and frank conversations and creating shared understanding across all parties. This ultimately forms your transformation strategy, and it should help your organization avoid the pitfalls of the 70 percent of those entities that fail in their bid to transform. If you have been keeping your reflections from previous chapters, you may find it easier to fill out your canvas.

> ### Reflection
>
> How much alignment is there around the vision, values, and success criteria on your transformation? Is it clear to all stakeholders what changes are required in each of the six enablers? Are the key risks, stakeholders, and obstacles visible and being actively managed? Could visualizing all of these factors on a single page improve collaboration and alignment?

Working with the Canvas: Change as the New Normal

Working through the canvas tends to lead to an initial set of steps to be walked through before the change picks up speed. These are outlined here:

1) Educate all senior leaders
2) Align on vision and values
3) Gather the driving team

4) Define success measures

5) Commit to the change

6) Begin communicating the vision

7) Plan the high-level changes

8) Experiment, inspect, and adapt

The Business Agility Canvas is specifically designed to facilitate steps 2–8, with steps 7 and 8 being the majority of the focus over time. In reality, they are far from linear and each step will be iterated on several times as more is learned. Many a failed transformation has begun on step 7. These organizations pick a preferred framework and begin implementing it with no clarity over the vision, desired outcomes, success criteria, or cultural fit. Worse still, they tend to ignore five of the six enablers and spend their time focused on processes, practices, and frameworks. When these approaches are incompatible with the prevailing organizational operating system, they abandon their efforts and blame everything but themselves and their advisers. The canvas is there to prevent this wasted time, effort, and money.

Over the years, I have found that success is more likely when a single individual is ultimately accountable for realizing the transformation vision and driving the change. For best results, such as in the cases I have discussed (and many others), this person should be the most senior person in the area in which the change is taking place. He or she must have the authority to make big changes to structures, policies, and cultures across all six enablers. For that reason, the point person tends to be the CEO—but with the relevant delegated authority, that needn't always be the case.

Having a single owner can help with difficult prioritization and trade-off decisions. It often also makes sense to have an owner for each enabler—for example, the finance director leading the Governance and Funding enabler and the HR director leading on People and Engagement. This team, along with many other enthusiastic volunteers, will form the powerful guiding coalition described by Kotter in *Leading Change*. This team will craft the vision and strategic approach and commit to seeing it through. Some will focus predominantly on a single enabler; others will have a broader view.

As every element is highly interconnected with all of the others, team members will need to come together frequently to coordinate, track progress, remove roadblocks, and plan the next steps. For example, it will not be possible to change the governance approach to enable many safe-to-fail experiments without the corresponding structural changes to create cross-functional teams, the cultural changes to create the safety to experiment, the HR policies to incentivize collaboration, and the decentralized decision-making model of leadership. Initially, the guiding coalition should meet at least monthly to ensure alignment and to track progress. Those working within a specific enabler may plan and meet more frequently. There will, of course, be much interaction among members of this coalition and others in the wider organization on a daily basis.

The process of working with the canvas is not a linear one. There will be many iterations over time. Nor will the canvas remain static. The canvas is a living document that evolves as more is learned about the transformation. The canvas must therefore be revisited frequently. Simply printing out as large as possible a copy of the canvas and working with sticky notes will yield maximum flexibility. It should live somewhere public so that anyone can become familiar with it.

One of the big errors described by Kotter in this process is declaring victory too soon. A real risk is that organizations will take their foot off the pedal after a few months. But a transformation of this kind will likely be a multiyear journey for a medium-to-large organization. And in reality, it never ends. Change as a process of continuous evolution is the new normal in organizations of all stripes.

There is also a real risk that when leaders move on, the changes will be undone. This could happen deliberately, as a new leader seeks to make his or her mark in a break with the old, or merely by inertia. For this reason, it is vital to anchor the change deeply in the culture and structure early on and to continue to build on it. There will always be improvements to be made, and changes in the business climate will necessitate constant evolution. Thus, even when the big-ticket items, like changing organizational structures, have been completed, it will be worth revisiting the canvas to ensure that the vision, values, and success criteria are still aligned. Keeping an organization primed to thrive is a never-ending endeavor that should never be considered done.

> ### Reflection
>
> How are the high-level changes coordinated and tracked in your transformation? At what cadence do the driving team get together to synchronize and coordinate? How are these changes communicated to the wider stakeholders?

Chapter Summary

- Most large-scale organizational change fails. Business agility change initiatives are no different.

- The causes of failure range from a lack of true commitment to change, to a lack of authority to drive change, to a lack of a coherent set of coordinated actions to effect change.

- Most organizations focus narrowly on one, and sometimes two, enablers but fail to step back and consider the wider picture.

- The Business Agility Canvas can be used to create a shared understanding around vision and success measures, as well as to plan a set of coordinated actions to be undertaken across the 6 Enablers.

Key Practices for Business Agility

- Understand the key reasons for seeking to increase business agility before beginning a transformation, then communicate these reasons widely.

- Any change or transformation initiative must be driven from the most senior levels of the organization to ensure the requisite authority to make changes and remove obstacles.

- Create a strong team that can work together frequently to drive change across all areas of the organization.

- Use the Business Agility Canvas to create alignment around the change, and take a strategic, holistic approach to designing changes that will form a coherent whole.

- Create a high-level implementation plan, but embrace experimentation and expect it to evolve as you progress. Transformation initiatives of this kind tend not to go exactly as expected. Take a data-driven approach.

- Avoid a one-size-fits-all approach. There are some common patterns from which organizations can learn, but each path will be different based on what is right for each unique context.

- Draw on a small number of deeply experienced experts to advise those driving the change. Be wary of bringing on large numbers of generalist consultants with minimal experience in guiding organizations along this path.

- Be sure to invest in building internal capability to ensure that the change can become self-sustaining as soon as possible.

Further Reading and Resources

Books

- John P. Kotter, *Accelerate: Building Strategic Agility for a Faster-Moving World* (Boston: Harvard Business Review Press, 2014)

- Scott D. Anthony, Clark G. Gilbert, and Mark W. Johnson, *Dual Transformation: How to Reposition Today's Business While Creating the Future* (Boston: Harvard Business Review Press, 2017)

- Mike Cohn, *Succeeding with Agile: Software Development Using Scrum* (Boston: Addison-Wesley, 2009)

- Simon Sinek, *Start with Why: How Great Leaders Inspire Everyone to Take Action* (London: Penguin, 2011)

Websites, Articles, and Videos

- Please see www.6enablers.com/resources for more on this topic, including a downloadable reading list.

Notes

Introduction

1. Charles A. O'Reilly and Michael L. Tushman, *Lead and Disrupt: How to Solve the Innovator's Dilemma* (Stanford, CA: Stanford Business Books, 2016).

Chapter 1: The Changing Business Climate

1. J. Clement, "Amazon Web Services, Annual Revenue 2013–2019," Statista, May 25, 2020, https://www.statista.com/statistics/233725/development-of-amazon-web-services-revenue/.

2. "The Moving Assembly Line and the Five-Dollar Workday," Ford, accessed October 28, 2020, https://corporate.ford.com/articles/history/100-years-moving-assembly-line.html.

3. Frederick Winslow Taylor, *The Principles of Scientific Management* (n.p.: Dover Publications Inc., 1998), 41.

4. Gary Hamel, *The Future of Management*, with Bill Breen (Boston: Harvard Business School Press, 2007), 128.

5. Pablo Tovar, "Leadership Challenges in the V.U.C.A World," Oxford Leadership, accessed October 28, 2020, https://www.oxfordleadership.com/leadership-challenges-v-u-c-world/.

6. CNN Arabic Staff, "How a Fruit Seller Caused Revolution in Tunisia," CNN, January 16, 2011, http://edition.cnn.com/2011/WORLD/africa/01/16/tunisia.fruit.seller.bouazizi/index.html.

7. Bob Simon, "How a Slap Sparked Tunisia's Revolution," *60 Minutes*, February 22, 2011, https://www.cbsnews.com/news/how-a-slap-sparked-tunisias-revolution-22-02-2011/.

8. Richard Dobbs, James Manyika, and Jonathan Woet, "The Four Global Forces Breaking All the Trends," McKinsey, April 1, 2015, https://www.mckinsey.com/business-functions/strategy-and-corporate-finance/our-insights/the-four-global-forces-breaking-all-the-trends.

9. Rick Rieder, "Tech Adoption Rated Have Reached Dizzying Heights," Market Realist, accessed October 28, 2020, https://marketrealist.com/2015/12/adoption-rates-dizzying-heights/.

10. Laura Montini, "Then and Now: How Long It Takes to Get to $1 Billion Valuation," Inc., accessed December 7, 2020, https://www.inc.com/laura-montini/infographic/how-long-it-takes-to-get-to-a-1-billion-valuation.html.

11. "The Speed of a Unicorn," fleximize, accessed December 7, 2020, https://fleximize.com/unicorns/.

12. James Gleick, *Chaos: Making a New Science,* rev. ed. (New York: Open Road Media, 2011), 20–21.

13. Innosight, *Creative Destruction Whips through Corporate America,* Executive Briefing, Winter 2012, https://www.innosight.com/wp-content/uploads /2016/08/creative-destruction-whips-through-corporate-america_final2015 .pdf.

14. Mark J. Perry, "Fortune 500 Firms 1955 v. 2017: Only 60 Remain, Thanks to the Creative Destruction That Fuels Economic Prosperity," AEI, October 20, 2017, https://www.aei.org/carpe-diem/fortune-500-firms-1955 -v-2017-only-12-remain-thanks-to-the-creative-destruction-that-fuels -economic-prosperity/.

15. Pierre Nanterme, "Digital Disruption Has Only Just Begun," World Economic Forum, January 17, 2016, https://www.weforum.org/agenda/2016/01 /digital-disruption-has-only-just-begun/.

16. Innosight, *Creative Destruction Whips through Corporate America.*

Chapter 2: Introducing Business Agility

1. *Encyclopaedia Britannica Online,* s.v. "Ignaz Semmelweis," accessed October 28, 2020, https://www.britannica.com/biography/Ignaz-Semmelweis.

2. "Ignaz Semmelweis."

3. Craig Silverman, "The Backfire Effect: More on the Press's Inability to Debunk Bad Information," *Columbia Journalism Review,* June 17, 2011, https:// archives.cjr.org/behind_the_news/the_backfire_effect.php.

4. Max Planck, *Scientific Autobiography and Other Papers* (London: Williams & Norgate, 1950), 33.

5. Winston Walker Royce, "Managing the Development of Large Software Systems," 1970, http://www-scf.usc.edu/~csci201/lectures/Lecture11/royce1970 .pdf.

6. Royce, "Managing the Development of Large Software Systems," 2.

7. "DOD-STD-2167A, Military Standard: Defense System Software Development (29 FEB 1988) [S/S BY MIL-STD-498]," EverySpec, accessed October 28, 2020, http://everyspec.com/DoD/DoD-STD/DOD-STD-2167A_8470.

8. Jim Highsmith, "History: The Agile Manifesto," 2001, https://agilemani festo.org/history.html.

9. Margaret Heffernan, *Uncharted: How to Map the Future* (London: Simon & Schuster UK, 2020), 297.

10. Manifesto for Agile Software Development website, accessed October 28, 2020, https://agilemanifesto.org.

11. Craig Larman and Bas Vodde, *Scaling Lean and Agile Development: Thinking and Organizational Tools for Large-Scale Scrum* (Boston: Pearson, 2009).

12. Clara Moskowitz, "Bigger Is Better, Until You Go Extinct," Live Science, July 17, 2008, https://www.livescience.com/2713-bigger-extinct.html.

13. Greg Sandoval, "Blockbuster Laughed at Netflix Partnership Offer," CNET, December 9, 2010, https://www.cnet.com/news/blockbuster-laughed-at-netflix -partnership-offer/.

14. Michael Liedtke and Mae Anderson, "Blockbuster Tries to Rewrite Script in Bankruptcy," Boston.com, September 23, 2010, http://archive.boston.com /business/articles/2010/09/23/blockbuster_tries_to_rewrite_script_in _bankruptcy/.

15. Bloomberg News, "Blockbuster's IPO Raises $465 Million," *Los Angeles Times*, August 11, 1999, https://www.latimes.com/archives/la-xpm-1999-aug-11 -fi-64598-story.html.

16. Minda Zetlin, "Blockbuster Could Have Bought Netflix for $50 Million, but the CEO Thought It Was a Joke," Inc., September 20, 2019, https://www.inc .com/minda-zetlin/netflix-blockbuster-meeting-marc-randolph-reed-hastings -john-antioco.html.

17. Rick Munarriz, "Blockbuster CEO Has Answers," The Motley Fool, last updated April 15, 2017, https://www.fool.com/investing/general/2008/12/10 /blockbuster-ceo-has-answers.aspx.

18. Amy Watson, "Netflix Subscribers Count Worldwide 2011–2020," Statista, October 21, 2020, https://www.statista.com/statistics/250934/quarterly-num ber-of-netflix-streaming-subscribers-worldwide/.

19. Michael Hiltzik, "Kodak's Long Fade to Black," *Los Angeles Times*, December 4, 2011, https://www.latimes.com/business/la-xpm-2011-dec-04-la-fi -hiltzik-20111204-story.html.

20. Oliver Kmia, "Why Kodak Died and Fujifilm Thrived: A Tale of Two Film Companies," PetaPixel, October 19, 2018, https://petapixel.com/2018/10/19 /why-kodak-died-and-fujifilm-thrived-a-tale-of-two-film-companies/.

21. Jordan Weissmann, "What Killed Kodak," *Atlantic*, January 5, 2012, https://www.theatlantic.com/business/archive/2012/01/what-killed-kodak /250925/.

22. Hiltzik, "Kodak's Long Fade to Black."

23. Kmia, "Why Kodak Died."

24. Kmia, "Why Kodak Died."

25. "Highly Functional Materials," Fujifilm, accessed October 28, 2020, https://www.fujifilm.com/about/profile/business_fields/highly_functional _materials/.

26. Walter Isaacson, *Steve Jobs* (New York: Simon & Schuster, 2011), 946.

Chapter 3: The 6 Enablers of Business Agility

1. Boris Ewenstein, Wesley Smith, and Ashvin Sologar, "Changing Change Management," McKinsey, July 1, 2015, https://www.mckinsey.com/featured -insights/leadership/changing-change-management.

2. *The 13th State of Agile Report*, version 1 (Collabnet, 2019), https://www .stateofagile.com/#ufh-i-521251909-13th-annual-state-of-agile-report/473508.

3. Pim, "Employee Engagement; The Business Case," Corporate Rebels, accessed October 28, 2020, https://corporate-rebels.com/employee-engagement
-the-business-case/.

4. *State of the Global Workplace*, 2017, p. 3, https://www.gallup.com/work
place/238079/state-global-workplace-2017.aspx.

5. "The 8 Trends," Corporate Rebels, accessed October 28, 2020, https://
corporate-rebels.com/trends/.

6. Joost Minnaar and Pim de Morree, "The 8 Habits of Companies You Wish
You Worked For," HuffPost, April 17, 2017, https://www.huffpost.com/entry/the
-8-habits-of-companies-you-wish-you-worked-for_b_58f53598e4b048
372700dac0.

7. This does not mean we do not need to make a profit; we absolutely do. It's
just that we inspire people through a common purpose, and profits are the *result* of great products and services.

Chapter 4: Leadership and Management

1. Gary Hamel, *The Future of Management*, with Bill Breen (Boston: Harvard Business School Press, 2007), 16.

2. Len Boselovic, "Steel Standing: U.S. Steel Celebrates 100 Years," *Pittsburgh Post-Gazette*, February 25, 2001, http://old.post-gazette.com/business
news/20010225ussteel2.asp.

3. Robert Kanigel, "R. Frederick Taylor's Apprenticeship," *Wilson Quarterly*,
Summer 1996, p. 49, http://archive.wilsonquarterly.com/essays/frederick-tay
lors-apprenticeship.

4. *Encyclopaedia Britannica Online*, s.v. "Frederick W. Taylor," accessed October 28, 2020, https://www.britannica.com/biography/Frederick-W-Taylor.

5. Frederick Winslow Taylor, *The Principles of Scientific Management* (n.p.:
Dover Publications Inc., 1998), 20.

6. Peter Drucker, *Management: Tasks, Responsibilities, Practices* (New
York: Harper & Row, 1974), 181.

7. Robert Kanigel, *The One Best Way: Frederick Winslow Taylor and the
Enigma of Efficiency* (New York: Viking, 1997), 206–207.

8. Frederick Winslow Taylor, *Scientific Management* (New York: Harper &
Row, 1911), 121.

9. Henri Fayol, *Critical Evaluations in Business and Management,* vol. 2
(London: Routledge, 2002), 146.

10. Abraham H. Maslow, *The Psychology of Science* (New York: Harper and
Row, 1966), 15.

11. Peter F. Drucker, *The Effective Executive* (New York: Harper & Row,
1967).

12. Ricardo Semler, *The Seven-Day Weekend: Changing the Way Work
Works* (New York: Portfolio), 60.

13. George A. Miller, "The Magical Number Seven, Plus or Minus Two: Some Limits on Our Capacity for Processing Information," *Psychological Review* 63 (1956): 81–97.

14. Nelson Cowan, "The Magical Number 4 in Short-Term Memory: A Reconsideration of Mental Storage Capacity," *Behavioral and Brain Sciences* 24, no. 1 (2001).

15. "Steve Jobs Talks about Managing People," June 12, 2010, YouTube video, https://www.youtube.com/watch?v=f60dheI4ARg.

16. E. Mazareanu, "Monthly Users of Uber's Ride-Sharing App Worldwide 2017–2020," Statista, August 7, 2020, https://www.statista.com/statistics/833 743/us-users-ride-sharing-services/.

17. Stephen Bungay, *The Art of Action: How Leaders Close the Gaps between Plans, Actions and Results* (London: Nicholas Brealey Publishing, 2011), 60.

18. Eric Schmidt and Jonathan Rosenberg, *Trillion Dollar Coach: The Leadership Handbook of Silicon Valley's Bill Campbell* (New York: Harper Business, 2019), 9.

Chapter 5: Organizational Culture

1. "NUMMI (2015)," This American Life, July 17, 2015, https://www .thisamericanlife.org/561/nummi-2015.

2. Kim S. Cameron and Robert E. Quinn, *Diagnosing and Changing Organizational Culture: Based on the Competing Values Framework*, 3rd ed. (San Francisco: Jossey-Bass, 2011), 16.

3. Edgar Schein, *Organizational Culture and Leadership,* 3rd rev. ed. (San Francisco: Jossey-Bass, 2004), 10–11.

4. "About the Organizational Culture Assessment Instrument (OCAI)," OCAI Online, accessed October 28, 2020, https://www.ocai-online.com/about -the-Organizational-Culture-Assessment-Instrument-OCAI.

5. Cameron and Quinn, *Diagnosing and Changing Organizational Culture.*

6. "Culture Change Is Free," Vanguard, accessed October 28, 2020, https:// vanguard-method.net/library/systems-principles/culture-change-is-free/.

7. John Shook, "How to Change a Culture: Lessons from NUMMI," *MIT Sloan Management Review*, January 1, 2010, https://sloanreview.mit.edu/arti cle/how-to-change-a-culture-lessons-from-nummi/.

8. David Marquet, Create Leaders at Every Level Course, Lesson 6, January 30, 2015, https://www.davidmarquet.com/2015/01/30/coming-soon-create -leaders-at-every-level-online-course/.

9. Ben Horowitz, *What You Do Is Who You Are: How to Create Your Business Culture* (New York: HarperBusiness, 2019), 68.

10. It is, of course, never possible to make a proper assessment from the outside.

11. Ed Catmull and Amy Wallace, *Creativity, Inc.: Overcoming the Unseen Forces That Stand in the Way of True Inspiration* (New York: Random House, 2014), 192–193.

12. Simon Sinek, "Performance vs Trust," November 18, 2019, https://youtu .be/YPDmNaEG8v4.

13. Netflix Culture, on Netflix Jobs website, accessed December 8, 2020, https://jobs.netflix.com/culture.

Chapter 6: Organizational Structure

1. Tim McNeese, *The Progressive Movement* (Broomall, PA: Chelsea House, 2008), 26.

2. McNeese, 26.

3. Tara-Nicholle Nelson, "Obsess Over Your Customers, Not Your Rivals," *Harvard Business Review*, May 11, 2017, https://hbr.org/2017/05/obsess-over -your-customers-not-your-rivals.

4. Peter Drucker, *The Practice of Management,* Classic Drucker Collection ed. (London: Routledge, 2007), 31.

5. Steven Denning, *The Age of Agile: How Smart Companies Are Trans-forming the Way Work Gets Done* (New York: AMACOM / American Management Association, 2018), 74.

6. George Day and Christine Moorman, *Strategy from the Outside In: Profiting from Customer Value* (New York: McGraw Hill, 2010).

7. Jeff Bezos, interview, *Business Week*, April 28, 2008.

8. Steve Denning, "The Alternative to Top-Down Is Outside-In," *Forbes*, February 13, 2011, https://www.forbes.com/sites/stevedenning/2011/02/13/the -alternative-to-top-down-is-outside-in/#1793eab91b1d.

9. This generally means people, a word I much prefer in this context.

10. This quotation is also often attributed to Don Berwick or Paul Batalden.

11. Mary Poppendieck and Tom Poppendieck, *Lean Software Development: An Agile Toolkit* (Boston: Addison-Wesley Professional, 2003), 4.

12. Hirotaka Takeuchi and Ikujiro Nonaka, "The New New Product Development Game," *Harvard Business Review,* January 1986, https://hbr.org/1986/01 /the-new-new-product-development-game.

13. For practitioners of the agile framework Scrum, this is the origin of the term.

14. Stanley McChrystal, *Team of Teams: New Rules of Engagement for a Complex World*, with Tantum Collins, David Silverman, and Chris Fussell (New York: Penguin Portfolio, 2015), 382.

15. Peter Turchin, *Ultrasociety: How 10,000 Years of War Made Humans the Greatest Cooperators on Earth* (Chaplin, CT: Beresta Books, 2015).

16. Gary Hamel and Michele Zanini, "Busting Bureaucracy," Gary Hamel's website, accessed October 28, 2020, http://www.garyhamel.com/blog/busting -bureaucracy.

17. Gary Hamel and Michele Zanini, "Assessment: Do You Know How Bureaucratic Your Organization Is?," *Harvard Business Review*, May 16, 2017, https://hbr.org/2017/05/assessment-do-you-know-how-bureaucratic-your-organization-is.

18. Brad Stone, *The Everything Store: Jeff Bezos and the Age of Amazon* (Boston: Little, Brown, 2013), 379.

19. Robin Dunbar, "Neocortex Size as a Constraint on Group Size in Primates," *Journal of Human Evolution* 22, no. 6 (June 1992): 469–493.

20. McChrystal, *Team of Teams*, 256.

21. Ori Brafman, *The Starfish and the Spider: The Unstoppable Power of Leaderless Organizations* (New York: Penguin Portfolio, 20016), 54–55.

22. Gary Hamel, *The Future of Management*, with Bill Breen (Boston: Harvard Business School Press, 2007), 84.

23. Pim, "Buurtzorg's Healthcare Revolution: 14,000 Employees, 0 Managers, Sky-High Engagement," Corporate Rebels, accessed October 28, 2020, https://corporate-rebels.com/buurtzorg/.

24. Doug Kirkpatrick, "Haier Elevation," Business Agility Institute, accessed October 28, 2020, https://businessagility.institute/learn/haier-elevation/.

25. Minnaar and de Morree, *Corporate Rebels* (Corporate rebels Nederland B.V, 2019), Kindle location 763.

26. Frans Johansson, *The Medici Effect,* revised ed. (Boston, MA: Harvard Business Review Press, 2017).

27. Walter Isaacson, *Steve Jobs* (New York: Simon & Schuster, 2011), 996–997.

28. "Inside Google Workplaces, from Perks to Nap Pods," CBS, January 23, 2013, https://www.cbsnews.com/news/inside-google-workplaces-from-perks-to-nap-pods/.

29. Joseph L. Bowers and Clayton M. Christensen, "Disruptive Technologies: Catching the Wave," *Harvard Business Review*, January–February 1995, https://hbr.org/1995/01/disruptive-technologies-catching-the-wave.

30. Charles A. O'Reilly and Michael L. Tushman, *Lead and Disrupt: How to Solve the Innovator's Dilemma* (Stanford, CA: Stanford Business Books, 2016), 175.

31. Martin Reeves et al., "Ambidexterity: The Art of Thriving in Complex Environments," BCG, February 19, 2013, https://www.bcg.com/en-gb/publications/2013/strategy-growth-ambidexterity-art-thriving-complex-environments.aspx.

32. McChrystal, *Team of Teams*.

Chapter 7: People and Engagement

1. Eric Schmidt and Jonathan Rosenberg, *How Google Works* (London: John Murray, 2014), 49.

2. *State of the Global Workplace*, 2017, https://www.gallup.com/workplace/238079/state-global-workplace-2017.aspx.

3. *State of the Global Workplace*, 2017.

4. Jacob Morgan, *The Employee Experience Advantage: How to Win the War for Talent by Giving Employees the Workspaces They Want, the Tools They Need, and a Culture They Can Celebrate* (Hoboken, NJ: Wiley, 2017), 160.

5. Naz Beheshti, "10 Timely Statistics about the Connection between Employee Engagement and Wellness," *Forbes*, January 16, 2019, https://www.forbes.com/sites/nazbeheshti/2019/01/16/10-timely-statistics-about-the-connection-between-employee-engagement-and-wellness/#2e89653522a0.

6. David Rock, *Your Brain at Work: Strategies for Overcoming Distraction, Regaining Focus, and Working Smarter All Day Long* (New York: Harper Business, 2009), 8.

7. Rock, 6.

8. Rock, 105.

9. Matthew Lieberman and Naomi Eisenberger, "The Pains and Pleasures of a Social Life," *Science* 323, no. 5916 (February 13, 2009): 890–891.

10. Daniel Goleman, *Emotional Intelligence: Why It Can Matter More Than IQ*, 1st ed. (London: Bloomsbury Publishing, 1996), 203.

11. David Rock, "SCARF: A Brain-Based Model for Collaborating With and Influencing Others," *Neuro Leadership Journal*, no. 1 (2008): 3–6.

12. Gary Hamel, *The Future of Management*, with Bill Breen (Boston: Harvard Business School Press, 2007), 58.

13. Hamel, 58.

14. Daniel Pink, *Drive: The Surprising Truth about What Motivates Us*, main ed. (Edinburgh: Canongate Books, 2018).

15. Nick Howard, "Edelman Trust Reveals Employee Trust Divide," Edelman, April 4, 2016, https://www.edelman.co.uk/research/edelman-trust-data-reveals-employee-trust-divide, 8.

16. Patrick Lencioni, *The Five Dysfunctions of a Team: A Leadership Fable* (San Francisco: Jossey-Bass, 2002).

17. Joel Gascoigne, "Why We Have a Core Value of Transparency at Our Startup, and Why the Reasons Don't Matter," Joel Gascoigne's website, September 21, 2014, https://joel.is/why-we-have-a-core-value-of-transparency-at-our-startup/.

18. David Allen, *Getting Things Done: The Art of Stress-Free Productivity* (London: Piatkus, 2015), 68.

19. SHRM/Globoforce, *Employee Recognition Survey, Fall 2012 Report: The Business Impact of Employee Recognition* (Society for Human Resource Management / Globoforce, 2012), http://go.globoforce.com/rs/globoforce/images/SHRMFALL2012Survey_web.pdf.

20. Robert Sutton and Ben Wigert, "More Harm than Good: The Truth about Performance Reviews," Gallup, May 6, 2019, https://www.gallup.com/workplace/249332/harm-good-truth-performance-reviews.aspx.

21. Edward L. Deci, *Why We Do What We Do: Understanding Self-Motivation* (New York: Penguin Books, 1996).

22. Avraham N. Kluger and Angelo DeNisi, "The Effects of Feedback Interventions on Performance: A Historical Review, a Meta-Analysis, and a Preliminary Feedback Intervention Theory," *Psychological Bulletin* 119, no. 2 (1996), https://mrbartonmaths.com/resourcesnew/8.%20Research/Marking%20and%20Feedback/The%20effects%20of%20feedback%20interventions.pdf.

Chapter 8: Governance and Funding

1. Marc Gunther, "Better Place: What Went Wrong for the Electric Car Startup?," *Yale Environment 360*, March 5, 2013, https://e360.yale.edu/features/gunther_why_israel_electric_car_startup_better_place_failed.

2. David Lavenda, "Is The Dream of the Electric Car Headed to a Better Place?," *Fast Company*, May 30, 2013, https://www.fastcompany.com/3010169/is-the-dream-of-the-electric-car-headed-to-a-better-place.

3. Simon Kucher and Partners, *Global Pricing Study 2014*, https://www.simon-kucher.com/en/resources/perspectives/global-pricing-study-2014.

4. Gary Hamel and Nancy Tennant, "The 5 Requirements of a Truly Innovative Company," *Harvard Business Review*, April 27, 2015, https://hbr.org/2015/04/the-5-requirements-of-a-truly-innovative-company.

5. The Business Agility Institute, *Business Agility Report: Responding to Disruption,* 3rd ed. (2020), 6.

6. Gary Hamel, *The Future of Management*, with Bill Breen (Boston: Harvard Business School Press, 2007), 152.

7. Frank T. Anbari, *The Story of Managing Projects: An Interdisciplinary Approach* (Westport, CT: Greenwood, 2005), 1.

8. John W. Swain and B. J. Reed, *Budgeting for Public Managers* (Abingdon, UK: Routledge, 2010), 18.

9. Adam L. Penenberg, "How Flickr Made It to the Next Level," *Fast Company*, May 7, 2012, https://www.fastcompany.com/1835525/how-flickr-made-it-next-level.

10. Liz Gannes, "Flickr Co-founder Stewart Butterfield Turns to Workplace Communication Tools with Slack," All Things D, August 14, 2013, http://allthingsd.com/20130814/flickr-co-founder-stewart-butterfield-turns-to-workplace-communication-tools-with-slack/.

11. Dominic Rushe, "Slack IPO: Stocks Sell at 50% Higher than Expected as Company's Value Tops $24bn," *Guardian*, June 20, 2019, https://www.theguardian.com/technology/2019/jun/20/slack-ipo-stocks-app-public-latest-share-prices-beat-expectations.

12. Peter Drucker, *Innovation and Entrepreneurship* (New York: Harper Collins, 1985), 189.

13. Stephen R. Covey, *The 7 Habits of Highly Effective People: Powerful Lessons in Personal Change*, anniversary ed. (New York: Simon and Schuster, 2013), 229.

14. Steve Blank, "No Business Plan Survives First Contact with a Customer—The 5.2 Billion Dollar Mistake," Steve Blank's website, November 1, 2010, https://steveblank.com/2010/11/01/no-business-plan-survives-first-contact-with-a-customer-%E2%80%93-the-5-2-billion-dollar-mistake/.

15. Ingrid Torjesen, "Drug Development: The Journey of a Medicine from Lab to Shelf," *Pharmaceutical Journal*, May 12, 2015, https://www.pharmaceutical-journal.com/publications/tomorrows-pharmacist/drug-development-the-journey-of-a-medicine-from-lab-to-shelf/20068196.article.

16. John LaMattina, "Drug Prices Defy Gravity—Until the Patent Expires," *Forbes*, May 1, 2014, https://www.forbes.com/sites/johnlamattina/2014/05/01/drug-prices-defy-gravity-until-the-patent-expires/#669a73632639.

17. "How Gold Is Mined," World Gold Council, accessed October 29, 2020, https://www.gold.org/about-gold/gold-supply/how-gold-is-mined.

18. "How Gold Is Mined."

19. Steve Blank, "What's a Startup: First Principles," Steve Blank's website, January 5, 2010, https://steveblank.com/2010/01/25/whats-a-startup-first-principles/.

20. "Seahorse Fathers Take Reins in Childbirth," *National Geographic*, June 14, 2002, https://www.nationalgeographic.com/news/2002/6/seahorse-fathers-take-reins-in-childbirth/.

21. Ken Robinson, "Do Schools Kill Creativity?," filmed February 2006 in Monterey, California, TED video, 19:06, https://www.ted.com/talks/sir_ken_robinson_do_schools_kill_creativity.

22. Torjesen, "Drug Development."

23. Charles A. O'Reilly and Michael L. Tushman, *Lead and Disrupt: How to Solve the Innovator's Dilemma* (Stanford, CA: Stanford Business Books, 2016), 51.

24. Gary Hamel, *What Matters Now: How to Win in a World of Relentless Change, Ferocious Competition, and Unstoppable Innovation* (San Francisco: Jossey-Bass, 2012), 91.

25. Thomas L. Friedman, "Advice for China," *New York Times*, June 4, 2011, https://www.nytimes.com/2011/06/05/opinion/05friedman.html.

26. Eric Ries, *The Lean Startup: How Constant Innovation Creates Radically Successful Businesses* (London: Portfolio Penguin, 2011).

27. Malcolm Gladwell, "Choice, Happiness and Spaghetti Sauce," filmed in February 2004 in Monterey, California, TED video, 17:26, https://www.ted.com/talks/malcolm_gladwell_choice_happiness_and_spaghetti_sauce.

28. There is little evidence that he ever actually said this. For more, see Patrick Vlaskovits, "Henry Ford, Innovation, and That 'Faster Horse' Quote," *Harvard Business Review*, August 29, 2011, https://hbr.org/2011/08/henry-ford-never-said-the-fast.

29. Andy Reinhardt, "Steve Jobs: 'There's Sanity Returning,'" *Business Week*, May 25, 1998.

Chapter 9: Ways of Working

1. Thomas J. Allen, *Managing the Flow of Technology* (Cambridge, MA: MIT Press, 1977).

2. Ben Waber, Jennifer Magnolfi, and Greg Lindsay, "Workspaces That Move People," *Harvard Business Review*, October 2014, https://hbr.org/2014/10/workspaces-that-move-people.

3. Donald Reinertsen, *Managing the Design Factory: A Product Developers Tool Kit,* illustrated ed. (New York: Free Press, 1998), 113.

4. Denise Grady, "The Vision Thing," *Discover*, June 1, 1993, https://www.discovermagazine.com/mind/the-vision-thing-mainly-in-the-brain.

5. Donald G. Reinertsen, *The Principles of Product Development Flow: Second Generation Lean Product Development* (Redondo Beach, CA: Celeritas, 2009), xxx.

6. Stefan Thomke and Donald Reinertsen, "The Six Myths of Product Development," *Harvard Business Review*, May 2012, https://hbr.org/2012/05/six-myths-of-product-development.

7. Fred Lambert, "Tesla Starts Pushing Fix to Its 'Dog Mode' in Incredible Turnaround," *electrek*, August 2, 2019, https://electrek.co/2019/08/02/tesla-pushing-fix-dog-mode/.

8. Donald Reinertsen, *The Principles of Product Development Flow: Second Generation Lean Product Development* (Redondo Beach, CA: Celeritas, 2009).

9. Michael I. Norton, Daniel Mochon, and Dan Ariely, "The 'IKEA Effect': When Labor Leads to Love," Harvard Business School working paper, 2011, https://www.hbs.edu/faculty/publication%20files/11-091.pdf.

10. Gary Hamel, *The Future of Management*, with Bill Breen (Boston: Harvard Business School Press, 2007), 23.

11. "Tidy Tape Exercise 'Is Madness,'" BBC News, January 4, 2007, http://news.bbc.co.uk/1/hi/england/tyne/6230629.stm.

12. Taiichi Ohno, *Taiichi Ohno's Workplace Management* (New York: McGraw-Hill Education, 2012), 142.

13. Paul Krugman, *The Age of Diminishing Expectations U.S. Economic Policy in the 1990s,* 3rd ed. (Cambridge, MA: MIT Press, 1997), 11.

14. Jeffrey K. Liker, *The Toyota Way: 14 Management Principles from the World's Greatest Manufacturer,* 2nd ed. (New York: McGraw-Hill Education, 2020), 548–549.

15. Jon Miller, "Toyota's Top Engineer on How to Develop Thinking People," Gemba Academy (blog), last updated May 15, 2017, https://blog.gembaacademy.com/2008/08/04/toyotas_top_engineer_on_how_to_develop_thinking_pe/.

Chapter 10: Leading the Change

1. Peter Tollma et al., "Getting Smart about Change Management," BCG, January 5, 2017, https://www.bcg.com/en-us/publications/2017/change-manage ment-getting-smart-about-change-management.aspx.

2. Michael Bucy et al., "The 'How' of Transformation," McKinsey, May 9, 2016, https://www.mckinsey.com/industries/retail/our-insights/the-how-of -transformation.

3. Behnam Tabrizi et al., "Digital Transformation Is Not about Technology," *Harvard Business Review*, March 13, 2019, https://hbr.org/2019/03/digital -transformation-is-not-about-technology.

4. He said this to me many times, but I cannot find it written down anywhere.

5. Simon Sinek, "How Great Leaders Inspire Action," TED Talk, 17:49, filmed September 2009 at TEDxPuget Sound.

6. John P. Kotter, *Leading Change* (Boston: Harvard Business School Press, 1996), 48.

7. Richard Rumelt, "The Perils of Bad Strategy," *McKinsey Quarterly*, June 1, 2011, https://www.mckinsey.com/business-functions/strategy-and-corporate -finance/our-insights/the-perils-of-bad-strategy.

8. Denise Fournier, "The Only Way to Eat an Elephant," *Psychology Today*, April 24, 2018, https://www.psychologytoday.com/gb/blog/mindfully-present -fully-alive/201804/the-only-way-eat-elephant.

9. The canvas, plus a 20-page guidebook, can be downloaded for free at https://www.agilecentre.com/the-business-agility-canvas/.

10. John P. Kotter, "Leading Change: Why Transformation Efforts Fail," *Harvard Business Review*, May–June 1995, https://hbr.org/1995/05/leading -change-why-transformation-efforts-fail-2.

Acknowledgments

There is not a chance I would have written this book without so many people playing their part. First and foremost, thanks to my wife, Aileen, for encouraging me to write a book when I didn't even begin to imagine I could, for holding together our family while I spent days at a time writing, then becoming my most valuable reviewer. It just would not have been possible without your support.

I have stood on the shoulders of so many giants it's hard to include them all. Thanks to the Snowbird 17, who wrote the *Manifesto for Agile Software Development* back in 2001 and changed the world. Thanks to Craig Larman and Bas Vodde, who shaped my thinking through their work and our subsequent collaborations as part of the Large-Scale Scrum trainer community. Thanks to the Scrum Alliance trainer and coach community, from whom I have learned so much.

Thanks to Mike Beedle, whose vision, passion, friendship, and mentorship inspired me to apply my knowledge and experience beyond large-scale agile implementations and toward helping to create truly innovative, engaging, agile organizations. Thanks also to Pete Behrens, who has taught me so much along the way, and to Adam Furgal for challenging my thinking about early versions of the 6 Enablers model.

Thanks to my dad, Glen Harbott, Evan Leybourn, Simon Roberts, Pia Maria Thorén, and Perry Timms, who took the time to read my early drafts and provide invaluable feedback, as well as Kel Pero for cleaning up my engineer's language. Thanks to the Berrett-Koehler team, who have been a joy to work with.

Thanks to my Agile Centre colleagues, who put up with me being all over the place for a year. I do hope my response times improve going forward.

Thanks to my SPPI agile support group, who always understand the challenges of this role and make things just a little easier.

Finally, thanks to the agile community at large for the endless engagement and contributions through which I have grown so much. It is one of the best, and most generous, communities in the corporate space and I hope it continues to flourish.

Index

Page numbers for figures are followed by "f"; page numbers for tables are followed by "t."

Author the Author

Karim Harbott is a world-leading business agility and leadership consultant, entrepreneur, author, and international keynote speaker. He has been involved with software development for 20 years with over a decade of experience helping organizations with business agility, working with some of the most complex transformations in the world. Karim's work involves advising on business agility, agile  at scale, leadership development, culture change, strategy, and innovation.

Karim has taught, coached, and delivered keynotes to thousands of leaders and practitioners across five continents, from start-ups to *Fortune* 500 companies. He stresses pragmatic, context-appropriate approaches over rigid out-of-the-box solutions. He has held several senior roles in the agile space, including building out the Agile at Scale practice in Europe, the Middle East, and Asia for global strategy consultancy McKinsey. He helped to craft the learning objectives for several leading agile certifications, which have been taken by over a million people globally. He also serves on the board of directors at the Scrum Alliance, the agile industry's leading certifying body.

Karim is one of only a handful of people globally to hold the Certified Agile Leadership Educator, Certified Scrum Trainer, and Certified Enterprise Coach status. He is also a Professional Certified Coach with the International Coach Federation, and Certified Leadership Agility 360 Coach.

In 2016, Karim cofounded Agile Centre (www.agilecentre.com), a leading provider of training and consulting based in London. In 2020, he cofounded the Business Agility Academy (www.business-agility.academy), the world's leading certification body in the business

agility and innovation space. Find out more about Karim at www
.karimharbott.com, and head over to www.6enablers.com to download some free resources described in the book.

Karim lives in North London with his wife and two lively
daughters.

Berrett–Koehler
Publishers

Berrett-Koehler is an independent publisher dedicated to an ambitious mission: *Connecting people and ideas to create a world that works for all.*

Our publications span many formats, including print, digital, audio, and video. We also offer online resources, training, and gatherings. And we will continue expanding our products and services to advance our mission.

We believe that the solutions to the world's problems will come from all of us, working at all levels: in our society, in our organizations, and in our own lives. Our publications and resources offer pathways to creating a more just, equitable, and sustainable society. They help people make their organizations more humane, democratic, diverse, and effective (and we don't think there's any contradiction there). And they guide people in creating positive change in their own lives and aligning their personal practices with their aspirations for a better world.

And we strive to practice what we preach through what we call "The BK Way." At the core of this approach is *stewardship,* a deep sense of responsibility to administer the company for the benefit of all of our stakeholder groups, including authors, customers, employees, investors, service providers, sales partners, and the communities and environment around us. Everything we do is built around stewardship and our other core values of *quality, partnership, inclusion,* and *sustainability.*

This is why Berrett-Koehler is the first book publishing company to be both a B Corporation (a rigorous certification) and a benefit corporation (a for-profit legal status), which together require us to adhere to the highest standards for corporate, social, and environmental performance. And it is why we have instituted many pioneering practices (which you can learn about at www.bkconnection.com), including the Berrett-Koehler Constitution, the Bill of Rights and Responsibilities for BK Authors, and our unique Author Days.

We are grateful to our readers, authors, and other friends who are supporting our mission. We ask you to share with us examples of how BK publications and resources are making a difference in your lives, organizations, and communities at www.bkconnection.com/impact.

Dear reader,

Thank you for picking up this book and welcome to the worldwide BK community! You're joining a special group of people who have come together to create positive change in their lives, organizations, and communities.

What's BK all about?

Our mission is to connect people and ideas to create a world that works for all.

Why? Our communities, organizations, and lives get bogged down by old paradigms of self-interest, exclusion, hierarchy, and privilege. But we believe that can change. That's why we seek the leading experts on these challenges—and share their actionable ideas with you.

A welcome gift

To help you get started, we'd like to offer you a **free copy** of one of our bestselling ebooks:

www.bkconnection.com/welcome

When you claim your **free ebook**, you'll also be subscribed to our blog.

Our freshest insights

Access the best new tools and ideas for leaders at all levels on our blog at ideas.bkconnection.com.

Sincerely,

Your friends at Berrett-Koehler

Certified

Corporation